The Economics of the Long Period

This book provides a non-technical introduction to
that is, the study of history as a succession of economic regimes. It first focuses on the
canonical example of regime shift: the transition from the regime of Malthusian
stagnation to the modern regime of sustained economic growth. Then, it broadens
the perspectives on historical change by examining other regime shifts involving
institutional and environmental forces. This book fills a gap in the market by providing a more accessible treatment of UGT and invites readers to explore ideas of
continuity and discontinuity in history.

Gregory Ponthiere is Professor of Economics and Philosophy at the Hoover Chair in
Economic and Social Ethics, Université catholique de Louvain.

The Economics of the Long Period

GREGORY PONTHIERE

Université catholique de Louvain

CAMBRIDGE
UNIVERSITY PRESS

CAMBRIDGE
UNIVERSITY PRESS

University Printing House, Cambridge CB2 8BS, United Kingdom

One Liberty Plaza, 20th Floor, New York, NY 10006, USA

477 Williamstown Road, Port Melbourne, VIC 3207, Australia

314–321, 3rd Floor, Plot 3, Splendor Forum, Jasola District Centre, New Delhi – 110025, India

103 Penang Road, #05–06/07, Visioncrest Commercial, Singapore 238467

Cambridge University Press is part of the University of Cambridge.

It furthers the University's mission by disseminating knowledge in the pursuit of
education, learning, and research at the highest international levels of excellence.

www.cambridge.org
Information on this title: www.cambridge.org/9781009169769
DOI: 10.1017/9781009169752

First published 2022

A catalogue record for this publication is available from the British Library.

Library of Congress Cataloging-in-Publication Data
Names: Ponthière, Grégory, author.
Title: The economics of the long period / Gregory Ponthiere.
Other titles: Economie de longue période. English
Description: Cambridge, United Kingdom ; New York, NY : Cambridge University Press, 2022. |
    Includes bibliographical references and index.
Identifiers: LCCN 2022011822 (print) | LCCN 2022011823 (ebook) | ISBN 9781009169769 (hardback) |
    ISBN 9781009169745 (paperback) | ISBN 9781009169752 (epub)
Subjects: LCSH: Economic development–Econometric models. | Economic development–History. |
    Economic history–Mathematical models. | BISAC: BUSINESS & ECONOMICS / Development /
    Economic Development
Classification: LCC HD75.5 .P6713 2022 (print) | LCC HD75.5 (ebook) | DDC 338.9–dc23/eng/20220318
LC record available at https://lccn.loc.gov/2022011822
LC ebook record available at https://lccn.loc.gov/2022011823

ISBN 978-1-009-16976-9 Hardback
ISBN 978-1-009-16974-5 Paperback

Contents

Part III Unified Growth Theory: Microeconomics of Regime Shift

Figures

Tables

Introduction

What can economic analysis teach us about the "long period", those times whose duration is such that nothing (or almost nothing) can be treated as a constant – neither population, nor knowledge, nor political and economic institutions? What concepts and tools can allow economists to think about the movements of the economy over a horizon of several centuries, or even millennia?

Because of the specificity of the time spans under consideration, the long period requires its own analytical tools. We are very far here from the relatively short time horizons usually studied by economists. The time for transactions between agents – that is of the adjustment of allocations – is limited to a few moments. The time for price adjustment, in order to level out supply and demand for goods and services, is generally not much longer. The time for the movement of capital from one sector of the economy to another – a movement that tends to level out profit rates between sectors – has for its part greatly diminished in the last decades.

An economic analysis of the long period examines much longer time spans, the spans needed to adjust the entire economy: adjustments in population, technologies, institutions. Ideally, adopting a long-period perspective means that nothing is taken as a given, neither the number of individuals, nor their level of knowledge, nor their production techniques, nor the institutions within which they operate. From the perspective of the long period, the theoretical framework should only include our planet – Earth and its resources – its inhabitants (men and women), as well as a stock of knowledge; and it should study the relationships between these elements over time. It would be a study of the *rhythms* at which humans, their techniques and resources accumulate.

Do humans "accumulate" too fast in relation to knowledge, thus threatening the population with the plights of poverty and misery? Or, conversely, does knowledge accumulate more rapidly than humans, thus creating prospects for lasting prosperity? These accumulation processes cannot be dissociated from the institutional frameworks in which they take place (the State, the market), which leads us to another fundamental question: namely the links that exist between these rhythms of accumulation and institutional dynamics. Does the improvement in the institutions provide a necessary condition, or even a sufficient condition, for economic take-off? Finally, the environmental damage caused by human activities (global warming, threats to biodiversity) give rise to many questions, such as: are population growth and economic growth sustainable on a finite planet?

The purpose of this book is to provide answers to these complex questions by exposing the recent developments of the economic theory of the long period.

Unified Growth Theory

The economic analysis of the long period has undergone a major theoretical revolution in the twenty-first century, with the development of "Unified Growth Theory". We owe this theoretical revolution to Oded Galor and his co-authors, as well as to an increasing number of economists of the "long period".

Unified Growth Theory is a class of varied dynamic models, whose common denominator is to *formalise the economic development processes (population, technology, output per capita) as a whole in one analytical framework,* hence the term "unified" growth.[1]

More specifically, Unified Growth Theory aims to account for the different phases of the economic development process – phases labelled as "economic regimes" – as well as the mechanisms of transition between these regimes.[2] It theorises the existence and succession, over the centuries, of different economic regimes, with the transition between regimes explained from *within* the model.

From the perspective of the long period, one major stylised fact is the birth of an era of output per capita growth, which occurred at the time of the industrial revolution, after millennia of economic activity experiencing a trend of (near) stagnation.

Each of these phases of history – stagnation and growth – can be explained or "rationalised" by economic thought. In his *An Essay on the Principle of Population* (1798), Malthus affirmed that no social progress was sustainable: improving living conditions necessarily led to demographic pressure, thus cancelling any possibility of lasting expansion, hence stagnation. More recently, modern growth theory – as exemplified by Solow's (1956) model – sees output per capita growth in the nineteenth and twentieth centuries as the result of the increase in capital intensity (the amount of capital (machines, tools) per worker). Each theory helps, in its own way, to shed light on a part of history, *but only on a part:* the Malthusian doctrine could not foresee the emergence of sustainable growth, and Solow's model cannot explain the long pre-industrial era of (near) stagnation preceding the phase of growth.

Whereas these analytical frameworks can be mobilised separately to account for the economic dynamics of distinct segments of history, Unified Growth Theory offers a *single* theoretical system to explain the shift from an economic regime of stagnation – as analysed, notably by Malthus – to a regime of output per capita growth – which Solow analysed. Within this unified analytical framework, the transition from one

---

[1] This is the very definition proposed by Galor (see Galor 2011, p. 5). Other presentations of Unified Growth Theory can be found in Galor (2005, 2010). The unified growth models include, in particular, those of Galor and Weil (1999, 2000) and of Galor and Moav (2002, 2005).

[2] This second definition, which emphasises the endogenous nature of the transition between regimes, is also proposed by Galor (2011, p. xvi of the Preface).

economic regime to another is not caused by some "exogenous" shock, but rather results from latent mechanisms present in the economy ("latent dynamics"). The expression "unified growth" is used to name this theoretical attempt to gather, within a single model, several distinct economic regimes, with each regime characterised by its own laws or regularities.

The theory of unified growth is presented in detail in *Unified Growth Theory* (Galor, 2011). That book is more of a treatise than it is a textbook, in so far as it presents this theory at a level of detail comparable to that of specialised journals. Galor studies a dynamic system with four dimensions (physical capital, size of population, technology and human capital), a system that enables him to account for the shift from a "Malthusian" regime (stagnation of output per capita and lack of education) to a "post-Malthusian" regime (in which output per capita grows slightly, while education remains absent) to, finally, the "modern" regime (high growth driven by mass education).[3]

The Objectives of This Book

This book offers an introduction to Unified Growth Theory and to the concepts and tools that this theory mobilises in thinking about the long period. It aims to make Unified Growth Theory more accessible and, in so doing, this book adds to the "classical" textbooks on economic growth, such as Barro and Sala-I-Martin (1996), Jones (1998), Foley and Michl (1999), de la Croix and Michel (2002), Weil (2005) and Acemoglu (2009), books which do not touch upon Unified Growth Theory, or only do so in passing.

The audience for this book is wide: it includes undergraduate students in economics and social sciences who are interested in the dynamics of human societies over the long period, as well as more advanced students in a master's program.

This book aims to familiarise students with the fundamental concepts of Unified Growth Theory, that is, mainly;

- the notion of economic regime;
- the notions of quantitative change and qualitative change;
- the notion of critical threshold;
- the notion of latent dynamics.

This book also aims to familiarise students with modelling:

- microeconomic mechanisms that lead to the existence of distinct economic regimes;
- microeconomic mechanisms at the root of the transition from one economic regime to another.

---

[3] The stylised facts covered by *Unified Growth Theory* also include other stylised facts, such as the demographic transition and the emergence of mass education.

There is an obvious contradiction between, on the one hand, trying to analyse the long period using Unified Growth Theory and, on the other hand, the demands of simplicity expected from an "introduction". Since Unified Growth Theory is the most advanced form of analysing the long period, it can hardly be simple. It is that very challenge which this book takes on: how to make Unified Growth Theory accessible to as many people as possible, including undergraduate and graduate students from economics and the other social sciences. The demands of simplicity are the reason why this book focuses on what we could call "reduced-form models", that is, modelling that has been pared down in relation to the works of Galor (2005, 2010, 2011). Simplification revolved around two aspects. First, in order to remain within a one-dimensional dynamic system, we have simplified the hypotheses regarding accumulation processes. Second, the book studies phenomena of size or scale and leaves out problems related to the structure of economies (production structures, population structures, etc.).[4]

The need for simplicity has another consequence: this book does not aim to cover all of the possible applications of Unified Growth Theory. We now have access to a wealth of statistical data: new "stylised facts" or "empirical regularities" are discovered every day in economics, in sociology, in demography, etc. Each one of these stylised facts could be considered from the perspective of a different theory. This book does not provide an overview of the various different applications of Unified Growth Theory, but rather tries to present its principal concepts and tools. To that end, this book focuses on the "core variables", such as total production, size of population, output per capita and technological progress; then, in a second step, widens the analytical framework to other aspects, such as institutions and natural environment.

Layout of the book

The book is organised in three parts. An undergraduate course could only cover Parts I and II (the first six chapters). A master's level course should ideally cover Part I, Part II (Chapters 3 and 4) and Part III.

Part I offers a few reference points by way of a contextual introduction, both theoretically and empirically, that help set milestones in the wide field of the economic analysis of the long period.

Chapter 1 mobilises fragments from the history of economic thought in order to sketch out a few of the influential theories of the long period: those of Malthus, Marx, Marshall, Kondratiev, Rostow and Solow. This initial perspective enables us to situate

---

[4] This is a broad simplification: Rostow (1960) considers that growth is inseparable from changes in the sectoral structure of the economy. Ignoring the age structure of the population deprives us of a potential determinant of economic take-off: the demographic transition. For an analysis of interactions between age structure and growth, see Challier and Michel (1996) and de la Croix and Michel (2002).

Unified Growth Theory in relation to its "ancestors" and to identify some of its inherited theoretical traits. Chapter 2 studies the evolution over the last two millennia of total production, population size and output per capita. It shows that the growth of output per capita is a recent phenomenon on the scale of human history. This structural break is the main stylised fact that we will attempt to explain in the rest of this book.

Part II presents the major concepts of Unified Growth Theory: economic regime, quantitative and qualitative change, latent dynamics and critical threshold. To that end, we will study reduced-form models that do not include microeconomic foundations, but do make it possible to "rationalise" the stylised facts of Part I.

Chapter 3 models an economic regime of output-per-capita stagnation. This stagnation is Malthusian in nature, that is, it is linked to an excessive reactivity of the population size to productivity gains, which prevents a sustained growth of the output per capita. This model accounts for the stagnation in living conditions during the pre-industrial era. Chapter 4 studies, by using a variant of Kremer's model (1993), the transition from a stagnation regime to a growth regime. Population size, which was the cause of stagnation according to Malthus, constitutes for Kremer the variable that leads, beyond a certain threshold, to an acceleration of technological progress (thanks to scale effects) and, therefore, offers a way out of stagnation. Chapter 5 analyses the relationships between economic dynamics and the institutional framework. It explores the role played by institutions in the transition from a stagnation regime to a growth regime and studies the links between inequalities and the occurrence of revolutions. Chapter 6 examines one of the major limitations to economic expansion: the natural environment (the finite dimensions of Earth). This leads to adding to the two above-studied regimes – stagnation and growth – three more regimes: those of congestion, non-regeneration and depopulation.

Part III mobilises the concepts introduced previously in order to construct unified growth models that explain, *based on assumptions about individual behaviours,* the transition from one economic regime to another. The use of microeconomic foundations enables the critical thresholds that determine changes in regime to become endogenous: the evolution of the macroeconomic environment encourages individuals to modify their behaviours, thus leading to regime change.

Chapter 7 develops a model that explains, from individual decisions of investing in education, the transition from a stagnation regime (in which the population is uneducated) to a growth regime (in which the population is educated). Introducing microeconomic foundations makes it possible to analyse the two-way interactions between individuals and the macroeconomic environment. Chapter 8 presents a microeconomic theory of the emergence of new institutions. It highlights the influence of citizen participation on the improvement of the institutional framework, an improvement that is the prerequisite for economic take-off. Chapter 9 re-examines the issue of limits to growth, by modelling how lifestyles adapt to environmental damage. These analyses result in the existence of an intermediate regime, the adaptation regime, which, by slowing the growth of pollution, pushes back the depopulation regime further into the future.

Acknowledgements

Above all, I wish to thank Hubert Kempf, the scientific director of the collection *Corpus Economie* that published this work in its original French version (*L'économie de longue période*, Editions Economica, Paris, 2020). The book owes much to his remarks, comments and suggestions, thanks to his careful proofreading and critiques. I can safely say that this book project would probably have remained a mere project without his involvement and enthusiasm. I would also like to thank Jean Pavlevski for his remarks and comments on the manuscript.

I also wish to extend my thanks to my colleagues and co-authors in the field of the economic analysis of the long period. I am thinking of Pierre Pestieau who introduced me more than twenty years ago – when I was still a student – to the analysis of dynamic economic models and with whom I have since written many articles on that topic. I also want to thank Hippolyte d'Albis and David de la Croix for our fruitful collaborations on long-run economic dynamics.

This book is the result of a decade of teaching the economic analysis of the long period. Therefore, it indirectly has been enriched by multiple interactions with students, notably with the students who participated in the courses *Economic Demography*, later called *Population Economics*, of the Master in APE – Economic and Political Analysis – of the École des Hautes Études en Sciences Sociales (2008–2019).

I would like also to thank Colette J. Windish for the translation from French to English.

Part I

The Long Period

Some Milestones

1 A Brief History of Long-Run Economic Analysis

The economic analysis of the long period is not recent, and its roots can be traced to the middle of the eighteenth century. In his *Reflections on the Formation and Distribution of Wealth* (1766), Turgot describes his theory of wealth over a long period of time. He studies the mechanisms through which societies of farmers and artisans saw, over the centuries, the birth of a new class: the class of landowners. At first, this social class did not exist, each farmer worked on his own land, as labour was the only way to keep ownership over his land in a time when "public rule" was less powerful than "private rule". As arable land was abundant enough, this two-class society remained in place for many centuries. Nonetheless, as a consequence of population growth, some farmers found themselves at times landless. The only solution for these individuals was to offer to work for farmers who did have land. It is at that precise moment that property was separated from agricultural labour: thus appeared the landowning class, a class earning revenue without working, hence its name of *classe disponible* or "available class" (available for war and justice). The birth of this class, according to Turgot, profoundly transformed how economies functioned.

Since Turgot, numerous economic theories of the long period have emerged and have proposed a vision of history as the struggle of societies in the face of resource scarcity. Each of these theories – whether using natural or mathematical language, whether predicting a convergence towards a steady state or the existence of long cycles – has an empirical basis as its starting point that it proposes to clarify through its own specific concepts. To that end, each theory of the long period disregards numerous elements so that it can showcase a "driving force" that is pushing the historical process forward. Each of these theories can be regarded as a different "lens" through which we can look at the past, the present and the future of our societies.

To write a history of economic theories of the long period would force us to take a long detour and, ultimately, would imply writing a new history of economic thought, alongside the monumental achievements of Gide and Rist (1944), Schumpeter (1954), Denis (1966) and Blaug (1985). Such a task would require elucidating the relationship of economic thought to time, as well as the incremental evolution of that relationship as economic thought has developed, and it would go beyond the scope of this book.

This chapter does not plan to undertake such a complex task, but it proposes, more modestly, to sketch out a *brief* history of economic analyses of the long period. This foray into the history of economic ideas aims to offer a double perspective on Unified Growth Theory.

First of all, Unified Growth Theory is but one theory amongst many of the evolution of societies over time. Its presentation requires us to clarify its concepts and to study its inner workings, its internal mechanics. But such a task – which lies at the heart of this book – can be supplemented by presenting *other* theories of the long period. Theories are like human beings: it is often by looking at the other that one can better know oneself. In that respect, studying other economic theories of the long period will enable us to place greater emphasis on the *specificities* of Unified Growth Theory.

Second, Unified Growth Theory is the most recent form of long-run economic thought. That thought did not spring from a blank canvas: it *borrowed* elements from previous theories and positioned itself within the field of economic knowledge in relation to those theories. A brief foray into the history of thought can be useful in identifying those inherited traits. By drawing the "family tree", so to speak, of this contemporary theory, we should be able to better determine its position with regard to previous theories – its ancestors – and to shed new light on its contents.

Because of space constraints, this chapter has to make a choice among the many existing theories. This selection retained six "masters" of the economic theory of the long period: Malthus, Marx, Marshall, Kondratiev, Rostow and Solow. This chapter will present their theories with respect to the long term, by emphasising their key concepts, the (assumed) "driving force" of historical change, as well as the form taken by the dynamics of the long period (stagnation, growth, cycles, etc.).

1.1   Malthus

Malthus published the first version of *An Essay on the Principle of Population* anonymously in 1798. The anonymous nature of the publication may seem surprising, especially considering the tremendous impact of that work during the nineteenth century, which extended well beyond economic thought alone.[1] Malthus wrote the essay with a clear political objective in mind: achieve the repeal of the Poor Laws, which had been in effect in England since the sixteenth century. In his *Essay*, Malthus defended the thesis that the very mechanism that was meant to help the destitute, organised at the parish level and financed by a land tax (the poor tax), did not contribute to diminishing the extent of poverty but, on the contrary, contributed to making the phenomenon even more widespread. Malthus boldly recommended a highly unpopular measure – that the Poor Laws be abolished.

Beyond the general context around the writing of the *Essay*, what is most interesting here is the *dynamic* nature of Malthus's argument. Indeed, from a static

---

[1] Darwin based himself in particular on the work of Malthus to write his famous treatise *On the Origin of Species* (1859), the founding work of modern biology. Darwin identified two conditions necessary for the existence of a natural selection mechanism for species: first, the existence of heterogeneity in living organisms (species variants); second, the existence of a struggle for life due to the limited means of subsistence, which brings us back to the Malthusian principle of population.

perspective, we would be hard-pressed to conclude that a redistribution from the wealthier to the poorer members of society could contribute to an increase in the extent of poverty. From a static perspective, such a redistribution should necessarily reduce – rather than increase – poverty. In order to understand Malthus's argument, one must reason within a dynamic framework: according to Malthus, the Poor Laws do not increase poverty immediately; it is only *once a whole series of adjustments take place within the economy* that poverty increases beyond the level that it would have reached in the absence of these laws.

Malthus presents a two-part argument. The first part deals with the adjustment of the size of what the economy produces: by helping the poorest, the Poor Laws contribute, according to Malthus, to discouraging entrepreneurship and reducing the level of production. This first argument – the perverse incentive effects of redistribution – is a traditional one in economics, which was then called political economy. The second part of Malthus's argument suggests adjusting the population size. This second argument is the one we will focus on. It is based upon what Malthus called the principle of population.

1.1.1   The Principle of Population

According to Malthus, every society meets two postulates: on the one hand, survival demands food, or a "means of subsistence"; on the other hand, the passions between the sexes do not vary over time.[2] Although Malthus uses both premises in his line of argument, at its core lies what he calls the principle of population, a principle that supposedly has prevailed everywhere and in every time period, whichever society you consider. Malthus thus made this one of the "great" laws of economics.

The principle of population states that there exists a fundamental imbalance between, on the one hand, a society's ability to produce human beings and, on the other, that society's ability to produce means of subsistence, with the former far exceeding the latter:[3]

Assuming then my postulata as granted, I say, that the power of population is indefinitely greater than the power in the earth to produce subsistence for man.

This major imbalance happens, according to Malthus, everywhere and in every time period, regardless of the type of institution (the form of government), geography or climatic conditions. More specifically, Malthus states the following two propositions:[4]

---

[2] See Malthus (1798), chapter 1, p. 70.

[3] See Malthus (1798), chapter 1, p. 71. Two centuries before Malthus – well before the concept of "population" first appeared – Botero (1588) had theorised an imbalance between what he called *virtus generativa* (the capacity of a society to produce new members) and *virtus nutritiva* (the capacity of a society to produce the means of subsistence). The latter, being limited, prevented a sustainable growth of cities.

[4] See Malthus (1798), chapter 1, pp. 71–72. A quantity follows a geometrical ratio when its size is multiplied by a constant at the passing of each time period (for example, 2, 4, 8, 16, 32, . . .). Conversely, a quantity follows an arithmetical ratio when its size increases by a constant at the passing of each time period (for example, 2, 4, 6, 8, 10, . . .).

Population, when unchecked, increases in a geometrical ratio. Subsistence increases only in an arithmetical ratio.

Since the power of the geometrical ratio outweighs that of the arithmetical ratio, it follows that, sooner or later, the population will lack the means of subsistence. Two corrections will pull down the population size. Malthus called them "population checks":[5] first a so-called preventive check, with parents reducing the number of their progeny in anticipation of future hardships in feeding their children; and second, a so-called positive check, that is premature deaths within the poorer classes, due to an over-mortality linked to famine and disease. Unfortunately, the positive check mechanism is much more prevalent than is the preventive check. Malthus does not endorse the perspective of humans as rational beings: he considers them as "compound subjects", subject to passion they cannot control.

Let us return to the justification of the two propositions that form the principle of population. The first proposition deals with the natural tendency of a population to increase, in the hypothetical case that no correction is present (as Malthus puts it, "if left unchecked"). Malthus asserts that no population has ever found itself in such a hypothetical situation. He relies, for this first proposition, on observations on the growth of population in the eighteenth century in the United States, a country where land was abundant in comparison to the size of the population.[6] The second proposition, for its part, found its justification in the fixed nature of the land. Malthus did not reject a priori the possibility of technical progress. Nevertheless, such a progress could only have limited effects on the means of subsistence produced from any given land area, leading to the limited growth embodied by the means of subsistence's arithmetical ratio.

1.1.2   An Oscillatory Dynamic

In spite of the absence of any mathematical equation in the *Essay*, the principle of population has clear implications on economic and demographic dynamics. The imbalance between the reproductive power of humans and their capacity to produce their means of subsistence is such that a society will inevitably experience cyclical dynamics and oscillate, in Malthusian terms, between periods of progress and periods of regression, between periods of expansion and periods of contraction.

The mechanism that governs these long-run oscillations is implacable. As an illustration, let us suppose that, at a given time, a technical advancement allows for an increase in the level of production of the means of subsistence. Will it be possible to maintain this increase in the standards of living and therefore escape fluctuations?

---

[5] Well before the *Essay* was written, the adjustment of population size was the foundation of the Smithian theory of "natural" wage (Smith 1776). In the case of a labour shortage, the market wage exceeds the natural wage (which is equal to the living wage), that leads to an increase in the size of the population in order to meet excess demand for labour. Conversely, in the case of a recession, the market wage drops below the living wage, which makes the population contract. As with Malthus, the time horizon is long enough to allow an "adjustment" in the size of the population.

[6] See Malthus (1798), chapter 2, pp. 73–74. Malthus did not take into account indigenous populations.

The answer is no. Indeed, the very fact that the constraints on resources are temporarily lifted will bring about, in accordance with the first proposition of the principle of population, a sharp growth in the size of the population. Considering that land is a fixed asset, demographical growth will sooner or later push down the output per capita and lead to positive and preventive checks, which will slow the demographical increase. It is therefore impossible, according to the principle of population, for an economy to benefit from a sustained increase in output per capita. The economy invariably experiences oscillations, without being able to profit from a lasting improvement in living conditions.[7]

In the absence of any mathematical equation in the *Essay*, it is impossible to ascertain whether such cyclical dynamics bring about, with time, a convergence of the economy towards a kind of steady state in which population size and output per capita stabilise or whether, on the contrary, cyclical dynamics lead to long cycles or to cycles of increasing magnitude. The theory outlined by Malthus does not provide an answer to this question.

It is clear however that, for Malthus, the imbalance between a society's capacity to beget humans and its capacity to produce the means of subsistence (from a given area of land) hinders any sustained progress. As this is a universal imbalance, all societies will be confronted with periods of progress followed by periods of regression. An endless improvement of the standard of living is unthinkable: the only possible long-term trend is stagnation.[8] Malthus believed that no society could ever escape this cruel fate, thus pitting himself squarely against thinkers such as Godwin in England or Condorcet in France, for whom lasting progress was possible for societies, provided that they reform their unjust or ageing institutions.[9]

1.2   Marx

1.2.1   Malthus and the Misleading Abstraction

According to Marx, the Malthusian population theory suffers from an improper use of abstraction. In his *Grundrisse*, Marx does not shy from calling Malthus's theory "false and childish". Marx claims that the Malthusian theory exhibits two main shortcomings. The first is formulated in these words:[10]

---

[7] These oscillatory dynamics are described by Malthus, particularly in chapter 2, pp. 76–77.

[8] The Malthusian doctrine is not the only theory that uses demographic pressure to explain long-term stagnation. Ricardo (1817) also states the impossibility of sustainable economic expansion. According to Ricardo, population growth pushes people to cultivate land of increasingly lower quality, with the effect of mechanically increasing the share of land rent in wealth. This growth in rent – and the accompanying fall in the rate of profit – hinders the process of capital accumulation that, for Ricardo, was the main engine for the enrichment of nations. We shall return to the Ricardian approach in Chapter 5.

[9] A large part of the *Essay* is devoted to refuting the ideas of Condorcet (chapters 8 and 9) and Godwin (chapters 10–15). We will revisit the critiques of the Malthusian doctrine in Chapter 3.

[10] See Marx (1858), pp. 605–606.

His conception is altogether false and childish 1) because he regards *overpopulation* as being *of the same kind* in all the different historic phases of economic development; does not understand their specific difference, and hence stupidly reduces these very complicated and varying relations to a single relation, two equations, in which the natural reproduction of humanity appears on the one side, and the natural reproduction of edible plants (or means of subsistence) on the other, as two natural series, the former geometric and the latter arithmetic in progression.

In that first criticism, Marx accuses Malthus of ignoring – even of forgetting – the different phases in the economic evolution of societies and of overly generalising by applying to *all* stages of the historical process relationships that are dominant in only a certain point in history.

The second part of the critique of the Malthusian doctrine deals with the very concept of the "means of subsistence", which is at the core of his doctrine:[11]

2) He stupidly relates a specific quantity of people to a specific quantity of necessaries. Ricardo immediately and correctly confronted him with the fact that the quantity of grain available is completely irrelevant to the worker if he has no *employment*; that it is therefore the means of employment and not of subsistence that put him into the category of surplus population. But this should be conceived more generally, and relates to the *social mediation* as such, through which the individual gains access to the means of his reproduction and creates them; hence it relates to the *conditions of production* and his relation to them.

Here Marx is once again denouncing a misuse of abstraction in economic analysis: focusing on the bulk of the means of subsistence without discussing the use and distribution of wealth makes little sense to him. Overpopulation cannot be absolute, but must necessarily be *relative* to the manner in which wealth is distributed at that point in time.

The critique of the *Essay on the Principle of Population* by Marx constitutes an ideal entry point to get an understanding of Marx's theory of history: historical materialism.

1.2.2   Historical Materialism

Marx's theory of history is too often summarised as the first lines of the *Manifesto of the Communist Party* (1848):[12]

The history of all hitherto existing societies is the history of class struggles. Freeman and slave, patrician and plebeian, lord and serf, guild-master and journeyman, in a word, oppressor and oppressed, stood in constant opposition to one another, carried on an uninterrupted, now hidden, now open fight, a fight that each time ended, either in a revolutionary reconstitution of society at large, or in the common ruin of the contending classes.

Although this representation of history as a struggle between the classes does account for an essential dimension of historical materialism – the antagonism resulting from social groups holding different positions of power – it does not come close to conveying its whole meaning.

---

[11] See Marx (1858), p. 607.   [12] See Marx (1848), p. 1.

It is in *The German Ideology* that Marx and Engels (1846) give the most detailed presentation of historical materialism.[13] In that text, they show that historical materialism is the thesis according to which the history of human societies is above all the history of the production, by humans, of their material conditions of life, as well as the history of the social and political relationships associated with that production process:[14]

The first premise of all human history is, of course, the existence of living human individuals. Thus the first fact to be established is the physical organisation of these individuals and their consequent relation to the rest of nature. [...] The writing of history must always set out from these natural bases and their modification in the course of history through the action of men. Men can be distinguished from animals by consciousness, by religion or anything else you like. They themselves begin to distinguish themselves from animals as soon as they begin to *produce* their means of subsistence. [...]. By producing their means of subsistence men are indirectly producing their actual material life. [...]

History is therefore mainly the history of the production, by humans, of their own means of existence. That production may take on different and varied forms. In order to account for the variety and complexity of that production, one of the key concepts of historical materialism is the concept of *mode of production*.[15]

The way in which men produce their means of subsistence depends first of all on the nature of the actual means of subsistence they find in existence and have to reproduce. This mode of production must not be considered simply as being the production of the physical existence of the individuals. Rather it is a definite form of activity of these individuals, a definite form of expressing their life, a definite *mode of life* on their part. [...] What they are, therefore, coincides with their production, both with what they produce and with how they produce. The nature of individuals thus depends on the material conditions determining their production.

For Marx, the mode of production cannot be reduced to a relationship between humankind and nature. The production by humans of their own existence is a social production and, within the framework of that production, humans enter into social and political relationships that are imposed upon them.[16] The description of a mode of production is not limited to the study of the developmental stage of the productive forces (such as the number of workers and machines), it must also include production relationships, that is to say relationships that determine how the productive forces interact within the production process. These interactions include in particular the relationships of ownership.

One of the most fundamental aspects of historical materialism resides in the primacy of material bases (the development of productive forces and production relationships) over all other forms of determination of the historical process. Production produces humans, their thoughts, their representations and their beliefs:[17]

---

[13] That manuscript, which long remained unpublished (for lack of a publisher), was not published until 1932.

[14] See Marx and Engels (1846), p. 61.   [15] See Marx and Engels (1846), pp. 61–62.

[16] See Marx and Engels (1846), p. 63.   [17] See Marx and Engels (1846), pp. 68–69.

> The production of ideas, of conceptions, of consciousness, is at first directly interwoven with the material activity and the material intercourse of men, the language of real life. [...] Men are the producers of their conceptions, ideas, etc. – real, active men, as they are conditioned by a definite development of their productive forces and of the intercourse corresponding to these[...] Life is not determined by consciousness, but consciousness by life.

This aspect of historical materialism – that it is the material activity of production that determines consciousness – plays an essential role in the description of the historical process. For Marx, a change in the mode of production takes place when the productive forces come to be "in conflict" with the existing production relationships (the relationships of property). This is when a "period of social revolution" starts.[18] A social transformation takes place when the mode of production produces the conditions of its own disappearance.

In the case of the disappearance – foretold by Marx – of the capitalistic mode of production (characterised by private property of the means of production and division of labour), the social transformation originates in the fact that such a mode of production leads, as the productive forces develop, to the creation of a specific social class – the proletariat – which becomes conscious of the fact that it is being crushed by the capital and is, in a way, "forced" to revolt against the inhumaneness of this crushing.

To summarise, if the "class struggle" is an essential aspect of history according to historical materialism, it is important to underline that the conditions of that antagonism, as well as its influence upon social transformation, are determined by the developmental stage of the productive forces. Historical dynamics cannot be understood without studying the accumulation of productive forces over the centuries.

1.3   Marshall

The theories of Malthus and Marx propose, each in their own way, a certain vision of history. Their analyses are of a *dynamic* nature. Time plays a fundamental role for them: Malthus believes that a certain lapse of time is necessary for population to adjust to a size that fits the level of the means of subsistence, whereas Marx claims that a certain amount of time is necessary for the productive forces to develop and that this development is a prerequisite for any social transformation.

In spite of the central role time plays in these analyses, neither Malthus nor Marx give any precisions about the time horizon needed for such processes of adjustment or development. Malthus does not explain whether the adjustment of population to the constraints of resources is a rapid process. As for Marx, he does not venture a guess on the speed of the social transformation process linked to the development of the productive forces, nor on the necessary time horizon for resolving the contradictions of the capitalistic mode of production.

---

[18] See Marx (1859), p. 12.

It was one of the founding fathers of neoclassical economic analysis, Marshall, who, by introducing the notion of period analysis, thought about time more precisely. Marshall's contribution to the economic analysis of the long period is not in the form of a new "theory of history", but is rather a methodological contribution. It implies outlining a method that can analyse the evolution of societies over time *by breaking things up*.

1.3.1 Period Analysis

In his *Principles of Economics*, Marshall (1890) insists upon the central role time plays in economic reasoning and the errors that can occur when that dimension is not properly clarified. Such analytical errors notably occur when studying complex economic issues:[19]

> The element of time is a chief cause of those difficulties in economic investigations which make it necessary for man with his limited powers to go step by step; breaking up a complex question, studying one bit at a time, and at last combining his partial solutions into a more or less complete solution of the whole riddle. [. . .] The study of some group of tendencies is isolated by the assumption other things being equal: the existence of other tendencies is not denied, but their disturbing effect is neglected for a time. The more the issue is thus narrowed, the more exactly can it be handled: but also the less closely does it correspond to real life.

Marshall approaches economic problems by breaking history up into periods, that is by drawing a distinction between the "short period" and the "long period". When an economist limits his reasoning to the "short period", he deliberately leaves out a whole range of tendencies or effects, for the sake of simplifying. He is then reasoning *ceteris paribus* or "all other things being equal". Leaving out those tendencies and effects has a cost in terms of realism, but it makes it possible to better determine the interactions between the deciding factors of the phenomenon being studied. Then, the economist may shift to a "long period" analysis by reintroducing into his line of reasoning the effects that had been left out. Such a time-slicing technique between "short period" and "long period" is an analytical tool that allows for the separation of different types of effects, thanks to the virtues of abstraction, in order to later reassemble them once their contributions and interactions have been studied within a simplified framework.[20]

Marshall uses this period analysis method to study how the prices of goods and services come to be, thus highlighting his theory of value. The distinction between "short period" and "long period" is a crucial one to understand why the determining factors of prices are different according to the different time horizons. Whereas in the "short period" the production capacity is fixed – quantity of work, of aptitudes, of

---

[19] See Marshall (1890), Book V, chapter 5, p. 304.
[20] The distinction Marshall (1890) draws between "short period" and "long period" is the source of Keynes's *The General Theory of Employment, Interest and Money* (1936), which focuses on an economy in which "adjustments" are limited, much more so than in the theories of classical economists. It is this economic theory of the short period that Hicks (1937) will reformulate in his IS-LM model.

knowledge, of machines, etc. – this does not hold true when looking at the "long period", during which all of those quantities have time to adjust. Consequently, whereas an increase in demand for a productincreases its price in the "short period", it may not be the case in the "long period" because, in the long period, the capacities of production have had the time to adjust, leading to the increasing supply of that good.[21] A theory of value cannot afford not to recognise the distinction between "short period" and "long period".

The division between "short period" and "long period" is not, according to Marshall, decided once and for all but, on the contrary, depends on the phenomenon being studied.[22]

Of course there is no hard and sharp line of division between "long" and "short" periods. Nature has drawn no such lines in the economic conditions of actual life; [...] If it is necessary for the purposes of any particular argument to divide one case sharply from the other, it can be done by a special interpretation clause [...].

In the case of value analysis, Marshall makes a distinction between four types of prices, with each price being dependent on both supply and demand. By focusing on the analysis of prices within different periods, it becomes possible to isolate the price of certain determining factors. *Market price* is the norm when demand is equal to stocked supply. *Normal price* insures that supply and demand remain equal when the former can adjust over a period of a few months to one year (by an adjustment of the cadences of production for a given number of workers, machines and factories). A second *normal price* ("normal" taking on here a different meaning) is the name of the price that equalises supply and demand, supply being adjustable over periods of several years thanks to the mobility of the production factors between sectors. Finally, Marshall touches on the *secular movements* in prices that are linked to the growth of knowledge, population and capital.

1.3.2 The Fiction of the Stationary Equilibrium

Whereas Marshall recommends that we draw a distinction between "short period" and "long period", economic analysis relies usually – since Smith (1776), Ricardo (1817) and Mill (1848) – on what is called a stationary equilibrium or steady state. That (purely fictitious) state of the economy is reached when the general conditions of production, consumption, distribution and exchange stop changing, that is when all those conditions are no longer in motion.[23]

In this steady state, the prices of goods are equal to their "normal" or "natural" level – the level that, according to Smith (1776), can compensate all of the production factors at their normal rate. This "normal" compensation of the production factors

---

[21] See Marshall (1890), pp. 307–308.   [22] See Marshall (1890), p. 314.

[23] Such a fiction is obviously not devoid of all movement: it is possible, for example, for some companies to disappear while others replace them, or for some individuals to die while others are born, but the general conditions of production, consumption, distribution and exchange, in this fictitious economic state, remain *by definition* on average unchanged.

(labour, capital, land) insures the stability of the sectoral structure of the economy: since the production factors are paid at the same rate for *all* sectors, there is no motivation to reallocate factors from one sector to another.

Marshall recognises that this theory has the advantage of being simple, but he nonetheless highlights a major problem: this theory only holds true in the steady state, not outside of it. The steady state is but a theoretical fiction, which diminishes the descriptive scope of that theory of value.[24]

> But nothing of this is true in the world in which we live. Here every economic force is constantly changing its action, under the influence of other forces which are acting around it. Here changes in the volume of production, in its methods, and in its cost are ever mutually modifying one another; they are always affecting and being affected by the character and the extent of demand. Further all these mutual influences take time to work themselves out, and, as a rule, no two influences move at equal pace. In this world therefore every plain and simple doctrine as to the relations between cost of production, demand and value is necessarily false [...]

According to Marshall, the stationary equilibrium presents the major inconvenience of placing the economy "outside of time" by erasing time from the analysis. By concentrating on the study of the stationary equilibrium, a fictitious state in which all variables have had the time to adjust, we are missing the most important element: *the different adjustments that lead to that equilibrium.* Rather than studying the steady state, Marshall instead recommended to analyse the adjustments of elements towards the steady state, with each adjustment retaining its own temporality.[25]

1.4   Kondratiev

If we were to choose but one economist among those who have attempted to go beyond the study of the stationary equilibrium in order to analyse the evolution of economic elements over time, Kondratiev would be a rather obvious choice. In his very first writings, Kondratiev likened the stationary equilibrium to a purely static equilibrium:[26]

> [Economic research] is not interested in the material constitution of the economy but in production capacity and management, the nature of consumption and demand, prices, etc. But, from a purely economic viewpoint, in a stationary economy, all these elements are assumed, by definition, to be invariant. This being the case, what new findings can be provided by the theory of a stationary economy in comparison with the theory of a static economy? In our opinion, precisely none. It seems to us that, from the economic point of view, the static and stationary theories are of necessity coincident.

---

[24] See Marshall (1890), p. 306.

[25] This criticism of the steady state was adopted and further developed in the twentieth century by Kaldor (1985).

[26] See "The Concepts of Economic Statics, Dynamics and Conjuncture" (1924), in Kondratiev, p. 8.

Kondratiev's work aims to free economic analysis from the limits imposed by the stationary equilibrium. In *Long Cycles of Economic Conjuncture*, Kondratiev (1928) offered an empirical and theoretical study of the movements of prices and production volumes over a period going from the end of the eighteenth century to the beginning of the twentieth century.

1.4.1 Quantitative and Qualitative Changes

In a 1924 text, Kondratiev introduces a whole series of conceptual distinctions with the goal of clarifying the analysis of the change of economic elements over time. A first fundamental distinction is made between "quantitative changes" and "qualitative changes":[27]

We essentially divide these into processes of qualitative and quantitative change. When the elements of economic life or the connections between these are subject to changes which are not limited to changes in their number or size and cannot, in general, be reduced to quantitative changes, we shall talk of the presence of qualitative changes.

The "qualitative changes" account for the idea that, over time, it is not solely the level of the variables that change, but that the *shape of the relationships* that link these variables also evolves.[28] Kondratiev gives several examples of "qualitative changes": changes in production techniques, in the organisation of the economy and in social needs. The technical evolutions modify the relationships between the production factors, whereas the changes in the organisation of the economy influence relationships between individuals.[29]

If one is reasoning over a short period, these elements remain constant, so that there are no "qualitative changes", only variations in the levels of economic quantities, that is to say only "quantitative" changes. But the long period is precisely where "qualitative changes" occur, and those changes need to be studied.

1.4.2 Reversible and Irreversible Processes

Alongside the distinction between "quantitative changes" and "qualitative changes", Kondratiev (1924) also introduced a second distinction, the one that exists between "irreversible" economic processes and "reversible" economic processes:[30]

[by] dividing dynamic processes into evolutionary processes (that is, non-repeatable or irreversible processes) and wave-like processes (repeatable or reversible). By *evolutionary* or

---

[27] Kondratiev (1924), p. 9.

[28] Kondratiev (1924), p. 9. Kondratiev (1924) does not a priori reject the possibility that any qualitative change may, after multiple analyses, be in the end "reduced" to a sum of quantitative changes. The possibility of such a reduction does not alter the scope of the distinction proposed by Kondratiev, which would then take the form of a distinction between quantitative changes of various orders.

[29] The analysis in Marx of the sequence of modes of production corresponds to a study of qualitative changes in Kondratiev.

[30] See Kondratiev (1924), pp. 9–10.

irreversible processes, we understand those changes which, in the absence of abrupt external perturbing effects, take place in a specific single direction. As an example, we may point to the constant tendency of population size to increase, the increasing overall production capacity, etc. [...].

By wave-like processes (repeatable or reversible), we understand those change processes having a direction at a given time, which they subsequently vary constantly, so that from being in a given state at a given time and then a changing state, a phenomenon may sooner or later return to the original state. Examples of such processes include changes in market prices, interest rates on capital, the percentage of unemployed, etc.

Although many variables may change direction at any time, there generally is a *general orientation* of these changes, a kind of concordance between these variations. It is this general orientation of the changes, this concordance in the direction of the variations that Kondratiev defines as the "economic conjuncture".[31]

In *Long Cycles of Economic Conjuncture*, Kondratiev (1928) studies the reversible economic processes and, specifically, the general orientation of the movements of the elements with respect to their previous positions. For this purpose, Kondratiev develops the method of deviations from the normal trend, a trend represented by an estimated function using the least squares method. Focusing his analysis mainly on England and France, Kondratiev estimates this normal trend – which he calls "theoretical series" – for statistics such as prices, wages, interest rates, production volumes and foreign trade revenues. The study of the deviations in these theoretical series reveals the existence of long cycles that last more than fifty years.

1.4.3 Long-Run Cycles

Kondratiev's calculations lead him to identify two cycles and the beginning of a third one:[32] a first long cycle, whose upward wave took place between the end of the 1780s and the years 1810–1817 and whose downward wave lasted from the years 1810–1817 to the years 1844–1851; a second long cycle, whose upward phase covered the years 1844–1851 to the years 1870–1875, while its downward phase occurred between the years 1870–1875 and the years 1890–1896. Kondratiev's third cycle is only partly identified: its upward wave was thought to have begun around the years 1891–1896, ending around the years 1914–1920, while its downward phase was thought to have begun after 1920.

Alongside the identification of these long cycles, Kondratiev also lays down several "empirical principles".[33] First, before and at the start of each upward wave, the economy undergoes profound changes, in terms of inventions and technical changes, but also in terms of currency circulation or trade relations. Second, it is during upward waves that major social upheavals take place (notably wars and revolutions). Third, the period of the downward wave is accompanied by a great agricultural recession.

Kondratiev offers an explanation for the existence of long cycles. According to him, long cycles are associated with the movement of investment linked to the renewal

---

[31] See Kondratiev (1924), p. 20.   [32] See Kondratiev (1928), p. 36.   [33] See Kondratiev (1928), p. 38.

and expansion of large basic equipment that is durable and characterised by long life spans. Each upward wave is linked to a large investment in these basic facilities (such as railways), whereas these investments do not take place during the downward waves.

Kondratiev's work has been the subject of much criticism since its publication. A fundamental criticism, formulated by Oparine (1928), concerns the lack of robustness of the "theoretical curve" around which long cycles are measured. This lack of robustness affects not only the magnitude of the cycles or their dating, but also their number. Oparine also questions the existence of long cycles for volume variables. Closer to home, Solomou (1987) has used the modern tools of econometric time series analysis to re-evaluate Kondratiev's work and he draws some rather critical conclusions regarding the existence of such long cycles.

1.5   Rostow

Kondratiev's analyses have been innovative in many ways, both at the conceptual and applied levels. However, they leave unexplored a fundamental question: what determines the famous "theoretical trend" around which cyclical movements take place? Is it possible to construct a general theory of the economic development of human societies?

In *The Stages of Economic Growth*, Rostow (1960) proposed a general theory of the economic history of societies. This meant carrying out an ambitious "generalization", by constructing an economic theory of the long period that includes as specific cases *all* societies and *all* periods of history:[34]

This book presents an economic historian's way of generalizing the sweep of modern history. This form of generalization is a set of stages-of-growth.

I have gradually come to the view that it is possible and, for certain limited purposes, it is useful to break down the story of each national economy – and sometimes the story of regions – according to this set of stages. They constitute, in the end, both a theory about economic growth and a more general, if still highly partial, theory about modern history as a whole.

According to Rostow, the development process of societies includes five stages:

(1) the traditional society;
(2) setting up the pre-conditions for growth;
(3) the economic take-off;
(4) the maturity;
(5) the mass consumption society.

Any society, regardless of its geographical location or the period under consideration, is at one of these stages along the economic development process.

---

[34] See Rostow (1960), p. 1.

1.5.1   From the Traditional Society to the Economic Take-off

A traditional society is a nearly static society where the standard of living is low, where production techniques are limited and where the size of the population cannot, due to the reduced possibilities of consumption, grow significantly. Inventions can certainly take place in this nearly static society, but technical progress remains limited. In a traditional society, the level of productivity is low, so that the population has to spend a significant part of its income on subsistence alone.

Agricultural activity occupies about 75% of the workforce in a traditional society. Economic and political power is held by landowners. A traditional society is also characterised by very low level of social mobility: family ties and clans play a key role in the organisation of society. This society is also in a state of great vulnerability: the size of the population as well as the standard of living adjust according to the sequence of harvests, epidemics, conflicts and wars.

Rostow gives several examples of these traditional societies: the world of medieval Europe, the Chinese dynasties, the civilisations of the Middle East and the Mediterranean. This first stage in the process of the economic development of societies can last several centuries or even several millennia.

It is only when certain transformations occur that societies enter the second stage of the development process. These transformations provide the pre-conditions for economic take-off. In the case of Europe, Rostow situates these transformations towards the end of the seventeenth century and the beginning of the eighteenth century.

Transformations occur at several levels. First of all, the presence of important scientific progress makes new production techniques possible. The agricultural sector – the most important sector in a traditional economy – benefits from substantial technical progress, which increases production yields. This is one of the pre-conditions for the later possibility of a take-off of the economy. During this transitional phase, knowledge becomes more widespread among the population, thanks to a wider dissemination of education, geared to accompany the changes in technology.

However, other fundamental transformations also take place. At the institutional level, a centralised and efficient national state is gradually being built. The building of the national state will encourage the implementation of policies that will promote take-off, such as the construction of public infrastructure and of facilities, particularly in the transport sector. This is a second pre-condition for the process of economic take-off.

During this transition phase, national trade strengthens, as does international trade, which leads to an increase in export-related revenues. These transformations are linked to the development of the transport infrastructure, which in turn leads to the emergence of a larger market economy. Another pre-condition for economic take-off is the development of a banking sector that will later enable the mobilisation of significant funds for investment. In the face of all these changes, the social structure undergoes changes: with the process of urbanisation, the city bourgeoisie seizes power from the landowners.

These conditions at the technical, institutional and cultural levels lead to the advent of the third stage of the development process: the economic take-off. The economic take-off consists of the establishment of a *sustainable* growth in the production per capita:[35]

We come now to the great watershed in the life of modern societies: the third stage of this sequence, the take-off. The take-off is the interval when the old blocks and resistances to steady growth are finally overcome. The forces making for economic progress, which yielded limited bursts and enclaves of modern activity, expand and come to dominate the society. Growth becomes its normal condition. Compound interest becomes built, as it were, into its habits and institutional structure.

This great "watershed" evoked by Rostow occurs once the transformations mentioned above have reached a certain critical threshold.[36] Often, a particular *stimulus* will promote the emergence of this "watershed": this *stimulus* may take the form of a major technological breakthrough or a new (more favourable) international environment. In the cases of England, France and the United States, the economic take-off is associated with a major technological revolution: the mechanisation of production. This technological revolution had major consequences in the transportation sector, with the introduction of railways. The railways contributed to the economic take-off in those countries, allowing the extension of the size of markets (and therefore of trade), while driving entire industrial sectors: coal mining, mechanics, metallurgy.

The take-off process has several facets:[37]

For the present purposes the take-off is defined as requiring all three of the following related conditions:

(1) a rise in the rate of productive investment from, say, 5 per cent or less to over 10 per cent of national income (or net national product (NNP));
(2) the development of one or more substantial manufacturing sectors, with a high rate of growth;
(3) the existence or quick emergence of a political, social and institutional framework that exploits the impulses to expansion in the modern sector and the potential external economy effects of the take-off and gives to growth an ongoing character.

Achieving sustainable growth in production requires an expansion of production capacity, which is achieved through an unprecedented investment effort. The economic take-off is also a phase during which new industries develop and the industrial sector becomes increasingly important in relation to the agricultural sector (the dominant sector in the traditional economy). In the case of England, France, Germany or the United States, the take-off was accompanied by strong growth in the mechanical engineering, mining and metallurgical industries. As for the third dimension of take-off, it concerns the emergence of a political, social and institutional framework that is favourable to growth and that will make seeking growth a sustainable objective for those societies.

According to Rostow, the first economic take-off took place in Great Britain around the years 1783–1802. Then came the take-off in France (1830–1860), Belgium

---

[35] See Rostow (1960), p. 7.   [36] See Rostow (1960), p. 36.   [37] See Rostow (1960), p. 39.

(1833–1860), the United States (1843–1860) and Germany (1850–1873). Rostow dates Japan's take-off period to the period between 1878 and 1900. Then came Russia (1890–1914), Canada (1896–1914), Argentina (1935), India (1952) and China (1952).[38]

1.5.2 Economic Growth as a Succession of Take-offs

After the take-off stage, which generally lasts about twenty years, the economy enters a fourth phase: the march towards maturity. During this phase, which lasts about three generations (sixty years), modern technology is disseminated to all economic sectors and output per capita continues to grow steadily.

One of the main characteristics of the move towards maturity is that the sectors that had driven the take-off in the past enter into crisis and lead to a reallocation of resources to new sectors. These sectors then develop and gradually take the place of the sectors that had contributed to the take-off of the economy:[39]

Once having overshot the mark in the key sectors of a first take-off surge, it is necessary for the economy to regroup and re-allocate its resources for a resumption of growth in new leading sectors. Structurally this is the nature and the historic function of a trade depression. It has been normal, therefore, for the take-off to end with a trade depression; and one measure of take-off having been achieved is a society's ability to regroup its resources effectively and to accelerate expansion in a new set of leading sectors.

In the case of Europe, the main activities thus shifted during the twentieth century from the coal, steel and mechanical engineering sectors to those of chemical industry, electrical installations and machine tools.[40] Once these sectoral changes have taken place, the phenomenon of output per capita growth becomes robust: at first driven by certain sectors of activity, it is then fed by the development of other sectors. Rostow depicts the growth process as a succession of take-offs, in the sense that flagship sectors hand over to other flagship sectors, and so on.

The fifth – and final – stage is the era of mass consumption. In this last stage, improved standards of living and sustainable income growth drive individuals to spend their money on more than just meeting their basic needs. Most of the population is urban, educated and has high aspirations.

To meet these new expectations, the sectors driving growth change towards consumer durables (cars, household appliances) and services. These are the sectors that will drive the growth process into the era of mass consumption. Rostow illustrates this change with the diffusion of the automobile in different societies around the world over the period 1900–1958.[41]

---

[38] See Rostow (1960), p. 40.   [39] See Rostow (1960), pp. 62–63.

[40] It should be noted that this is not the only change in the sectoral structure of the economy. Rostow also explains that the share of agricultural employment in total employment, which was 75% before take-off and 40% after take-off, continues to fall and reaches 20% in the mature stage.

[41] Over this period, the number of private cars in the United States increased from 8,000 to 56,645,000, from one car per 10,000 inhabitants in 1900 to about one car per 3 inhabitants in 1958.

In short, for Rostow, the analysis of the long term is, above all, the study of the gradual *modernisation* of economies. It examines the different stages of diffusion of new techniques and new goods or services within populations. The starting point for this analysis is the exiting from a traditional society model – the take-off phenomenon – and then the succession of new take-offs that ensure sustainable growth for the economy. It should be noted, however, that Rostow warns the reader against reducing the stages of growth to a simple study of the output per capita curve:[42]

It would have made my task much easier in *The Stages* if I could have accepted GNP per capita as a legitimate measure of stages of growth and proceeded to associate that measure with changing structures and leading sectors as Colin Clark, Kuznets, and Chenery [...] have done. There are statistical associations to be made on that basis; but the averages that emerge with such statistical elegance are flawed.

They are flawed because GNP per capita is determined by a number of variables that do not link to the degree to which technologies are absorbed in the economy.

For Rostow, while output per capita growth does account for part of the development process over the long period, that process is by no means reducible to that growth alone. The latter is a highly aggregated way of measuring a complex process of change, the core of which is the dynamics of the sectoral structure of the economy, as well as societal and cultural changes.

Rostow's work has attracted a great deal of criticism. Myrdal (1968) denounces an almost "mechanical" view of the historical process, while Kuznets (in Rostow, 1963) considers growth to be primarily a global phenomenon and not a sectoral process as Rostow argues. Other criticisms relate to the dating of periods of take-off, as well as to the impossibility of including each national economic history in a broad theoretical generalisation (see Rostow, 1963).

1.6   Solow and the Modern Theory of Growth

One the most important criticisms of *The Stages of Economic Growth* is to be found at the methodological level and it is the work of Solow (1963), one of the fathers of the modern theory of economic growth. According to Solow (1963):[43]

Any model designed to describe the behaviour of an economic system over time generally comprised three important components: rules of behaviour, parameters, and initial conditions.

Solow (1963) regrets that Rostow's theory is not formulated in these terms, that is, it does not take the form of a dynamic mathematical system that, starting from the initial conditions of the variables, would allow for the study of the evolution of these variables according to the structural parameters of the economy. This approach, inspired by physics, has become the standard approach adopted by economists when studying the long period.

---

[42] See Rostow (1960), p. 197.   [43] See Solow in Rostow (1963), pp. 468–476.

Rostow (1963) replied to Solow that it was possible, in part, to translate his theory in those terms. To do so, modelling the take-off would require, as initial conditions, a prior accumulation of collective equipment allowing modern techniques to diffuse to the whole economy. Moreover, the parameters could include the population growth rate, as well as a certain state of technology. But Rostow did not believe that such a reformulation of his theory would be useful:[44]

In sum, the ultimate reasons the approach to growth via mainstream economics is misleading are that cultural, social, and political factors are all at work as well as economic factors; and that the process of growth is inherently interactive, yielding not only changes in the parameters but even in the rules of behavior. In a sense, there can be no formal theory of growth of the kind held up as a goal by Solow until there is a unified theory of both human beings and the societies they construct out of their multi-dimensional complexity. This is what Alfred Marshall, a mathematician by training, understood better than any modern economist.

Rostow stresses the need for a "unified" theory that takes into account the complexity of interactions of humans with their social environment. The remainder of this book is devoted to the presentation of such a "unified" theory of the long period. But before presenting such a theory, let us look at the modern approach to economic growth defended by Solow: the modelling of economic dynamics using a mathematical model that includes initial conditions, rules of evolution and parameters. To do so, we will study Solow's growth model (1956).

1.6.1 Initial Conditions, the Production Function and the "Race" between Factors

Solow's model (1956) aims to explain the growth of the output per capita in the nineteenth and twentieth centuries. The two variables in this model are, on the one hand, the stock of physical capital, that is the set of tools and machines available for production, and, on the other hand, the size of the population that, in this model, corresponds to the number of workers. The description of the economy includes initial conditions for these two variables.

In Solow's economy, the production process is represented with the help of a production function that assigns a quantity of output to each quantity of capital and labour. In the spirit of Walras (1874), Solow supposes that the production function has constant returns to scale, that is, that the multiplication of the quantities of capital and labour by the same constant C leads to an *output* that is also multiplied by this constant C. Solow writes the production function in intensive terms: the output per capita as an increasing and concave function of the ratio of capital per worker, that is, as a function of the capital intensity of the economy.

Let us now present the rules for the evolution of that economy. In the discrete-time version of this model, it is assumed that the population size grows at a rate n (considered, in the main part of the paper, as a constant), while the capital stock accumulates according to a simple rule; the capital stock at time t is equal to the sum

---

[44] See Rostow (1960), p. 247.

of the non-depreciated part of the capital stock at time $t - 1$ and investment, which here is equal to savings. Solow rewrites the capital accumulation equation in intensive terms, by dividing the left and right sides of this equation by the size of the population at time t, and thus obtains an equation that describes the dynamics of the capital to labour ratio.

At this stage, it is useful to specify that Solow's model is part of the debate about the possibility or impossibility of "balanced growth", that is, growth in which labour and capital grow at the same rate, leading to a stationary capital to worker ratio. Harrod (1939) had demonstrated the impossibility, under a function of production with perfect complementarity of factors, of a "balanced" growth of output. Solow, thanks to a production function allowing for a certain substitution between factors, shows on the contrary that balanced growth is possible.

For Solow, the growth process takes the form of a "race" between the "capital" and "labour" factors. When capital accumulates faster than labour, the capital intensity increases and output per capita grows. The stock of capital per worker is constant only when the actual investment in the economy is exactly equal to the investment that ensures the constancy of the capital intensity, that is, the hypothetical investment that exactly compensates for both population growth and depreciation of existing capital stock.

Solow shows that, under general assumptions, there exists a stationary equilibrium, a value of the capital to labour ratio that will reproduce itself exactly the same over time. For this level of the capital to labour ratio, the actual investment in the economy is equal to the investment that ensures the constancy of capital intensity. Solow also shows that, under general assumptions, an economy will, whatever the initial conditions, converge in the long term towards this stationary state. Starting from a low capital intensity, the economy initially has an actual level of investment higher than the hypothetical level of investment required to keep the capital intensity constant, so that the capital to labour ratio increases. Such an increase will last until a stationary state is reached. Once the stationary state is reached, output per capita is constant, while output growth is balanced: capital stock and population size grow at the same rate.

Solow's model proposes an explanation for the growth in output per capita: this phenomenon finds its source in an increase in the capital intensity of the production process. In other words, the growth of the output per capita comes from the fact that workers are endowed with an increasingly important quantity of capital.

1.6.2   Beyond the Stationary State: Endogenous Growth Theory

In Solow's economy, the total output grows, in the long run, at an exogenous rate: the population growth rate (taken, in the basic model, as a constant). It is that result that will be called into question in the 1980s and 1990s, with the emergence of the so-called "endogenous growth" theory – in contrast to the "exogenous growth" theory attributed to Solow. The objective of this reformulation of the growth theory is to represent the rate of growth of the output in the long term as an endogenous variable explained by the functioning of the economy.

The endogenous growth theory also aims to depart from one of the predictions of Solow's model in its basic version: in the long term, the output per capita is constant, so that there is no longer any economic growth. This new theory of growth, which will be developed by Lucas (1988), Romer (1990), Barro (1990), Kremer (1993) and Aghion and Howitt (1998), puts forward various mechanisms at work in the economy (positive externalities linked to capital accumulation, technological progress, accumulation of human capital, scale effects), mechanisms that make the *self-reinforcement of growth* possible and guarantee that the economy will experience a sustainable expansion of the output per capita over the long run.

While endogenous growth theory has enriched the mathematical models of economic dynamics, the distinction between "exogenous growth" theory and "endogenous growth" theory should not be overstated. This is the first lesson that Solow (2000) draws from his assessment of half a century of growth studies:[45]

First of all, I think that it is a mistake to dichotomize growth theory into an "exogenous" and an "endogenous" branch. Every area of economic theory will have to stop somewhere; it will rest on some exogenous elements. Some of those exogenous elements will be sociological in character, and some will even be economic. Physics may be able to contemplate a "theory of everything" without smiling, but that will not be so of economics for as far as the eye can see, and maybe forever.

Solow (2000) draws a second lesson about the excessive attention growth theorists pay to the steady state. Solow considers that growth theory has not paid enough attention to the trajectories taken by economies that are not in a state of equilibrium or are in a state of transition.[46] It is true that growth theory has not only studied the steady state, but has also examined its uniqueness and stability; it answers the question of why the economy tends to converge towards this equilibrium regardless of the initial conditions. This study of stability leads to the exclusion of certain trajectories as theoretically impossible. However, very often the models only admit a single steady state that is also stable, so that the study of trajectories that are outside the equilibrium generally takes a back seat.

Solow invites theorists to further study out-of-equilibrium trajectories, in a spirit reminiscent of Marshall's critique of the stationary state. Although formulated in different contexts (before and after the mathematisation of economic thought), these criticisms point in the same direction: from the point of view of the economic analysis of the long period, the study of the transition is as important as that of the long-term equilibrium. This desire to orient the analysis more towards trajectories rather than towards the long-term equilibrium naturally leads us to the Unified Growth Theory. Over the last twenty years, this theory has sought to fulfil a wish shared by both Marshall and Solow.

---

[45] See Solow (2000), pp. 180–181.   [46] See Solow (2000), pp. 181–182.

1.7   Towards a Genealogy of Unified Growth Theory?

This chapter has presented several economic theories of the long period. Each theory proposes a global vision of the long-term evolution of societies, a vision developed with the help of a very specific conceptual apparatus: "means of subsistence", "production modes", "long cycles", "take-off", etc.

This diversion through the history of ideas brings to light some "features" that Unified Growth Theory has received "as a legacy". As always in matters of inheritance, time has made a certain selection of inherited traits. No theoretical framework – neither Unified Growth Theory nor any other theory – could synthesise all at once the analyses of Malthus, Marx or Solow. As the latter pointed out, a theory – even a theory of the long period – cannot be a "theory of everything". An inventory of the "inherited traits" of Unified Growth Theory will enable us to draw *a first outline of this theory* and its main characteristics.

The first salient feature of Unified Growth Theory can be found at the methodological level. Unified Growth Theory takes the form of a modern growth theory as Solow defines it. This theory is a study of dynamic mathematical systems describing the evolution of economic variables over time. It includes the three "basic materials" mentioned by Solow: initial conditions, rules of evolution and parameters.

At the methodological level, another major feature of Unified Growth Theory is that it pays great attention to the analysis of the trajectories taken by an economy, rather than to the study of stationary states alone. This emphasis on transitions – on their explanation, replication or "rationalisation" – is in line with Marshall's critiques and, more recently, the lessons drawn by Solow.

Another fundamental feature is that Unified Growth Theory does not limit itself to the study of quantitative changes, but also analyses qualitative changes as defined by Kondratiev (and as studied by Marx). As we shall see, Unified Growth Theory is a theory of the transition from one economic regime to another, each regime being characterised by its own laws or relationships between variables.

In addition to this methodological legacy – the study of a dynamic system, emphasis on transitions and qualitative changes – three other "inherited traits" of Unified Growth Theory concern the themes it addresses.

As an economic theory of the long period, Unified Growth Theory generally includes a so-called "Malthusian" regime, that is, a regime that explains economic stagnation by means of demographic pressure. In a sense, Galor's work has put the Malthusian doctrine back at the centre of growth theory, making it the first regime to be studied, the one that serves as the starting point for the evolution of all societies.[47]

Another "salient feature" of Unified Growth Theory lies in a theme that it explores: the take-off of the economy. The theme of take-off, key in Rostow, is at the heart of Unified Growth Theory, even if its formalisation is not always faithful to the way in

---

[47] We should note that Galor's (2011) modelling of the Malthusian regime is but one formalisation amongst others (such as Eltis 1984) of Malthus's thinking. We will revisit this question in Chapter 3.

which Rostow conceived it.[48] Take-off is here modelled as a regime change. Although Unified Growth Theory cannot be summarised by studying take-off alone, it is undeniable that take-off is the canonical example of regime change.

A final contribution, related to historical materialism, is worth highlighting. Unified Growth Theory has not borrowed that doctrine: although it may include antagonisms between social groups, it does not make it a central theme.[49] On the other hand, a feature of historical materialism does appear in Unified Growth Theory, but in a more general form. Within historical materialism, social transformations are related to the state of development of the "productive forces" that, at some point, reaches a critical threshold leading to transformations. Unified Growth Theory, for its part, also uses this type of explanation, under the term "latent dynamics", even if the dynamics at the origin of regime change do not necessarily concern the "productive forces".[50]

In short, the inventory of the "traits" that Unified Growth Theory shares with its "ancestors" reveals a first outline of that theory, although it remains largely incomplete. The reason for this incompleteness is simple: the highlighted "inherited traits" lead to an outline of Unified Growth Theory as a theoretical object. Such a description leaves aside an entire aspect of the theory: *its relationship to the facts*. Any theory is constructed as an attempt to describe and explain several (recorded) facts. The object of any theoretical construction is to tell us something about the world around us. What is true for a theory in general is also true for Unified Growth Theory.

The facts studied by scientists are certainly not independent of theories, as the empirical bases (recording of facts, measurement procedures) are conditioned by theoretical constructs. However, the presentation of a theory cannot dispense with the study of the facts that motivated its construction, the facts that it tries to explain. The next chapter will pursue this task.

---

[48] The variables included in Rostow's conception of take-off do not always correspond to the variables implied in the version of take-off found in unified growth models (chapters 4 and following).

[49] Marx (1858) described Smith's (1776) and Ricardo's (1817) analyses of "singularised" or isolated individuals (the examples of the hunter or the fisherman) as "Robinsonades", in which production relationships are ignored. As many unified growth models also ignore production relationships, they could be subject to this criticism. We are not arguing that historical materialism has been adopted by Unified Growth Theory but, more modestly, that the idea of latent process, present in Marx, can also be found in this theory.

[50] Within Unified Growth Theory, numerous variables, not only population size or physical capital stock, can act as latent dynamics (see Chapters 5 and 6).

2   Empirical Elements

The economic analysis of the long period, like any true "economic" analysis, studies the struggle of men and women against resource scarcity. The specificity of this field of study in relation to the discipline of economics in general concerns the *time horizon* studied.

As Marshall (1890) pointed out, there is no precise criterion for characterising the "long period".[1] The "long period" is defined as the time horizon that allows the adjustment of as many economic variables as possible: production, technology, population size, knowledge, lifestyles, etc. While it cannot be measured precisely, the time interval during which all these adjustments take place is necessarily long and extends over several centuries or even longer.

The starting point for the economic analysis of the long period is the study of statistical series presenting economic variables over a long time horizon. For many years, economists did not have access to such statistical series and based their analyses on a few tables of numbers that they had constructed by themselves.

The pioneers of seventeenth-century English political arithmetic, Petty (1687) and King (1699), based their study of the population of major English cities using data from parish registers that collected records of baptisms, marriages and burials. These sources allowed them to extrapolate aggregate figures and even general trends in population dynamics. For example, it was by comparing the number of burials in London in 1605, 1642 and 1682 that Petty (1687) was able to deduce, under some assumptions, that over that period the population of London was doubling every forty years.[2]

At the same time, Boisguilbert (1697, 1707) and Vauban (1707) proposed, in various writings, tax reforms designed to remedy the "ruin of France". According to these authors, that "ruin" was caused by heavy indirect taxation that reduced domestic demand, leaving much of the land uncultivated. The proposed tax reforms – replacing multiple indirect taxes with direct taxation – were based on figures (notably royal tax revenues or "Revenus du roi" over several reigns) scattered throughout their writings.[3]

---

[1] See Chapter 1.

[2] According to parish registers, the number of registered burials in London was 5,135 in 1605, 11,883 in 1642 and 22,331 in 1682. By assuming, as Petty (1687) did, a constant force of mortality, one can extrapolate from this series that London's population doubled in size approximately every forty years.

[3] Boisguilbert proposed to abolish internal and external customs and toll duties (*Douanes intérieures et extérieures*) and the indirect tax on the sale of wine (*Aides*), setting up instead an income tax. For his

The situation is quite different at the beginning of the twenty-first century when, conversely, a researcher is almost overwhelmed by the quantity of databases covering various dimensions of the economy. This reversal has its origins, on the one hand, in the creation of national statistical institutes in the mid-twentieth century and, on the other hand, in the emergence of information technology; this has facilitated the construction, and later the development, of very large databases.[4] As a result, the question facing researchers today is rather: which statistical series should be chosen from among the wealth of existing series? The answer to this question depends on which part of reality the researcher wishes to shed light on in his work.

Considering that this book aims at studying the struggle against resource scarcity, it is necessary to focus first on data that capture, as summarily as possible, what this struggle against scarcity is all about. In this chapter, we will consider the time series relating to:

- the production of goods and services by humans (Section 2.1);
- the production of humans themselves (Section 2.2).

We will then study the relationship between these two production processes, that is, the level of production per capita (Section 2.3). While Sections 2.1 to 2.3 will focus on the raw data, the next sections will attempt to go beyond a descriptive analysis of facts in order to propose a first "reading grid" to synthesise these trends. To do so, Section 2.4 will mobilise the distinction introduced by Kondratiev (1924) between "quantitative changes" and "qualitative changes". This analysis will lead us to introduce the notion of "economic regime" (Section 2.5). We will then be able, in Section 2.6, to explain the emergence of Unified Growth Theory as an attempt to theorise or "rationalise" the structural breaks observed in the statistical series of output per capita over the last few centuries.

2.1   Production

One way to approach, with the help of statistical series, the human struggle against scarcity is to study the most widely used indicator of production, gross domestic product (GDP), which summarises in a single figure the mass of goods and market services produced in an economy over a period of one year. As Nordhaus (2000) points out, GDP is a kind of "satellite" sent into space, giving us a global, synthetic picture of the scale of economic activity in a country. GDP is a global measure of the "economic performance of nations" as described by North (1994), that is, their ability to overcome scarcity in all its forms.[5]

---

part, Vauban favoured replacing most taxes with a single tax: the royal tithe (*Dîme Royale*), a direct tax, collected on all revenue sources and paid by the entire population (suppression of privileges).

[4] This evolution is described by Le Roy Ladurie (1973).

[5] However, it is worth noting the very imperfect nature of GDP as a measure of the economic performance of nations. This indicator focuses on the production of tradable goods and services, leaving aside many dimensions of the struggle against scarcity. Nordhaus and Tobin (1972) proposed that GDP should be corrected to incorporate leisure time, valued at the hourly wage rate.

GDP is an indicator that was developed in the middle of the twentieth century and has been calculated for each country on an annual basis from that period onward. This indicator has also subsequently been used retrospectively for estimations about earlier periods, in order to obtain a more accurate picture of the dynamics of production over a longer period of time.

2.1.1   The Global Trend

Figure 2.1 shows the evolution of world GDP between year 1 and the beginning of the twenty-first century, with all countries here grouped into one economy, the global economy. These data come from the statistical series developed by the historian-economist Maddison, who, during the twentieth century, was one of the pioneers in the compilation and analysis of long time series on production.[6]

As Figure 2.1 shows, we do not have an annual estimate for all the years between year 1 and the mid-nineteenth century, but only estimates for a few years, such as the years 1000, 1500, 1600, 1700 and 1820. Each point in Figure 2.1 presents the level of world production of market goods and services for the year under consideration, measured in a fictitious currency unit: the "1990 international Geary–Khamis dollar".

It is useful, at this point, to explain what this fictitious monetary unit, the "1990 international Geary–Khamis dollar", is and to clarify the functions that this fictitious monetary standard fulfils in the construction of an indicator of world production. In fact, the use of this fictitious currency responds to a double requirement of comparability of production in the different countries: *comparability in space and in time.*

Calculating a GDP for the world economy requires making the productions that take place in the different countries of the world *comparable,* in order to aggregate them into a single indicator of world production. In each country, the production of market goods and services is valued within the GDP on the basis of that country's market prices. The problem is that these prices differ from one country to another, making international comparison of production impossible. The exercise of aggregating the output of different countries into a global GDP requires, first, converting the nominal amounts of output per country into a common monetary standard.

Moreover, constructing a time series of world GDP also requires making countries' output *comparable* at different points in time, that is, correcting for price movements from one year to the next. The objective is to avoid that GDP estimates for two successive years reflect changes in the general price level (inflation) – rather than changes in the quantities produced.

This requirement of double comparability of production – in space and in time – is complex and there are many ways to reach this double objective. To obtain this double comparability, Maddison relies on a widely used technique that consists of measuring

---

[6] Source: Maddison Project (2010). Maddison's work collates, in a single database, estimates of statistical production series from all continents. In France, the pioneering work on the construction of long time series of production is that of Marczewski, Toutain, Markovitch and Fontvieille at the Institut de Sciences Mathématiques et Économiques Appliquées (ISMEA).

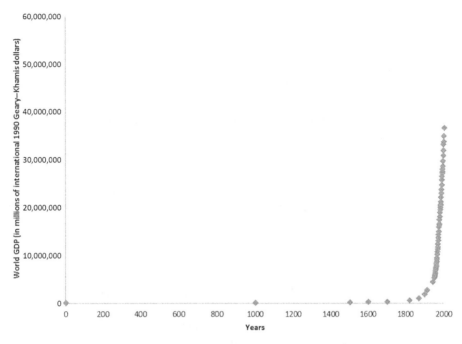

Figure 2.1 World GDP over the last two millennia
(*source*: Maddison Project 2010)

all the production of a country in a common fictitious monetary unit: the "1990 international Geary–Khamis dollar".

The use of this fictitious monetary unit makes it possible to solve the problem of the comparability of productions in space. Indeed, the way this fictitious monetary unit was conceived gives it, in any given country, the same purchasing power as the US dollar in the United States (see Geary, 1958). Valuing the production of national goods and services using the international Geary–Khamis dollar thus makes it possible to make the different productions comparable between countries. The second problem of comparability – that of the comparability of production over time – is solved by adopting the international Geary–Khamis dollar as the standard of measurement for a reference year, 1990.

The main lesson to be drawn from Figure 2.1 is that the phenomenon of GDP growth, which is much talked about at the beginning of the twenty-first century, is, historically speaking, a very recent phenomenon that has taken place over an extremely short period of time.

For centuries, world GDP remained at a relatively stable level and did not experience any growth. The estimated GDP for the year 1500 is thus very close to that of the year 1000, or even that of year 1. These figures are close, but not exactly equal: for example, the world GDP in the year 1000 is about 20% higher than the world GDP in year 1, but a 20% increase over a period of 1000 years is not much. As a first approximation, it can be said that the world economy experienced, until the beginning of the nineteenth century, a long period in which the trend was a near-stagnation of output.

This statement does not mean that there have not been temporary periods of boom and bust. The figures presented in Figure 2.1 do not make it possible for us to know the magnitude of changes in economic conditions, for example, during the first half of the second millennium. Historians' writings testify to very large fluctuations in the economic situation in certain cities.[7] By presenting only a few points for a few years here and there, Figure 2.1 obscures these economic fluctuations.

However, if we adopt a long period perspective, the general trend is what is most important and, from that point of view, the general trend is clearly, over the long period, one of overall stagnation of global GDP. Thus, economic activity has tended not to grow for much of history. On the contrary, there have been centuries of stagnation or near stagnation.

As shown on the right-hand side of Figure 2.1, world GDP grew only very slowly in the eighteenth century. It was not until the early nineteenth century that world GDP began to grow significantly, before experiencing much stronger growth after 1950. Economists generally refer to the process of GDP growth after a long period of stagnation as "economic take-off". This economic take-off at the beginning of the nineteenth century is intrinsically linked to the industrial revolution and the associated productivity growth.[8]

From the point of view of long-period analysis, the fundamental point to be stressed is that the series of world GDP shows a real "structural break" at the beginning of the nineteenth century: after centuries and millennia of near-stagnation, output experienced growth. This "break" in the world GDP series is a stylised fact of primary importance that we will return to at length in the rest of this book. How can we explain that an economy that had experienced a trend of centuries, or even millennia, of (near) stagnation in its total production can suddenly take off and enter a phase of growth? This is one of the fundamental questions addressed by the economic analysis of the long period.

2.1.2   International Comparisons

Figure 2.1 shows the long-term dynamics of global production. It is also possible to describe the evolution of production at less aggregated levels, at the level of continents, sub-continents and even countries. For illustrative purposes, Table 2.1 shows the evolution of GDP for several countries: the United Kingdom, France, the United States, Japan, China and India.

A first observation concerns the general shape of the trajectories of these economies. The countries under consideration originally experienced, for the first 1,500 years, a very long period of near-stagnation of the GDP, with very low GDP growth rates on an annual basis. Throughout this period, the hierarchy of economies in terms

---

[7] See Braudel (1990) on the cyclical variations in several European cities and regions over the 1450–1750 period.

[8] It is worth noting that we use the term "take-off" based solely on the GDP curve. In his analyses, Rostow (1960) used the term "take-off" in a different sense, that did not simply indicate a structural break in the GDP curve (see Chapter 1).

Table 2.1 GDP by country, in millions of 1990 international Geary–Khamis dollars (*source*: Maddison Project 2010)

Years	United Kingdom	France	United States	Japan	China	India
1	320	2,366	272	1,200	26,820	**33,750**
1000	800	2,763	520	3,188	27,494	**33,750**
1500	2,815	10,912	800	7,700	**61,800**	60,500
1700	10,709	19,539	527	15,390	82,800	**90,750**
1820	36,232	35,468	12,548	20,739	**228,600**	111,417
1900	184,861	116,747	**312,499**	52,020	218,154	170,466
1950	347,850	220,492	**1,455,916**	160,966	244,985	222,222
2000	1,211,451	1,248,521	**8,032,209**	2,628,056	4,319,339	1,899,526

of GDP varied little: India and China then had the highest GDPs, well ahead of France, Japan, the United Kingdom and the United States. In the year 1700, this hierarchy of economies around the world remained virtually unchanged.

Then, after this long period of virtual stagnation, the countries experienced a gradual take-off of output, but with significant differences in the timing of that take-off. The differences in the timing of the take-off explain the changes in the GDP hierarchy of those countries. The United Kingdom, France and the United States experienced strong GDP growth as early as the nineteenth century. As a result, in 1900, the hierarchy of economies was profoundly altered. In 1900, the largest economy in the world was the United States, ahead of China and the United Kingdom, with India falling to fourth place. In 1950, this hierarchy changed again slightly, with the United States ahead of the United Kingdom, while India fell further, to fifth place (behind France), with Japan at the bottom of our ranking. The early take-off of the European and North American economies led those countries to the top of the world economic hierarchy.

It was not until the second half of the twentieth century that the Asian countries – Japan, China and India – would in turn experience a take-off in their economies, enabling them to catch up and surpass, in terms of GDP, the United Kingdom and France. In the year 2000, while the United States remains the world's largest economy, China ranks second, Japan third and India fourth. The two European economies – France and the United Kingdom – have fallen back in the rankings, respectively to fifth and sixth place.

In other words, the global GDP curve in Figure 2.1 obscures significant changes over the centuries in the ranking of economies in terms of GDP, changes in hierarchy that are related to different timelines in their take-off.

2.2   Population

2.2.1   The Global Trend

How can we explain that an economy that has known near stagnation of its output for centuries can, at a given time, experience a take-off? When considering this question,

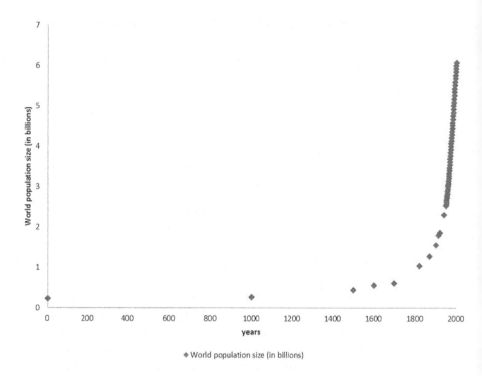

Figure 2.2 World population size over the last two millennia
(*source*: Maddison Project 2010)

the first answer would be to say that the growth in global output is closely linked to the growth in global population. Indeed, for much of history, the labour of men and women was, together with land, the main factor of production. Since land is (relatively) fixed over time, we might assume, as a first approximation, that the growth in the production of goods and services should be linked mainly to the growth in the number of people.

This brings us, intuitively, to studying the evolution in the size of global population. Figure 2.2 presents that evolution, based, once again, on Maddison's (2010) temporal series. Figure 2.2 also shows a kind of "structural break", with at first a long period of near-stagnation in population size, followed by a growth, first at a moderate rate, then at a higher rate.

Let us first examine the period of (near) stagnation. The total number of humans did not evolve much during the first millennium of the common era. In year 1, that number was around 225 million, and around 267 million in the year 1000. World population therefore had increased by 40 million between year 1 and year 1000. Such an increase may not seem negligible, but that growth is in fact paltry when you consider that one thousand years had gone by between those two dates. We can therefore speak of a trend of "near-stagnation" of the size of the global population over this period. This near-stagnation corresponds to a situation of extremely slow growth, so slow that one can almost speak of stagnation.

Once more, we must be careful when making such statements: stating that there was near-stagnation is a statement that refers to the overall demographic trend, and not to the local fluctuations around this trend. Historian-demographers, such as Wrigley (1969), have extensively documented the existence of large fluctuations in population size for various cities and periods; these are linked to economic conditions, among other things. Figure 2.2, by showing only estimates of world population for a few years, obscures those fluctuations. For example, between 1346 and 1351, a large part of the European population was decimated by the Black Death, an epidemic that affected approximately one third of the European population. The figures presented in Figure 2.2 tell us nothing about that specific period, but show that there has been a near-stagnation in the size of the world's population for centuries, with variations (in trend) that are small compared to the magnitude of the period under consideration.

Between 1500 and 1600, the world population went from 438 million inhabitants to 556 million. The gain here is more than 100 million, over a period of "only" one century. During this period, the world's population started emerging from its quasi-stagnation to experience more sustained growth. But between 1600 and 1700, that growth slowed down, with world population increasing from 556 million to 603 million, which represents a gain of only 47 million inhabitants over a century.

It is during the eighteenth century that we can witness a real take-off in global population: between 1700 and 1820, the population increased from 603 million to 1.041 billion. We are, therefore, as with the world GDP series, in the presence of a structural break. After centuries of virtual stagnation, the size of the world's population was taking off. Demographic growth then accelerated in the nineteenth century, before experiencing a real explosion during the twentieth century. There were 1.5 billion inhabitants on Earth in 1900. In 1950, the number of inhabitants rose to 2.5 billion, an increase of one billion in just fifty years. This number then rose to 3 billion in 1960, to 4 billion in 1975, to 5 billion in 1987 and to 6 billion in the year 2000. In 2020, the Earth had a population of about 7.8 billion.

We have therefore witnessed, after long centuries of virtual demographic stagnation, a gradual take-off in the size of the population in the eighteenth century, followed by increasingly strong growth in the nineteenth century, culminating in the demographic explosion of the twentieth century, with the number of Earthlings multiplied by a factor of more than 7 between 1800 and the present day.

2.2.2   International Comparisons

The curve presented in Figure 2.2 aggregates the populations of the different countries of the world into a single figure. A less aggregated view is provided by Table 2.2, which presents the demographic trends over the past two millennia in the six economies studied in Table 2.1.

Table 2.2 shows that, for each country, the first 1,500 years studied are characterised by slow, or very slow population growth. During this period, the hierarchy of countries did not change much: India had the largest population, ahead of China, Japan and France.

Table 2.2 World population size by country over the last two millennia, in millions of inhabitants (*source*: Maddison Project 2010)

Years	United Kingdom	France	United States	Japan	China	India
1	0.800	5.000	0.680	3.000	59.600	**75.000**
1000	2.000	6.500	1.300	7.500	59.000	**75.000**
1500	3.942	15.000	2.000	15.400	103.000	**110.000**
1700	8.565	21.471	1.000	27.000	138.000	**165.000**
1820	21.239	31.250	9.981	31.000	**381.000**	209.000
1900	41.155	40.598	76.391	44.103	**400.000**	284.500
1950	50.127	42.518	152.271	83.805	**546.815**	359.000
2000	59.522	61.137	282.158	126.729	**1,262.645**	1,004.124

Demographic growth accelerated in the following centuries, but with different times of take-off and different rates of growth in different countries. In the case of the United Kingdom, the period of strongest growth was between 1700 and 1820. In Japan, on the contrary, it was much later, between 1900 and 1950, that population growth was the greatest. Finally, in India, it was during the second half of the twentieth century that population growth was the most sustained. Therefore, while the general trajectory of population size has some common features across countries (a long period of virtual stagnation followed by growth), there are, however, important differences between countries.

2.3   Output per Capita

2.3.1   The Global Trend

Having studied the dynamics of total output and population size over the last two millennia, it seems natural to cross-reference those two time series to measure GDP per capita or output per capita. GDP per capita is obtained, for a given year, by dividing GDP by the size of the population in that year. The output per capita, which measures economic activity per capita, is very often used to quantify, as a first approximation, the standard of living of individuals. The intuition behind this use is that the output per capita also measures the average income available to individuals, an income derived from the activity quantified by GDP per capita. Dividing production by the size of the population is therefore a way of measuring the average material standard of living.[9]

Figure 2.3 shows that, during many centuries, the output per capita did not change much. In year 1, it was about 466 dollars. A thousand years later, it was 453 dollars. In the year 1500, the GDP per capita was only 566 dollars, which represents a gain,

---

[9] As only young adults work (children and older adults do not), the output per capita is dependent on the population's age structure. We refer to this phenomenon as the demographic dividend (Lee, 2003).

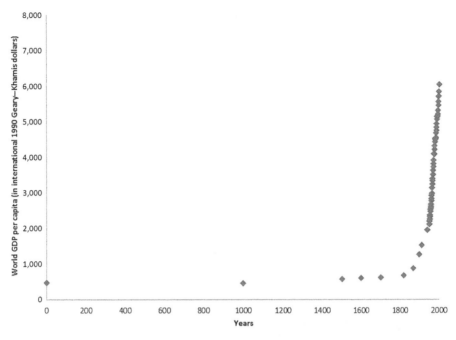

Figure 2.3 Global GDP per capita over the last two millennia
(*source*: Maddison Project 2010)

per inhabitant, of only 100 dollars in 1,500 years! Here we can say it is not near-stagnation, but plain stagnation. The output per capita continued to (nearly) stagnate during the following three centuries. In 1600, it was approximately 595 dollars, compared to 614 dollars in 1700 and 665 dollars in 1820.

However, the output per capita grew more significantly during the nineteenth century: in 1870, it amounted to 869 dollars. Between 1820 and 1870, there was an average gain of 200 dollars over a 50-year period, equivalent to the gain made over the previous 1,800 years, between year 1 and 1820. The GDP per capita clearly took off during the nineteenth century. After centuries of stagnation, the output per capita finally grew. This phenomenon of growth in per capita income is, on the scale of history, very recent. It covers at best two centuries, while stagnation had prevailed for millennia.

Figure 2.3 also shows that GDP per capita growth accelerated sharply after World War II. It rose from $2,110 in 1950 to $6,131 in 2000, (almost) tripling in 50 years. This strong growth in output per capita during the twentieth century is all the more remarkable because, over the same period, the size of the world's population really exploded, as we have already pointed out above (Figure 2.2).[10]

---

[10] This acceleration in output per capita growth during the twentieth century is one of the most studied stylised facts, both within and outside Unified Growth Theory. This stylised fact is particularly highlighted by Jones and Romer (2010) in their study of long time series of output per capita.

2.3.2   International Comparisons

In conclusion, it is useful to look, in a less aggregated way, at the evolution of GDP per capita over the last two millennia in a few large economies (Table 2.3). This table confirms, at a less aggregated level, what is shown in Figure 2.3: output per capita in each country initially experienced a long period of stagnation, followed by a recent short period of growth. It should be noted, however, that the different countries did not experience the take-off of GDP per capita at the same time. The United Kingdom had an earlier take-off, followed later by France and the United States.[11]

This difference in the timing of the take-off of the output per capita led to a real upheaval in the economic hierarchy of countries: while average standards of living were very close in year 1 to what they were in 1000 and 1500, this was no longer true in 1820, when per capita income was then three times higher in the United Kingdom than it was in Japan or in China. There was still a significant gap in 1900. However, the Asian economies, during the second half of the twentieth century, began a process of catching up. The classic example of convergence is Japan which started from an output per capita four times smaller than that of the United Kingdom in 1900, but exceeded that of the United Kingdom in the year 2000. Japan was the first Asian economy to enter this convergence process. The take-off there took place more than half a century before the take-offs in China and in India.

Table 2.3 GDP per capita per country over the last two millennia, in 1990 international Geary–Khamis dollars (*source:* Maddison Project 2010)

Years	United Kingdom	France	United States	Japan	China	India
1	400	**473**	400	400	450	450
1000	400	425	400	425	**466**	450
1500	714	**727**	400	500	600	550
1700	**1,250**	910	527	570	600	550
1820	**1,706**	1,135	1,257	669	600	533
1900	**4,492**	2,876	4,091	1,180	545	599
1950	6,939	5,186	**9,561**	1,921	448	619
2000	20,353	20,422	**28,467**	20,738	3,421	1,892

The different take-off timelines explain the gaps in output per capita between the economies. When less advanced societies finally started to take off, several decades later, their GDP per capita level started to grow and partly caught up with the richer economies. However, this convergence is not observed to the same extent in all countries. Convergence is neither universal nor automatic, and large differences between countries may remain. For example, despite rapid growth in the second half

---

[11] On differences in the timing of the take-off of economies, the classic work is that of Rostow (1960), discussed in Chapter 1.

of the twentieth century, India's GDP per capita in 2000 was still almost fifteen times smaller than that of the United States.[12]

2.4   A Major Qualitative Change

Let us now step back slightly away from the numbers, in order to better understand what they tell us about the economic dynamics over the long period. To do so, it is useful to return to the distinction, introduced by Kondratiev (1924), between *quantitative* changes and *qualitative* changes (Chapter 1).

Our interpretations have insisted on quantitative changes, changes that relate to the *level* of a given variable. For example, we have noted the virtual stagnation of output per capita for centuries, then its take-off from the nineteenth century onwards. Another example is that of population growth: at first it was extremely slow for a millennia, then it experienced an initial acceleration in the eighteenth century, before experiencing further, even greater accelerations in the nineteenth and twentieth centuries.

The description of economic dynamics over the long period requires highlighting the most important quantitative changes for the variables under study, therefore, those of the greatest magnitude, or those that have occurred most rapidly. This is what we have tried to do in the previous sections.

However, the description of long-term economic dynamics is not limited to the most striking quantitative changes. In fact, the study of the long period also requires highlighting changes of another nature, changes which Kondratiev (1924) called "qualitative changes". Qualitative changes do not relate to the level of a particular variable, but rather to the shape of the *relationships* between the variables. The idea is that, over time, it is not just the variable levels that change, but also the form of the relationships between the variables.

Identifying qualitative changes requires linking the different variables studied. The aim is to see whether the form of the relations between those variables has changed or not over the centuries. When the data on population size (Figure 2.2) and output per capita (Figure 2.3) are cross-referenced in this way, a qualitative change in the relationship between these two variables can be noted.

Indeed, between 1600 and 1820, the size of the population began to grow, leaving behind the centuries-old situation of near stagnation. However, during that same period, output per capita stagnated. It is therefore tempting, on the basis of these observations, to consider that demographic growth is *generally* associated with a stagnation of output per capita and a stagnation of material living conditions.

Such a conclusion is consistent with the theory of the long period advocated by Malthus. As discussed in Chapter 1, the *Essay on the Principle of Population* argues that population growth is a fundamental obstacle to economic progress and is associated with stagnating standards of living. That theory was based on the principle of population, according to which a society's capacity to produce people exceeds, in the absence of resource

---

[12] We shall return to the question of convergence – and the conditions necessary for its realisation – in the rest of the book, and in particular in Chapters 4 and 5.

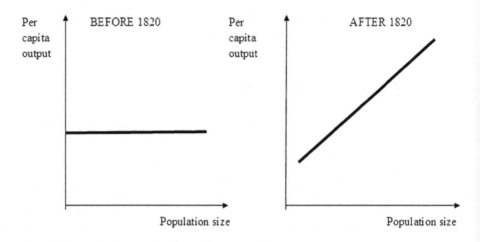

Figure 2.4 Qualitative change: the relationship between population size and output per capita

constraints, its capacity to produce means of subsistence.[13] Whenever technical progress made it possible to improve living conditions, thereby easing the resource constraint, the resulting population growth cancelled out that improvement. For Malthus, population growth is associated with a stagnation trend for living conditions, with all productivity gains being systematically "absorbed" by the increase in population size.

It should be noted, however, that from 1820 onwards – and even more so in the twentieth century – we witnessed both a growth in the size of the population and a take-off in output per capita. During this recent period, demographic growth is no longer associated with stagnation, but with a growth in output per capita and a substantial improvement in material living conditions. Over the last two centuries, productivity gains have not been offset by population growth.

The combined growth of output per capita and population size contradicts the principle of population and calls into question its validity. Here we are very far from a "law" that holds true everywhere and at all times. Above all, however, the transition from the relationship "population growth associated with output per capita stagnation" to the relationship "population growth associated with output per capita growth" constitutes, in itself, a major qualitative change. It would seem that the form of the relationship between these two variables – population size and output per capita – has changed over the centuries.

If the relationship between these two variables had remained unchanged, then economies could never have experienced an output per capita take-off. Indeed, if population growth acted as an impediment to GDP per capita growth between 1600 and 1820, it should have continued to do so beyond 1820.

Something has therefore changed qualitatively between the two periods under consideration, in the sense that the shape of the relationship between population size and output per capita has not remained the same. This qualitative change is shown in Figure 2.4.

---

[13] See Chapter 1.

It is quite possible that the change in the relationship between these two variables is linked to other variables and to changes within those variables. Stating the existence of a qualitative change between the pre-1820 and post-1820 periods does not, of course, rule out the possibility that other things may have varied and differed between those two periods, with more or less close links to both population size and output per capita.[14]

The relationship between population size and output per capita is but one example, among many, of a qualitative change. This example is nonetheless very important in order to understand how the nature of men's and women's struggle with resource scarcity has evolved over the centuries.

2.5   Towards the Concept of Economic Regime

2.5.1   North's (1981) Observation

The existence of qualitative changes in history creates a fundamental problem for the modelling of economic processes over the long period. The problem is that the existing theories and models – on the one hand, the classical theory of stagnation (Malthus) and, on the other, the neo-classical growth models (Solow) – are unable to explain *both* the long period of pre-industrial stagnation and the take-off that led to modern growth. This fundamental observation was made by North (1981, chapter 6):[15]

> Both the optimistic model of neoclassical economics and the pessimistic model of classical economics provide powerful insights into economic history. The former [...] approximates the unparalleled growth experience of western economics since the Second Economic Revolution (the Industrial Revolution). The latter sets economies history in a persistent tension between population and the resource base and is a far more useful starting point to explore the human experience in the millennia prior to the middle of the nineteenth century.

That observation, which Galor (2005, 2010, 2011) also later made, was at the root of Galor's developing Unified Growth Theory, as we shall see. However, before we examine the solutions that have been proposed to that problem, let us look at the origin of this fundamental observation, by returning to the relationship between the size of the population and the output per capita.

The Malthusian population doctrine can account, relatively easily, for the long period of stagnation of both the output per capita and the population size. It also explains why the population growth of the seventeenth and eighteenth centuries was an obstacle to the process of rising standards of living.

However, once the qualitative change had taken place, it appears that the Malthusian doctrine of population can no longer explain the facts, namely the combined growth of population size and of output per capita. We therefore need another theory.

---

[14] For example, it could be argued that the relationship between population size and output per capita depends on a third variable that has changed significantly between the pre-industrial and industrial periods, thus explaining the change in the relationship between population size and output per capita. We shall return to this issue later, particularly in Chapters 4, 5, 7 and 8.

[15] See North (1981), chapter 6, p. 60.

Modern growth theory has produced many models that can explain the combined growth of the GDP per capita and of the population size.[16] Let us examine Solow's (1956) model. In that model, the factor that explains the output per capita growth is the increase in the capital intensity of the production process.[17] Such growth is fully compatible with an increase in the size of the population. In fact, as long as the effective investment (given by the output per capita multiplied by the propensity to save) is higher than the investment required to keep the capital to labour ratio constant, this ratio grows and the output per capita grows. Solow's model applies easily to the industrial period, when both population size and GDP per capita have risen. This model makes it possible to "conform", at least qualitatively, to the paths observed for these variables during the nineteenth and twentieth centuries.

But the problem that then arises is how to explain, using Solow's model, the millennia of stagnation in output per capita and near-stagnation in population size that preceded the industrial period.

For example, it could be assumed that the economy was in a stationary equilibrium throughout the pre-industrial period, with actual investment being exactly equal to the investment required to keep the capital to labour ratio constant, thus leading to a stable output per capita. Admittedly, this is a possible explanation. But then how can we explain that, starting from an economy in a stationary equilibrium, and which has remained so for centuries, we can leave this state of equilibrium and move towards another state of equilibrium?

This kind of explanation contradicts the very essence of a stationary equilibrium. By definition, a stationary equilibrium is a state of the economy that, once reached, will reproduce itself in exactly the same way over time. There cannot, by definition, be a transition from a stationary equilibrium to something else.

In fact, the only way to explain, using Solow's model, both the period of pre-industrial stagnation and then the take-off of the nineteenth century, is to postulate the existence of a "shock" that hits a parameter, such as the propensity to save or the rate of depreciation of capital, and leading the economy away from its initial stationary equilibrium, towards another stationary equilibrium. The problem is that this type of "shock", while making sense in a short-run analysis, is difficult to use in a long-run analysis. The long period is defined precisely as the time horizon over which all the variables adjust, without any "shocks". The explanation of a "shock" causing the transition from stagnation to growth is not convincing.[18]

Solow's (1956) model alone cannot explain how a long period of output per capita stagnation was followed by a period of output per capita growth. That problem is not confined to Solow's model: as we have seen, the Malthusian doctrine cannot account for such a transition either. The existence of qualitative changes creates real difficulties for the economic analysis of the long period.

---

[16] See Chapter 1.   [17] See Chapter 1.

[18] It is worth noting that this problem does not only affect Solow's model or its variants. Endogenous growth models with multiple equilibria, such as Lucas's (1988), also need this type of "exogenous shock" to explain the "overcoming" of a poverty trap after centuries of stagnation.

In short, although the Malthusian doctrine can account for the long pre-industrial stagnation, and modern models of growth (such as the Solow model) are capable of explaining the growth of output per capita over the last two centuries, neither of these two theoretical frameworks is sufficient to rationalise the *entire development process*, including both the long period of stagnation and the period of growth.

2.5.2 Modelling History with Economic Regimes

These difficulties can be overcome if the existence of qualitative changes is taken into account and if these are placed at the centre of the analysis. A simple way to do this is to define what we will call an "economic regime". *An economic regime is defined as a given set of relationships between variables (economic, demographic, technological, etc.).*

The concept of economic regime does justice to the existence of qualitative changes. Indeed, when qualitative changes occur, it means that the shape of the relationships between certain variables changes from one period to the next: we are then dealing with a change of economic regime. The notion of qualitative change is therefore intrinsically linked to the notion of economic regime change.

In the example that we have chosen – the relationship between population size and GDP per capita – the change over time in the shape of the relationship between those variables indicates that the economic regime has changed. The pre-industrial economic situation, during which population growth was associated with a stagnation in output per capita, constitutes *a different regime* from the situation during and after the industrial revolution, which belongs to another economic regime.

Once we identify the presence of qualitative changes and, as a corollary, the existence of various economic regimes, with each one characterised by its own relationships between the variables studied, the main task of the economic analysis of the long period lies in studying the transition between the various economic regimes. This will involve constructing theoretical frameworks that will make it possible to explain or replicate all of the following elements:

- the regime of pre-industrial stagnation, during which population growth was an obstacle to growth in output per capita;
- the modern regime of growth, during which population growth is no longer an obstacle to growth in output per capita;
- the transition between those two regimes.

2.6 Conclusion: The Empirical Bases of Unified Growth Theory

Building on a study of long statistical series for production, population and output per capita, this chapter has given us a better understanding of the emergence of Unified Growth Theory. Unified Growth Theory was developed starting from a fundamental observation: *the impossibility for classical theoretical frameworks to explain or "rationalise" the existence of a long period of stagnation followed by a take-off and a sustainable growth of the output per capita.*

This observation led Galor (2005, 2010, 2011) to develop his Unified Growth Theory, a theory constructed precisely in order to account for the existence of various economic regimes and for the transitions between those regimes. The term "unified" reflects the desire to bring together, under the same theoretical framework, a theory of stagnation (to account for pre-industrial dynamics) and a theory of take-off and growth (to explain the economic dynamics of the last two centuries).

Appendix 1: Further Reading

Regarding the construction and study of long time series of GDP and GDP per capita, the inescapable reference is Maddison's monumental work, set out in several treatises (see Maddison 2001, 2003). These data are available on the website of the *Maddison Project* of the *Groeningen Growth and Development Center*: www.rug.nl as well as at www.ggdc.net. There are several other databases studying different aspects of the long run, such as the databases collected by the *Economic History Association* on the site: EH.net. In addition, the *Long-Term Productivity Database* (Bergeaud, Cette and Lecat, 2019) presents data on GDP per capita, labour productivity and machine obsolescence in twenty-three countries over the 1890–2016 period. This database is available at: longtermproductivity.com.

The succession of a long period of stagnation by a period of growth is studied by North (1981), who does not limit himself to the study of the last two millennia, but also considers the agricultural revolution (the "First Economic Revolution"). More recently, chapter 1 in Clark (2007) presents a detailed analysis of long time series of output per capita and other variables, as well as an interpretation of those series in light of the Malthusian theory. Chapter 2 in Galor (2011) also includes a detailed analysis of long time series of the main economic variables. That chapter makes the same observation as North (1981): the impossibility for traditional (classical or neoclassical) theoretical models and frameworks to explain both the long period of pre-industrial stagnation and the nineteenth-century take-off.

Part II

Unified Growth Theory
Foundations

3 The Stagnation Regime

Output per capita growth, commonly referred to as "economic growth", is, historically speaking, a recent phenomenon that extends over an extremely limited period of time. Most of history has not been a period of growth, but rather one of output per capita stagnation. This chapter is exclusively devoted to the study of the long reign of the stagnation regime.

This long period of output per capita stagnation is accompanied by a trend of relative *stability in standards of living*, living conditions that do not vary much over the centuries. During the pre-industrial era, generation after generation of humans faced a kind of "permanence" in the material constraints of their lives.[1] In order to document this long stagnation (in trend) in living conditions, historians use information coming from varied sources, but most notably data on food availability. Those statistics are particularly rich in information, because they highlight an essential component of material conditions: the everyday availability of food.

For example, Figure 3.1 shows the evolution in Britain and Wales of the average number of calories consumed per capita per day between 1700 and 1909–1913. This figure is based on the research of Harris et al. (2010) and shows that, during the first half of the eighteenth century, the average number of calories available for daily consumption remained virtually unchanged, around 2,200 calories per person per day. It was not until the second half of the eighteenth century that one can observe a rise in the quantity of available calories, a trend that becomes even more pronounced in the second half of the nineteenth century.

Similar analyses regarding the pre-industrial era, but using other statistical series, seem to confirm that the stability in output per capita reflects a stagnation in living conditions, regardless of the statistical indicators examined (see Clark 2007). The phenomenon of output per capita stagnation is therefore not a statistical artifice: stagnation had a real concrete consequence in the lives of successive generations during the pre-industrial era.

We should note that collecting all periods and all places of the pre-industrial era together under one and the same "stagnation regime" is simplistic. The pre-industrial

---

[1] This tendency of stability of living standards is true only if one focuses on long-run trends. Due to wars, famines and epidemics, there existed, locally, severe short-run fluctuations in standards of living. But we focus here on long-run trends, and not on short-run fluctuations.

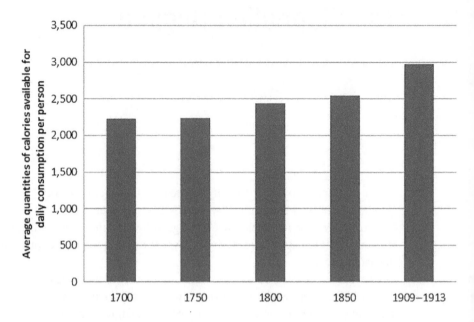

Figure 3.1 Average quantities of calories available for daily consumption per person, Britain and Wales, between 1700 and 1909–1913
(*source*: Harris et al. 2010)

era did experience (temporary) periods of economic expansion, mostly concentrated in certain urban centres, whose hierarchy changed over time.[2] Simplifying is, nonetheless, useful because it accounts for the important fact that output per capita growth *as a trend* was never sustainable before the industrial revolution, unlike what we have seen in the past two centuries.

In the eighteenth and nineteenth centuries, many theories were offered to explain this output per capita stagnation – and therefore the living conditions that went with it. One of the most influential theories is the one proposed by Malthus (1798) that we examined in Chapter 1. As a reminder, in his *Essay on the Principle of Population*, Malthus outlined a theory of long-term stagnation, which originated in the principle of population, that is the existence of an imbalance between, on the one hand, the economy's capacity for producing humans and, on the other hand, its capacity for producing the means of subsistence (the former exceeding the latter). According to Malthus, this imbalance is the cause of stagnation. As soon as living conditions improve, the population size grows too rapidly in relation to the means of subsistence, which brings the economy back to a less favourable condition. The ensuing degradation will slow population growth and thus increase standards of living, but that

---

[2] Braudel (1985, chapters 1 and 3) retraces the intersecting destinies over several centuries of a few "central cities" or "empire cities": Genoa, Venice, Antwerp and Amsterdam, cities that were successive centres of the European economy between the fourteenth and the eighteenth centuries. His research suggests that a wide diversity of local situations can be found within the global trends represented in the graphs of Chapter 2.

increase can only last until the population starts growing again, and so on. The *Essay* gives the outline of a theory of long-term cyclical oscillations, in which population growth is the only obstacle to economic progress.

Malthus believed that his principle of population could be applied universally and was true in all places and times: no society could escape this stagnation. There was no remedy according to Malthus and public policies (such as the Poor Laws) could only make the fluctuations more pronounced. Neither migration nor technical progress could provide a remedy. Indeed, overpopulation would eventually reach those who had migrated to other lands and, according to the principle of population, any improvement in agricultural yields would automatically lead to an expansion in population, thus cancelling the positive effects of the increase in yields on living conditions. Therefore, according to Malthus, stagnation was inevitable.

We know today that human societies did emerge from output per capita stagnation during the Industrial Revolution (see Chapter 2). The Malthusian doctrine was disproved by the facts: although the pre-industrial era data, as a trend, does not contradict the principle of population, it definitely did not prove valid for the nineteenth century, and even less so for the twentieth and twenty-first centuries. This principle is incompatible with the combined growth of output per capita and population size observed during the past two centuries. Malthus had overestimated the universality of his principle, but while writing his treatise at the end of the eighteenth century, he could not have predicted the future.

In spite of the limited scope of the principle of population – and its inability to rationalise the output per capita growth over the past two centuries – it is nonetheless useful, when doing an economic analysis of the long period, to develop a Malthusian stagnation model, in order to understand the period that preceded the Industrial Revolution. Any economic study of the very long run cannot analyse the few decades of growth, without first considering the long millennia of stagnation.

Whereas Malthus had only developed a (non-mathematical) theory of stagnation, this book shall propose a mathematical model of output per capita stagnation, expressed as a trend. The stagnation will here be of a Malthusian nature, in the meaning that, in this model, a sustainable growth of output per capita is impossible because of an excessive growth of population in relation to the means of subsistence. The theoretical framework studied in this chapter was not present in the *Essay* and one could create yet other models of Malthusian stagnation (see Eltis, 1984; Galor, 2011). However, the stagnation model analysed in this chapter will provide a useful starting point to study the transition to a growth regime (Chapter 4).

At this point, two preliminary remarks must be made. First of all, output per capita stagnation during the pre-industrial era had a large number of causes and the Malthusian doctrine offers just one way, amongst many, to explain this period of stagnation. The theory of stagnation inspired by Malthus is widely used in academic circles, not only in the field of Unified Growth Theory, but also notably in the works of historians such as Wrigley (1969), Clark (2007) and Allen (2011). Nonetheless, this theory has limits and the demographic dimension is just one cause of stagnation among others, such as, for instance, institutional factors.[3] We will later revisit these other causes of stagnation and we will show how they can be combined with demographic factors.[4]

Furthermore, the theoretical model presented in this chapter is deliberately simplified and pared down. It should be seen as an "abstract foundation" that we will gradually refine and modify throughout this book. Nevertheless, in spite of its simplicity, this theoretical framework has the advantage of illustrating the mechanism that underpins modern growth theories, as well as Unified Growth Theory. This mechanism is the "race" between factors: output per capita can only grow if the level of labour productivity, which is determined here by the level of knowledge, grows faster than the population size.

The rest of the chapter is organised as follows. Section 3.1 presents our model's assumptions regarding production, population growth and accumulation of knowledge. Section 3.2 studies the pre-conditions for output per capita growth. Section 3.3 offers a reformulation of the principle of population. Section 3.4 analyses the dynamics of long-run fluctuations. Section 3.5 revisits the international comparisons during the pre-industrial era, using the stagnation model. Section 3.6 outlines several critiques of this modelling.

3.1   Modelling Production

One should first examine the production process in the economy. The model chosen is that of a discrete time economy, where time t ranges from $t = 0$ to $t = +\infty$. In each period t, the economy is engaged in a production activity. To simplify, we adopt a macroeconomic perspective that considers the production of a single composite good, which is assumed to take into account all dimensions of material life. Focusing on the production of a single good in this way is a simplification: real economies are composed of millions of goods and services. However, studying the production of a composite basket of goods and services makes it possible to remain within a one-dimensional dynamic analytical framework.[5]

Throughout the book, the quantity of output per capita at period t will be represented by y_t. This single variable y_t summarises the entire economy's production activity relative to its population and can also be considered as describing the "material standards of living" of individuals living in period t.

In the economy under consideration, the production of goods and services requires three production factors: (1) labour; (2) land; (3) knowledge.

---

[3] This issue will be examined at the end of the chapter.   [4] See Chapters 5 and 8.

[5] Restricting the analysis to such a one-dimensional framework is a simplification. Some authors, such as Kondratiev (1926) and Rostow (1960), have linked the dynamics of the long period to the emergence of new capital goods eventually shared with the entire population (see Chapter 1).

3.1.1   Labour

When it comes to the labour factor, it will be assumed that all adults live for only one time period, during which they are working and N_t will represent the number of adults in period t, which corresponds to the number of workers in period t.

The size of the adult population in period t depends on the population size during the preceding period, that is to say their parents:

$$N_t = n_{t-1}N_{t-1}$$

in which n_{t-1} is the number of children who survived to adulthood per parent at $t-1$. n_{t-1} could also be interpreted as the growth factor of the adult population or of the number of workers, while the demographic growth rate corresponds to $n_{t-1} - 1$.[6]

The variable n_t accounts for two things: what can be called fecundity behaviours as well as infant mortality. It is important to make this distinction because it is well known that child mortality was very high during most of history. In his *Essay on the Nature of Trade in General* (1755), Cantillon insisted upon the fact that half of all children died before reaching the age of 17.

Demographic dynamics are crucially dependent on the n_t variable. Three cases can arise.

- When n_{t-1} is above 1, the number of workers increases from one period to the next (that is $N_t > N_{t-1}$). In that case, the cohort of workers is replaced by a larger cohort in the following period.
- When n_{t-1} equals 1, the number of workers is constant from one period to the next (that is $N_t = N_{t-1}$). In that case, the cohort of workers is replaced by a new cohort of equal size in the following period.
- When n_{t-1} is smaller than 1, the number of workers decreases from one period to the next (that is $N_t < N_{t-1}$). In this case, the cohort of workers is replaced by a smaller cohort in the following period.

To make things simpler, it will be assumed that all of the workers living at a given time period are identical (same productivity, same skills). However, Skills and work productivity can vary over time (that is from one generation to the next) due to knowledge accumulation, as will be discussed later in this chapter.

It will also be assumed that the whole population is working, so that output per capita y_t is defined by the ratio of total output Y_t to number of workers N_t.

3.1.2   Land

The production of goods and services does not only require labour, but also a certain amount of land. The quantity of land is represented by the variable L. Land is used here as a generic term that encompasses all so-called "natural" production factors.

---

[6] Generally speaking, for any variable x_t, the growth *factor* between periods t and $t+1$ is found through the ratio x_{t+1}/x_t, whereas the growth *rate* between periods t and $t+1$ is $(x_{t+1}/x_t) - 1$.

In this sense, "land" includes arable land as well as, more generally, the natural environment in which economic activity takes place.

We will first assume that the available amount of land is constant, that is to say the land quantity L remains the same for all periods. This assumption is a simplification: human activities can drive global warming and, therefore, can increase the rate of desertification or cause some land to be submerged by oceans. In reality, the quantity of land is neither constant not independent from human actions. However, as a starting point, we will assume that land is indeed a constant quantity that can completely regenerate from one period to the next. We will examine the effects of human activities on the natural environment in Chapter 6.

3.1.3   Knowledge

The third production factor is the stock of knowledge and techniques. Producing goods and services requires knowledge in addition to labour and land (or at least some type of natural environment).

Knowledge has evolved over the centuries. For millennia, humans survived thanks to their hunter-gatherer skills. Agriculture and the use of livestock only appeared 8,000 years before the common era, around 10,000 years ago. Other major technical changes appeared subsequently: the invention of the wheel (5,500 years ago), of the printing press (fifteenth century), of the steam engine (mid-eighteenth century), etc.

In our model, the variable A_t represents the state of production technology during period t. It is a simplifying modelling conceit to aggregate all knowledge into a single variable, to be able to study its dynamic; however, it is a very convenient way of summarising a complex phenomenon. As science historians have demonstrated, knowledge evolves in a manner that is not purely cumulative, because new paradigms replace those paradigms deemed to be outdated, by overcoming the anomalies encountered in those previous paradigms (see Kuhn, 1962). Since paradigms may, in some cases, be non-measurable and incomparable, the analysis is made easier here by thinking in terms of knowledge accumulation.

Nevertheless, simplifying things in this way proves useful when explaining how, over the centuries, a given quantity of labour and land may lead to production quantities that are more or less significant, depending on how advanced the "knowledge" was. The variable A_t thus provides a kind of theoretical shortcut to account for the considerable influence knowledge has on production activities, in particular on average labour productivity (which is equal to the output divided by the number of workers).

We will then assume, as a first approximation, that knowledge accumulates according to a process with a constant growth factor, which is represented by the parameter $a > 0$:

$$A_t = aA_{t-1}.$$

Parameter a is the knowledge growth factor or the factor of technical progress, whereas $a - 1$ is the knowledge growth rate or rate of technical progress.

As was true with the demographic dynamics, there can be three cases:

- when $a < 1$, knowledge tends to decrease over time (that is $A_t < A_{t-1}$). In this case, ignorance gradually takes hold and people forget the knowledge and techniques accumulated over the previous centuries.
- when $a = 1$, knowledge tends to reproduce itself exactly over time (that is $A_t = A_{t-1}$). In this case, human knowledge is frozen: as time passes, no new techniques are invented, but no knowledge is otherwise lost.
- when $a > 1$, knowledge tends to accumulate over time (that is $A_t > A_{t-1}$). In this case, ignorance recedes while humans acquire ever more knowledge about the surrounding world.

Clearly, the third case seems the most plausible of the three and it will be the assumption used in the rest of the book. There are several ways to justify hypothesis $a > 1$. For example, working helps humans broaden their skills and their knowledge through repetitive actions. This process of learning, defined by Arrow (1962), is called "learning by doing"[7] and explains that know-how automatically accumulates over time.

3.1.4   The Production Function

Generally speaking, a production function links certain quantities of production factors (or inputs) to a certain quantity of output, which is the maximum output quantity that can be obtained from those quantities of inputs.

In the economy under consideration, the production function links certain quantities of labour N_t, of land L and of knowledge A_t, to a certain quantity of output Y_t. This book adopts a simple hypothesis regarding the production of the composite good and assumes that the total output is determined by the interaction of labour N_t, land L and knowledge A_t in the following manner:

$$Y_t = A_t(L)^\beta (N_t)^\alpha$$

in which Y_t represents the total output, α the elasticity of the total output to the quantity of labour, while β represents the elasticity of the total output to the quantity of land.

This production function is very often found in the long-run economic literature. Kremer's (1993) model is based on this function.[8]

Parameter α measures the responsiveness, as a percentage, of the total product to a variation in the amount of work. This parameter is usually set at a positive value inferior to one ($0 < \alpha \leq 1$), so as to formalise the idea of diminishing marginal returns of labour. What is being intuited here is that the addition of a worker contributes to increasing output, but to a lesser extent than the addition of the previous worker, and

---

[7] Arrow (1962) gave a good illustration of this concept by using the example of aircraft manufacture. The time required to manufacture an aircraft decreases with the number of aircraft already produced.

[8] To be more precise, Kremer (1993) uses the production function $Y_t = A_t(N_t)^\alpha (L)^{1-\alpha}$ in which L is normalised to 1, whereas, in this book, the quantity of land L will vary in Chapters 6 and 9.

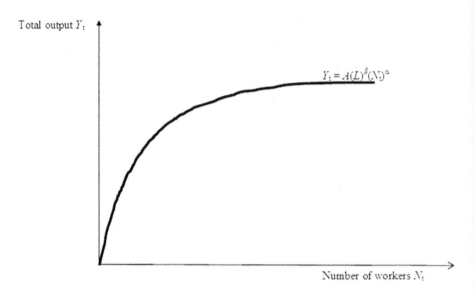

Figure 3.2 Production function for a given knowledge stock (A) and amount of land (L)

so on. Parameter β measures the percentage responsiveness of the total product to a percentage change in the amount of land. It often has a value inferior to one, to account for diminishing marginal yields of land.

It is important here to note an interesting characteristic of this production function. If you assume, as neoclassical analyses did, that the labour and land production factors are paid according to their marginal productivity (i.e. according to the contribution to the total product of the last unit of that factor), you find that the total wage bill equals $N_t \alpha A_t (L)^\beta (N_t)^{\alpha-1}$ and that the share of the total wage bill in the total output equals α, a constant.[9] This result is consistent with the stylised fact highlighted by Kaldor (1961).

For illustrative purposes, Figure 3.2 is a representation of the production function in the (N_t, Y_t) space. Figure 3.2 shows how the total output Y_t therefore changes relative to the number of workers N_t, for a given quantity of land L and a given knowledge stock A_t.

As shown in Figure 3.2, the produced output increases concavely with the increase in the number of workers. The concavity of the production function, which stems from the fact that $\alpha < 1$, reflects the idea of decreasing marginal returns to labour: as the number of workers increases, total production increases, but this increase gradually gets smaller. The marginal product – the change in total product created by one additional worker – is therefore positive, but decreases with the number of workers.

---

[9] It should be noted that this is one assumption on remunerations among other possible assumptions and that the arguments being developed in this book do not postulate a specific theory of remunerations (unless explicitly mentioned). The assumption that factors are paid at their marginal productivity only makes sense if returns to scale are constant, that is, in this model, if the condition $\alpha + \beta = 1$ holds true. Indeed, it is only under this assumption that the remuneration of all of the factors of production at their marginal productivity is exactly equal to the total output.

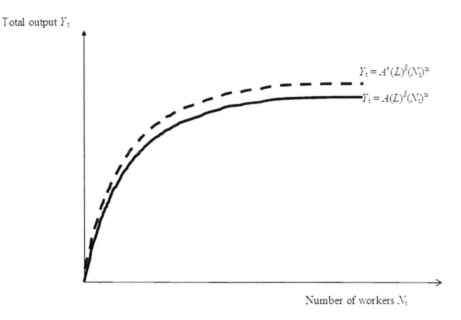

Total output Y_t

$Y_t = A'(L)^\beta (N_t)^\alpha$

$Y_t = A(L)^\beta (N_t)^\alpha$

Number of workers N_t

Figure 3.3 Effect on total output of an increase in the knowledge stock $(A' > A)$

Whereas Figure 3.2 shows the effect of an increase in the number of workers on total output as a function of time, Figure 3.3 shows the effect of a change in the knowledge stock A_t on the relationship between the number of workers and total output. A change in this knowledge stock results in a shift in the production function. Indeed, an increase in the knowledge stock leads to an increase in the output produced by a given number of workers.

3.2 The Conditions for Growth

3.2.1 Growth of Total Output

In order to study the growth in total output from one period to the next, it can be useful to write the level of production at period $t + 1$ by using the production function:

$$Y_{t+1} = A_{t+1}(L)^\beta (N_{t+1})^\alpha.$$

Dividing Y_{t+1} by the production at period t (i.e. Y_t) allows the growth factor of the total output between the period t and the period $t + 1$ to be deduced. Subtracting 1 from this growth factor gives the growth rate of the total output, denoted by G_{t+1}:

$$G_{t+1} = \frac{Y_{t+1}}{Y_t} - 1 = \frac{A_{t+1}(L)^\beta (N_{t+1})^\alpha}{A_t(L)^\beta (N_t)^\alpha} - 1 = a(n_t)^\alpha - 1.$$

Let us note that the growth rate of the total output does not depend on the land area L, as this is assumed to be constant over time.

Three situations may arise here:

- If $a(n_t)^\alpha > 1$, total output increases over time. This first case can occur if both knowledge and population experience growth $(a > 1, n_t > 1)$, or if only one of the two grows, but grows enough to compensate for any decrease of the other factor.
- If $a(n_t)^\alpha = 1$, total output stagnates. This case arises if both knowledge and population remain constant or if the growth of one factor is exactly compensated by the decrease in the other factor.
- If $a(n_t)^\alpha < 1$, total output decreases. This can happen if both knowledge and population experience a decrease $(a < 1, n_t < 1)$, or if only one of the two factors decreases enough to compensate any increase in the other factor.

3.2.2   Growth of Output per Capita

The most interesting variable in long-run economic analysis is output per capita. Output per capita can be rewritten, dividing the left and right sides of the total output equation Y_t by population size N_t, arriving to the following:

$$y_t = \frac{Y_t}{N_t} = A_t(L)^\beta (N_t)^{\alpha-1} = \frac{A_t(L)^\beta}{(N_t)^{1-\alpha}}.$$

Rewriting it this way makes it clear that output per capita at period t increases with land area L and with knowledge stock A_t, and decreases with population size N_t. That decrease of output per capita with population size is the corollary to our assumption of labour's diminishing marginal returns $(\alpha < 1)$.

In order to identify the determinants of the growth rate of the output per capita, the above equation can be rewritten for the following period $(t + 1)$ and then divide it by the output per capita in period t. The growth rate of output per capita is found by subtracting 1:

$$g_{t+1} = \frac{y_{t+1}}{y_t} - 1 = \left(\frac{A_{t+1}(L)^\beta}{(N_{t+1})^{1-\alpha}} \times \frac{(N_t)^{1-\alpha}}{A_t(L)^\beta} \right) - 1$$

in which g_{t+1} is the growth rate of the output per capita between periods t and $t+1$.

Considering that $A_{t+1} = a A_t$ and that $N_{t+1} = n_t N_t$, this expression can be rewritten in the following form:

$$g_{t+1} = \frac{a}{(n_t)^{1-\alpha}} - 1.$$

The growth rate of the output per capita is independent of the available land area L, simply because this area is assumed to be constant over time.

From the previous formula, it follows that the growth rate of the output per capita can be rewritten in this manner:

$$g_{t+1} = \frac{a - (n_t)^{1-\alpha}}{(n_t)^{1-\alpha}}.$$

This equation makes it clear that whether or not the growth rate of the output per capita is positive depends on the existence of a positive difference between, on the one hand, the factor of growth in knowledge, a, and, on the other, the factor of growth in population raised to the power of $1 - \alpha$.

Three situations can occur:

- if $a > (n_t)^{1-\alpha}$, the output per capita grows at a positive rate (i.e. $g_{t+1} > 0$);
- if $a = (n_t)^{1-\alpha}$, the output per capita remains constant (i.e. $g_{t+1} = 0$);
- if $a < (n_t)^{1-\alpha}$, the output per capita grows at a negative rate (i.e. $g_{t+1} < 0$).

The intuition behind these three cases is simple. For output per capita to increase, the accumulation of knowledge must be fast enough to compensate for population growth given the presence of declining marginal returns to labour. That condition is only verified if the knowledge growth factor a is higher than n_t raised to the power of $1 - \alpha$.

It should be mentioned that if there were no decrease in the marginal return on labour, that is if α were equal to 1, the output per capita y_t would be independent of the population size, so that the increase or decrease of the output per capita would only depend on the increase or decrease in knowledge (i.e. if $a > 1$ or $a < 1$).

However, in the presence of declining marginal returns on labour, output per capita decreases with population size, leading to a kind of "race" between the production of humans and the production of knowledge (which determines the productivity of each worker). This "race" between knowledge and population size is the deciding factor on whether output per capita increases or decreases.

When $a > (n_t)^{1-\alpha}$, knowledge is "winning" the race and output per capita increases. In that case, despite population growth and despite the fact that each worker contributes marginally less and less, technological progress is sufficiently high to allow an increase in output per capita.

Conversely, when $a < (n_t)^{1-\alpha}$, knowledge is "losing" the race, so to speak, and output per capita must decrease. In this case, technological progress is too low in relation to population growth to sustain a constant level in output per capita. A decrease in output per capita therefore follows.

The three cases considered above rely on a condition that is itself dependent on time, through the variable n_t. In order to think about the dynamics of output per capita over the long period *in general terms*, more precise assumptions need to be made about the variation in the intensity of population growth as a function of the level of output per capita. The Malthusian principle of population includes this type of assumption and we shall propose a reformulation of that principle in the following section.

3.3   A Reformulation of the Principle of Population

As we have seen previously, Malthus (1798) formulated the notion that every society faces a succession of periods of expansion and periods of regression. These fluctuations are due to the fact that the population size grows at a rate that depends on living conditions. When living conditions are bad, population growth slows down, through correction mechanisms ("population checks"), but when the economy is flourishing, population growth accelerates. The mechanism by which good living conditions enhance population growth is at the heart of the principle of population: it is because a society's capacity to produce people exceeds its capacity to produce means of subsistence that economic progress cannot be sustained.

A simple way to formalise Malthus's intuition within our model is by positing that the population growth factor n_t depends on the level of income per capita y_t, and that the population growth factor is increasing with income per capita. There are multiple ways to model that condition. So that our model remains as simple as possible, we will posit that: (1) there exists a threshold of output per capita $\hat{y}$ and (2) the population growth factor n_t can have two different values, depending on whether the output per capita is inferior or superior to the threshold $\hat{y}$.

[Hypothesis M1]
There exists a threshold of output per capita $\hat{y} > 0$ such that:[10]

$$n_t = \check{n} > 1 \quad \text{if } y_t < \hat{y}$$

$$n_t = \hat{n} > 1 \quad \text{if } y_t \geq \hat{y}$$

with $\check{n} < \hat{n}$.

Hypothesis M1 amounts to introducing a dependence of population growth on the material standards of living, represented here by the output per capita. This hypothesis affirms the existence of a very specific form of dependence: if the output per capita exceeds a certain threshold, population growth will be stronger, whereas if the output per capita is below that threshold, population growth will be weaker. This form of dependency, as set out in M1, is quite an assumption, but for the period considered by Malthus (the pre-industrial period) it is a satisfactory one as a first approximation.

It should be noted that, since output per capita is an increasing function of available land area, hypothesis M1 implies that economies with more land area will experience *ceteris paribus* a higher output per capita and, hence, are likely to experience higher population growth. This corollary corresponds exactly to what Malthus had in mind when he studied the case of the United States, which served as a "model" when he first proposed the principle of population.[11]

But hypothesis M1 is not enough, alone, to reformulate the Malthusian principle of population within our analytical framework. The principle of population refers to an *imbalance* between the capacity to produce people and the capacity to produce means of subsistence. That principle therefore does not solely touch upon the population

---

[10] It is assumed, with no loss of generality, that $\hat{n}, \check{n} > 1$. Indeed, the instances of population decrease ($n < 1$) could automatically lead to a permanent growth of output per capita even in absence of technical progress. Such a growth of output per capita "through depopulation" is a purely hypothetical consideration that would lead to human extinction. We will revisit this question in Chapter 6.

[11] See Chapter 1.

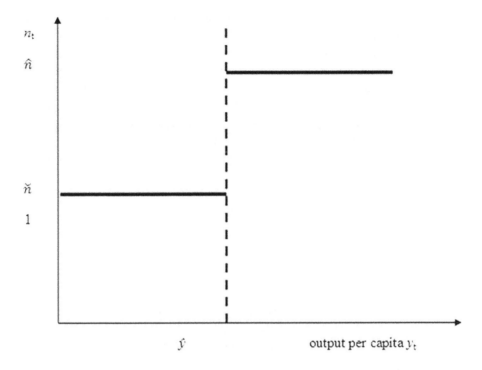

Figure 3.4 Hypothesis M1: population growth and output per capita

growth factor n_t, but must also include an assumption about the size of that factor in relation to the capacity of societies to produce means of subsistence.

A simple manner to account for that imbalance in our model is to posit that the growth factors $a, \check{n}$ are $\hat{n}$ are such that:

[Hypothesis M2]

$$(\check{n})^{1-\alpha} < a < (\hat{n})^{1-\alpha}.$$

Hypothesis M2 amounts to formulating that knowledge growth takes on an intermediate value: it is greater than the lower population growth factor raised to the power $1 - \alpha$, but smaller than the upper population growth factor raised to the power $1 - \alpha$.

Hypothesis M2 does not exclude the possibility of technological progress. In so doing, it remains in the spirit of the Malthusian doctrine, which also did not exclude improvements in production techniques. However, hypothesis M2 does posit that, even though technological progress can be positive, it remains nonetheless limited by the upper population growth factor raised to the power of $1 - \alpha$. The accumulation of knowledge is therefore not always enough to compensate for population growth.

Hypotheses M1 and M2 seem very plausible when considering the pre-industrial era. In the next section, we shall see that, when put together, they will lead to a dynamic of fluctuations and oscillations that makes reaching a sustainable increase in output per capita impossible.

As a conclusion, before looking at the consequences of hypotheses M1 and M2 for long-run dynamics, it should be noted that these hypotheses are merely specific reformulations, among other possible reformulations, of the Malthusian principle of population. Other mathematical reformulations of the Malthusian doctrine have been offered by Eltis (1984) and Galor (2011). However, our hypotheses account for the key elements of the Malthusian doctrine: on the one hand, a positive dependency of the population growth on the living conditions (even if it takes on a rudimentary form here, through a function with two values) and, on the other hand, the fact that technological progress is not always sufficient to compensate population growth.

3.4   Long-Run Fluctuations

This section examines the consequences of hypotheses M1 and M2 on the output per capita dynamics over the long period, showing that hypotheses M1 and M2 make it *impossible* for the output per capita to grow sustainably.

Let us posit that the output per capita in the initial period, denoted y_0, is lower than the threshold $\hat{y}$. It follows that, because of hypothesis M1, the population growth factor is given by $\check{n}$. Because of hypothesis M2, we can also deduce that the output per capita at period 1, y_1, will be greater than the output per capita at period 0, because hypothesis M2 gives us that $a > (\check{n})^{1-\alpha}$. We therefore have as a result that $y_1 > y_0$.

Let us now consider the following period ($t = 2$). Two situations can occur.

If y_1 is greater than the threshold $\hat{y}$, then, because of hypothesis M1, the population growth factor is now given by $\hat{n}$. Because of hypothesis M2, we have $a < (\hat{n})^{1-\alpha}$, which will lead to a decrease of the output per capita and will be lower at $t = 2$ than at $t = 1$. We therefore have $y_2 < y_1$, bringing a halt to the growth in output per capita.

If, conversely, y_1 is smaller than the threshold $\hat{y}$, we apply the same rationale as in period $t = 0$ and we get $y_2 > y_1$. In that case, growth carries on. But up to what point? Once again, if y_2 is greater than threshold $\hat{y}$, the associated increase in population growth will put an end to the growth in output per capita.

Considering these elements, which can be repeated for any period t, we can clearly infer that a sustained growth of the output per capita y_t is only possible if it remains below threshold $\hat{y}$. But since in our model, when y_t increases, it must increase at a constant rate, we are hard pressed to see how y_t could grow indefinitely without ever exceeding threshold $\hat{y}$. Sooner or later, that threshold will be crossed and output per capita will then drop. A permanent growth of the output per capita is impossible in this model: the economy will, sooner or later, necessarily experience a decrease in the output per capita.

Similarly, a permanent decrease in the output per capita is not possible in this model. Indeed, a decrease in the output per capita cannot prevail here if the output per capita is greater than threshold $\hat{y}$. But by decreasing at a constant rate, the output per capita will sooner or later fall below this threshold, which will lead to the end of the decrease and the return of the growth of the output per capita.

The effect of combining hypotheses M1 and M2 is that neither a sustainable growth nor a sustainable decrease of the output per capita is possible. The economy inevitably experiences oscillations in the output per capita around the critical threshold $\hat{y}$. Those oscillations are, in spirit, in line with the Malthusian doctrine, which, like our model, ruled out any possibility of a lasting improvement in living conditions. According to the Malthusian theory, the tendency of the economy is to experience a succession of periods of growth and decline in income per capita, the general trend being constant in the long term, in the sense that there is a lasting tendency for income per capita income to stagnate.

The term "near-stagnation" is perhaps more precise than the term "stagnation", because there are more or less long periods in our economy during which the output per capita will increase (or decrease). To be precise, our model excludes not only the possibility of a sustainable increase or decrease in output per capita, but also the existence of any kind of stationary equilibrium in output per capita. Indeed, for output per capita to remain constant, it would require that the condition $a = (n_t)^{1-\alpha}$ be satisfied for a certain t, something that hypothesis M2 excludes. We are therefore not in a situation of pure stagnation in which output per capita remains constant at all periods; rather, in the spirit of the Malthusian doctrine, we have an oscillatory movement of the output per capita around a constant trend, without any possibility of sustainable growth or decline.

Under hypotheses M1 and M2, our economy must necessarily experience fluctuations in output per capita around the threshold $\hat{y}$. The magnitude of these oscillations and the number of periods included in a cycle depend on the precise parameterisation of our model, thus on the values given to the parameters $a, \check{n}$ and $\hat{n}$. In other words, the size of the cycles (number of periods) and the size of the deviations between the minimum and maximum achieved values of the output per capita depend on the parameterisation.

Without going into all the details, let us examine the dynamics of variables such as output per capita, total product and population size, as well as knowledge that can be elicited by the model under hypotheses M1 and M2.

Considering that a is assumed to be greater than 1, knowledge A_t constantly accumulates in our economy. By further positing, as we did, that $\check{n}$ and $\hat{n}$ are greater than 1, population size N_t also experiences growth, although some periods will show higher growth and some lower growth, depending on whether output per capita is above or below the threshold $\hat{y}$.[12] Since knowledge and population size increase over time, total product Y_t also experiences growth, although some periods will show higher growth and some lower growth, depending on whether output per capita is

---

[12] This result of sustainable, unlimited growth in population size is the direct corollary of our M1 hypothesis, which will be replaced by more general hypotheses in the rest of this book.

above or below the threshold $\hat{y}$. So, we have increasing trends (but with fluctuations around the trend) for total product and total population, while output per capita fluctuates around a flat trend.

For illustration purposes, Figure 3.5 presents a numeric example of the dynamics of output per capita (y_t), population (N_t) and knowledge (A_t).

Since this book will often present numerical simulations as illustrations of the models studied, it is worth providing some details here about these simulations, their nature and main objectives.

The principle of these numerical simulations is simple enough: based on assumptions about the initial conditions of the economy, that is, the values taken by the variables in the model (y_t, A_t, etc.) at an initial period $t = 0$, and based on assumptions on the values of the structural parameters of the economy (a, $\check{n}$, $\hat{n}$, etc.), it is possible, on the basis of the equations describing the laws of accumulation (for knowledge, population size, etc.), to calculate the values taken by the variables of the model at the following periods $t = 1$, $t = 2$, $t = 3$, etc.[13] Numerical simulation consists, as it were, of setting initial values for all the variables in $t = 0$, and setting values for the structural parameters, then "letting the model run", so as to obtain the values of all the variables of the model for the future periods $t = 1$, $t = 2$, $t = 3$, etc.

In the models studied in this book, a time period corresponds to the career length of a cohort of workers.[14] Indeed, the cohort of workers active at period t of size N_t is replaced, at the following period $t + 1$, by a new cohort of workers of size $N_{t+1} = n_t N_t$, in which n_t is the number of surviving children per adult in period t. Therefore, each time period in our model corresponds to the career length of a cohort of workers, a period of about forty years. A numerical simulation thus shows us the dynamics of production and other variables in the model for periods of about forty years.[15] One consequence of this periodisation is that if we "let the model run" over twenty periods, as is the case in Figure 3.5, the total period covered by the numerical simulation is 800 years. The time horizon studied by the numerical simulations presented in this book is an extremely long one, extending over several centuries.

Each figure associated with a simulation presents the dynamics of a given variable over twenty periods of approximately forty years each, conditional on the initial values of the variables and the values taken by the structural parameters. Each graph could present both the number of the periods (0, 1, 2, etc.) – or even the corresponding dates (year 1200, year 1240, etc.) – and the values taken by the variables (10, 25, etc.). However, since the objective of these simulations is to illustrate the *qualitative* properties of the models studied, we have chosen not to indicate either

---

[13] As an example, the numerical simulation presented in Figure 3.5 is based on the following values: $a = 1.015$, $\alpha = 0.5$, $\beta = 0.5$, $\check{n} = 1.005$, $\hat{n} = 1.040$, $\hat{y} = 10.5$ and the model's initial conditions are: $A_0 = 10$, $L = 1$ and $N_0 = 1$. These hypotheses imply an initial level of output per capita equal to $y_0 = 10$.

[14] The expression "cohort of workers" is understood here as a set of people working during the same period t.

[15] There is no single way of translating the period lengths of our models into numbers of years. Instead of forty-year periods, one could consider periods lasting thirty-five or forty-five years. The forty-year figure is only to give an order of magnitude.

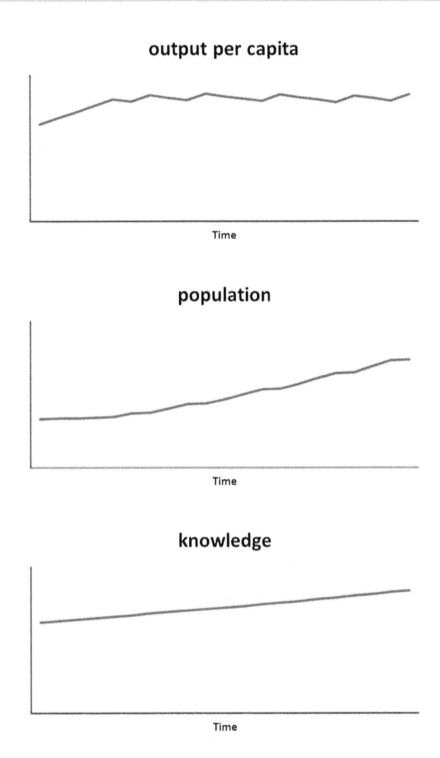

Figure 3.5 Dynamics of the output per capita, population size and stock of knowledge

dates or precise values for the variables on the axes. Such indications would be useful if our objective was one of quantitative replication of a specific temporal series (for example, the level of output per capita in a given country over a given period), which is not the case here. Our objective is simply to illustrate the qualitative properties of the models studied.[16]

In this book, these numerical simulations will serve to illustrate the robustness of the model when faced with changes in the initial conditions or in the values of the structural parameters. On the same graph, we will then present the product of two distinct numerical simulations, each relying on different assumptions.

If we examine Figure 3.5, it shows a simulation of our model over 20 generations, or approximately 800 years. The top graph of Figure 3.5 presents the oscillatory dynamic of the output per capita around threshold $\hat{y}$. Output per capita cannot experience a sustainable growth and is condemned to fluctuate around threshold $\hat{y}$. This inability to experience a sustainable take-off exists in spite of the growth of the knowledge stock at a constant rate (bottom graph of Figure 3.5). The mechanism underlying these long-term fluctuations of the output per capita in spite of a constant accumulation of knowledge is detailed below.

As shown in the middle graph of Figure 3.5, population size does not increase at a constant rate, but rather at a rate oscillating between two values, depending on whether the output per capita is above or below threshold $\hat{y}$. At first, output per capita is below the threshold, which leads to a very small population growth, that is dominated by the growth in the stock of knowledge (see bottom graph), such that output per capita increases.

However, that growth in output per capita is not sustainable: once output per capita reaches threshold $\hat{y}$, population growth strengthens, so that the slope of the population profile steepens on the middle graph in Figure 3.5. As a result, population growth dominates the accumulation of knowledge, so that output per capita declines.

It is worth mentioning that the decrease in output per capita does not necessarily imply that threshold $\hat{y}$ has been crossed in a straightforward manner. As shown in Figure 3.5 (top), it is possible for the output per capita to decline while staying above threshold $\hat{y}$ over several periods, thus leading to greater population size growth. The number of periods needed for the output per capita to cross the critical threshold $\hat{y}$ determines the length of the cycles. If the threshold is crossed rapidly, the cycles are short, whereas if the threshold is crossed after several periods, the cycles are longer. The trends shown in Figure 3.5 are the result of a special calibration of the parameters. Generally speaking, the duration of the cycles associated with Malthusian oscillatory dynamics depends ultimately on the precise values taken by the structural parameters of the economy (factors of demographic and technological growth, production parameters, levels of critical thresholds), as well as the initial conditions.

Figure 3.5 offers a numerical illustration of the Malthusian stagnation regime studied in this chapter. It shows that the output per capita experiences oscillations induced by the dependence of population growth on the level of output per capita.

---

[16] Similarly, we are not going to mention, for each simulation, the assumptions relating to the initial conditions and the values of the structural parameters.

In conclusion, this section demonstrates that, under the Malthus-inspired hypotheses M1 and M2, the economy cannot experience a sustainable growth of output per capita, even though there is permanent technical progress. The intuition behind this result is that, for a sustainable growth of the output per capita to be possible, knowledge must necessarily win the "race" between the accumulation of knowledge and the accumulation of people. However, this possibility is excluded by hypothesis M2, according to which, in the case of favourable living conditions, human accumulation is faster than knowledge accumulation, leading to a fall in output per capita. It follows that such an economy cannot experience sustainable growth in GDP per capita.

The model outlined in this section thus offers an explanation or "rationalisation", among others that are possible, of the stagnation economic regime that remained the norm during the pre-industrial era (discussed in Chapter 2). According to this model, the stagnation in trend of the output per capita derives from the fact that any improvement in the living conditions leads to boosting the population growth, thus bringing living conditions back down to their original level.

3.5   International Comparisons during the Pre-industrial Era

By formalising the Malthusian principle of population, we have been able to develop a theory of long-run stagnation. Within the model, the obstacle to sustainable growth of the output per capita comes from population growth that increases when the output per capita reaches a certain threshold and thus prevents any sustainable way of crossing that threshold. This is an appropriate theoretical framework to shed light on the economic dynamics of the pre-industrial era, which are characterised by an overall stagnation of the GDP per capita.

Can our model be also used to get a better understanding of international comparisons during the pre-industrial period?

In order to answer this question, it is necessary to re-examine the data presented in Chapter 2, specifically Table 2.3. Table 3.1 revisits these data for the period of stagnation in output per capita. Beyond the output per capita stagnation itself, another important observation is that the values of output per capita are extremely close together in the different economies considered. The differences are indeed minimal, especially for the years 1 CE and 1000 CE.

The small differences in output per capita levels may seem surprising at first glance, because the six economies considered in Table 3.1 are very different. While the United

Table 3.1 GDP per capita over the 1–1500 period in six major economies, in 1990 international Geary–Khamis dollars (*source*: Maddison Project 2010)

Years	United Kingdom	France	United States	Japan	China	India
1	400	473	400	400	450	450
1000	400	425	400	425	466	450
1500	714	727	400	500	600	550

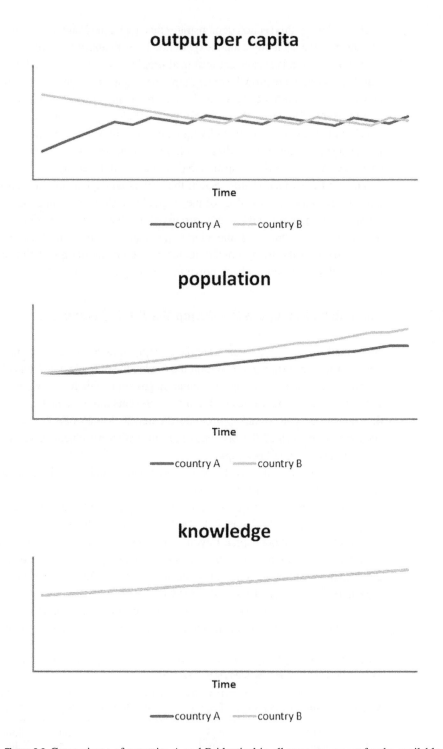

Figure 3.6 Comparisons of countries A and B identical in all respects, except for the available land area L ($L_B = 1.1\ L_A$)

Kingdom is relatively small, China and India are very large countries. Thus, in our model, variable L, the amount of land, is very different across countries. Therefore, based on our production function, one might expect much higher output per capita levels in China and India, compared to those in France or the United Kingdom. Table 3.1 shows that this is not the case.

This relative proximity of output per capita levels during the pre-industrial period, despite the existence of significant differences, in particular in terms of the land-based production factor, may at first glance seem counter-intuitive. However, it is fully compatible with the predictions of our Malthusian model of stagnation.

Indeed, our model predicts that output per capita stagnates at a level oscillating around threshold $\hat{y}$, regardless of the available quantity of land L. Whether a country's territory under consideration is vast or not, the level around which the output per capita oscillates does not vary: that level is equal to $\hat{y}$. Our model predicts that if different economies are characterised by the same output per capita critical threshold $\hat{y}$, then, regardless of the amount of land L, they will all experience fluctuations in output per capita around that threshold. Our model's predictions are therefore compatible with relative proximity in output per capita levels in pre-industrial economies.

Of course, this does not mean that the quantity of available land has no effect on international comparisons. Figure 3.6 illustrates the consequences of the variations in land area L by comparing the dynamics of output per capita, population size and knowledge accumulation for two countries A and B. They are equal in all respects, except that country B's territory is 10% larger than country A's ($L_B = 1.1\, L_A$).

Figure 3.6 shows that both countries will experience long-term oscillations around the same level of output per capita. During the first periods, country B, which has a larger land area, will present a higher output per capita than country A. But this is a temporary situation, because country B's larger output per capita also leads to higher population growth (middle graph). Country B will therefore be able to support a sustainably larger population size than country A. Nevertheless, once the levels of output per capita start fluctuating around the same threshold in both countries, the variation between their populations tends to stabilise.

In other words, Figure 3.6 illustrates that the only effect of having access to a greater land area is the ability to reach a larger population size, it has no influence of the long-term trend of the output per capita: in all cases, output per capita stagnates around critical threshold $\hat{y}$.

These theoretical predictions are compatible with the data presented in Chapter 2, that shows that China and India had greater population sizes than France and the United Kingdom, while their levels of output per capita were very close. This also seems to be consistent with our Malthusian modelling.

3.6   Criticisms of the Malthusian Stagnation Model

The model presented above allows for a simple explanation or rationalisation of the stylised fact according to which the economy experienced a trend of output per capita stagnation during the pre-industrial era, in spite of the constant accumulation of knowledge over time.

As we have emphasised, the Malthusian doctrine constitutes but one way among others to account for the long stagnation during the pre-industrial period. As soon as the *Essay* was published and for decades after that, the Malthusian doctrine was often criticised. The criticisms touched upon different aspects of the doctrine and we will only address here the criticisms that specifically questioned the *Essay* in its purely positive dimension.[17] We can identify several different lines of attack.

3.6.1   Accumulation of Humans versus Accumulation of Ideas

Some authors accuse Malthus of being too pessimistic regarding the possibilities for the economy to expand in the future. In his *Outlines of a Critique of Political Economy* (1844), Engels makes the point that scientific progress is necessarily as rapid as population growth and cannot be slower than demographic growth. The reason given by Engels is that knowledge is built by humans, so if population size increases, the knowledge stock must increase in similar proportions. It is therefore not possible, according to Engels, to have an imbalance between population growth and knowledge growth (as Malthus thought).

This criticism by Engels directly addresses our hypothesis M2, according to which population growth can be greater than knowledge growth. It should be noted that, if one follows Engels in assuming that both accumulation processes – knowledge and humans – are equally strong, one must assume that a equals n, which means that output per capita increases at a positive rate as a consequence. Population is therefore not a source of real economic stagnation according to Engels.

3.6.2   Absolute Overpopulation versus Relative Overpopulation

Marx (1858) was also one of the strongest critics of the Malthusian doctrine. His two criticisms of the principle of population were discussed earlier (see Chapter 1). On the one hand, Malthus's principle leads to absolute overpopulation, whereas overpopulation is necessarily *relative* to a given mode of production. On the other hand, the principle is based on the abstract concept of "means of subsistence", when it is not so much the quantity of food that matters, but rather the purchasing power of individuals and, therefore, the distribution of resources within the population.

---

[17] Criticisms also addressed the more normative aspect of the *Essay on the Principle of Population*, in particular Malthus's recommendation that the Poor Laws be abolished, a recommendation based on extremely questionable normative foundations. These criticisms will not be addressed here. It should however be noted that Malthus's political recommendations were in part based on his principle of population, and the criticisms of that principle also made his normative argument weaker.

In *Das Kapital*, Marx (1867) further expanded his criticism of the Malthusian population doctrine and made the case that each historical mode of production has its own population law:[18]

The labouring population therefore produces, along with the accumulation of capital produced by it, the means by which itself is made relatively superfluous, is turned into a relative surplus population; and it does this to an always increasing extent. This is a law of population peculiar to the capitalist mode of production; and, in fact, every special historic mode of production has its own special laws of population, historically valid within its limits alone. An abstract law of population exists for plants and animals only, and only in so far as man has not interfered with them.

According to Marx, population growth is not the true cause of misery and stagnation: that cause can rather be found in the institutions of the capitalist society, in its mode of production, that is, in the form taken by the relationships between the different factors that enter into the production process. The sources of stagnation must be sought on the distribution side, not on the side of population growth. The Malthusian idea that population growth plays a central role in long-term economic dynamics is therefore erroneous according to Marx.

If this criticism is well-founded, then the Malthusian doctrine of population – and the model inspired by it in this chapter – misses the explanation for stagnation that is not the result of a disproportion between population and resources, but of an institutional framework that is unfavourable to economic progress. This framework would be an "omitted variable" in the analysis. We will return to this criticism in Chapter 5, which will be devoted entirely to the effect of institutions on long-run economic dynamics.

3.6.3 Population Growth as the Driving Force of Economic Growth

While Engels and Marx reject the thesis that population growth is the factor preventing the economic progress of societies, other authors go even further in their criticism. These other critics of Malthus argue that population growth does play a central role in economic development, but not the one emphasised by Malthus: for these authors, rather than being an obstacle to progress, population growth is a real *driving force* in the development process.

In his *Principles of Population and Production* (1816), Weyland criticises the foundations and corollaries of the Malthusian population doctrine. According to Weyland, the principle of population is wrong and there are no mechanisms of preventive or positive checks, simply because a population has a natural tendency to stay within an interval compatible with its ability to produce means of subsistence.[19]

Population has a *natural* tendency to keep *within the powers* of the soil to afford it subsistence in every gradation through which society passes.

---

[18] See Marx (1867), pp. 692–693.   [19] Weyland (1816), p. 21.

More fundamentally, Weyland accuses Malthus of ignoring the fact that societies have, over time, taken on very different forms. In particular, Malthus has ignored the crucial role played by the population size in the development of societies. According to Weyland, the pressure of population and, with it, the threat of lack of means of subsistence (risk of famine), have played a key role in the development of human societies.[20]

> During the alternate progress of population and subsistence in the earliest and most advanced stages of society, a *previous* increase of people is necessary to stimulate the community to a farther production of food [...] It results from this proposition that the incipient pressure of population against the *actual* means of subsistence [...] instead of being the cause of most of the miseries of human life, is in fact [...] the cause of all public happiness, industry, and prosperity.

Weyland explains that the pressure of population has led humans to seek – and ultimately find – new production techniques, new ways of organising and cooperating. Weyland refers here to the mechanism of the "force of necessity": the fear of lack of resources pushes people along the paths of progress. It is this fear that has enabled human societies to progress, both technologically and institutionally. The historical process cannot be separated from demographic pressure. For Weyland, in the absence of demographic pressure, humans would have remained primitive cave-men and there would have been no economic development of societies.

Weyland's approach is diametrically opposed to Malthus's: for Malthus, population growth is the major impediment to the progress of societies, whereas Weyland believes the opposite: population growth constitutes the main driving force in the technical and institutional progress of societies.

Weyland was well aware that human societies have often faced food scarcity, and even famine. He did not see these phenomena as a result of demographic pressure, but rather of the poor quality of those economies' institutions. Weyland insisted on the role played by institutions and in his comparison of Britain and Turkey, he went as far as claiming that the high quality of British government more than compensated for the lesser quality of British land compared to Turkish land. Weyland considered that episodes of famine or food scarcity were not caused by some sort of principle of population, but were rather the consequence of the poor quality of institutions.

In short, these criticisms of the Malthusian doctrine are also criticisms that could be levelled at the theoretical model developed in this chapter. In the next chapters, we shall return to these different aspects: the relationship between the rate of technical progress and the rate of population growth and, in particular, the effect of demographic pressure on the accumulation of knowledge (Chapter 4) and the question of the role of institutions on stagnation – and, later, on take-off (Chapter 5).

3.7   Conclusions

This chapter has presented a theoretical framework to explain the long period of stagnation in output per capita during the pre-industrial era. The model proposed is

---

[20] Weyland (1816), p. 22.

inspired by Malthus: in this analytical framework, *demographic pressure constitutes the obstacle to sustainable growth in output per capita.*

The mechanism is as follows: on the one hand, population growth is low when the output per capita is below a certain threshold $\hat{y}$, and higher when the output per capita is above $\hat{y}$ (hypothesis M1). On the other hand, the accumulation of knowledge, which takes place at a constant rate, dominates the demographic pressure when it is low, but is dominated when the latter is higher (hypothesis M2). Taken together, hypotheses M1 and M2 make permanent growth in output per capita impossible. The "race" between knowledge accumulation and human accumulation is "won" by knowledge for low levels of output per capita, but is "lost" in all other cases. The economy is therefore subject, over a long period of time, to fluctuations in GDP per capita around the $\hat{y}$ threshold, with no hope of sustainable growth and, hence, of a lasting improvement in living conditions.

Those who criticised the Malthusian doctrine identified, quite accurately, its excessive pessimism, but the fact remains that Malthus's theory accounts for the lack of sustainable improvement in living conditions that was the norm during the pre-industrial era. The Malthusian doctrine thus offers an explanation for the long reign of the stagnation regime, despite the continuous accumulation of knowledge and the improvement of production techniques over the centuries.

While this "rationalisation" of the stagnation of GDP per capita during the pre-industrial period is often used by historians and economists, it nevertheless suffers from a number of limitations. In addition to theoretical criticisms (underestimating institutional and distributional influences, ignoring the driving role of population), other criticisms of an empirical nature are worth noting. For example, although the historian–demographer Wrigley (1967) uses a Malthusian model to describe the pre-industrial demographic regime, he also acknowledges that the doctrine faces a number of anomalies. One of the most striking anomalies concerns the period following the Black Death in Europe (1346–1351). The epidemic decimated about a third of the European population. In the century following the epidemic, real wage levels rebounded to a level unprecedented in history.[21] One might have expected, in the light of the Malthusian doctrine (and our hypothesis M1), strong demographic growth after this wage increase. However, when we look at the evolution of the size of the British population over the next 125 years, we do not see any demographic "rebound"; it was only later, in the sixteenth century, that this rebound took place. This anomaly illustrates that while the Malthusian doctrine makes it possible to rationalise pre-industrial stagnation, it can only offer a "first approximation". Other factors, of a non-demographic nature, are also at work behind this stagnation.

Fortunately, human societies were able, during the nineteenth and twentieth centuries to escape from the stagnation regime and enter a new regime, the regime of economic growth. The next chapter will use the model we have developed to analyse the drivers of the transition from a stagnation regime to a growth regime. As we shall

---

[21] See Allen (2011).

see, the explanation of this transition is not unrelated to elements put forward by critics of the Malthusian doctrine.

Appendix 3A.1 Further Reading

In order to reflect at greater length on the Malthusian population doctrine and its consequences for long-run dynamics, nothing comes close to reading Malthus, notably his *Essay on the Principle of Population* (Malthus 1798). The later editions (Malthus 1803) and the final synthesis of his work *A Summary View* (1830) are also recommended reading. The reader will see that this chapter presents only one particular mathematical formalisation of the Malthusian doctrine, among a large number of other possible formulations.

Clark (2007) defends a very Malthusian reading of the pre-industrial stagnation period. He describes a whole series of empirical elements that tend to support this particular way of explaining or rationalising the long period of stagnation in living conditions through demographic dynamics. In particular, Clark provides empirical evidence establishing a link between wealth and the number of surviving children, all of which is evidence in support of the Malthusian mechanisms of positive and preventive checks, thus justifying our hypothesis M1.

Concerning the mathematical reformulations of the Malthusian doctrine, two contemporary references bear mentioning. First of all, *Classical Theories of Economic Growth* (Eltis 1984) constitutes a bold attempt to translate into mathematical language, and in particular into the language of modern growth theory, not only the thought of Malthus, but also the works of Quesnay, Ricardo and Marx. A second reference concerning Malthusian modelling is chapter 3 of Galor's treatise (2011), which has already been widely referred to above. This chapter proposes an alternative formulation of the Malthusian doctrine. It differs in spirit from ours, which places greater emphasis on the fluctuating or cyclical nature of the economic dynamics associated with the principle of population. Since Malthus himself did not give a clear mathematical formulation to his theory, no modelling can claim to be "the best", neither that of Eltis, nor that of Galor, nor, of course, the one proposed in this chapter.

Concerning the criticisms of the Malthusian doctrine, many works can be cited. At the theoretical level, the criticisms of Weyland (1816), Engels (1844) and Marx (1858, 1867), mentioned above, deserve a careful reading of the theoretical frameworks within which these criticisms were formulated. It is indeed a simplification to extract this or that element from a broader theoretical construction. At the empirical level, demographers and historians have examined, in various places, the validity of the Malthusian doctrine of population and, thus, indirectly, his economic theory of the stagnation regime. This is true in particular of Wrigley (1969), but also of the works of Mokyr (1980), Clark (2007) and Crafts and Mills (2009), with rather varied results, the Malthusian doctrine being far from unanimously accepted. The question of the empirical validity of this theorisation of stagnation remains entirely open today.

Appendix 3A.2 Exercises

1. Recalling the production function:

$$Y_t = A_t(L)^\beta (N_t)^\alpha.$$

Assuming that $\alpha = \frac{1}{2}$, that $L = 1$ and that $A_0 = 1$ and $N = 4$ and assuming that the knowledge accumulation factor a is unique and equals 2, whereas the population growth factor n is unique and equals 4.
   a. Calculate the total product in $t = 0$, $t = 1$ and $t = 2$.
   b. Calculate the output per capita in $t = 0$, $t = 1$ and $t = 2$.
   c. Under these hypotheses, can such an economy experience a long-term output per capita growth? Justify your answer.

2. Considering an economy with the following production function:

$$Y_t = A_t(L)^\beta (N_t)^\alpha.$$

That economy experiences the following time series of output per capita:

Period	$t = 0$	$t = 1$	$t = 2$	$t = 3$
y_t	10	30	90	270

   a. If $\alpha = \beta = 1$ and $L = 1$, what is the initial level of the knowledge stock A_0?
   b. Under the same hypotheses, what is the knowledge accumulation factor?
   c. Repeat a. and b. if $L = 2$.

3. Let us examine once again the model developed in this chapter. The production function is:

$$Y_t = A_t(L)^\beta (N_t)^\alpha.$$

And we also have hypothesis M1:
There exists an output per capita threshold $\hat{y} > 0$ such that:

$$n_t = \check{n} > 1 \quad \text{if } y_t < \hat{y}$$

$$n_t = \hat{n} > 1 \quad \text{if } y_t \geq \hat{y}$$

$$\text{with } \check{n} < \hat{n}.$$

Let us replace hypothesis M2:

$$(\check{n})^{1-\alpha} < a < (\hat{n})^{1-\alpha}$$

by hypothesis M2':

$$a < (\check{n})^{1-\alpha} < (\hat{n})^{1-\alpha}.$$

a. Describe the dynamics of the total product.
b. Describe the dynamics of the output per capita.
c. Repeat a. and b. if hypothesis M2 is replaced by hypothesis M2″:

$$(\check{n})^{1-\alpha} < (\hat{n})^{1-\alpha} < a.$$

4. As noted by Bairoch (1993), p. 237:

Strong population growth does not have a minor role in the economic problems of the Third World.[22]

a. Is this remark by Bairoch concerning developing countries compatible with the model studied in this chapter? Justify your answer.
b. In that model, what mechanisms would contribute to population growth preventing the process of economic take-off?

---

[22] Translated by Colette J. Windish.

4 The Economic Take-Off

The previous chapter showed how we could account for the long stagnation in output per capita during the pre-industrial era, by using a production model of a composite good made up of labour, land and knowledge. This explanation was inspired by Malthus: in the model, any improvement in living conditions ends up generating demographic pressure that cancels it, so that the economy cannot make sustainable progress. Demographic pressure is at the root of the long stagnation regime.

The statistical series studied in Chapter 2 have shown that this period of stagnation, which lasted several millennia, came to an end at the beginning of the nineteenth century, and that a kind of "economic take-off" took place at that time. There are several ways to illustrate this take-off. While Chapter 2 used statistical series measuring total production (by country), the chronology of this take-off can also be studied using other, less aggregated data. As an example, Figure 4.1 shows the evolution of cast iron production in England between 1720 and 1850. By focusing on a single sector – but one that was a driving force of the industrial revolution – Figure 4.1 provides a less aggregated, and more concrete, picture of the take-off and its timing.

While cast iron production remained almost constant during the first half of the eighteenth century, a take-off began around 1780 and, by the end of the century, cast iron production was already four times higher than in 1720, but this was only the beginning of the take-off. The rhythm of growth was to accelerate: between 1796 and 1850, the production of cast iron was multiplied by twenty-two, from 109,000 tonnes to 2,249,000 tonnes. This substantial growth, in just five decades, reflects the speed and scale of the take-off that took place in Britain at the beginning of the nineteenth century.

Economic take-off can obviously not be explained by the model used in the previous chapter, because that model makes explicit the conditions for the existence of a regime of perpetual stagnation (from which the economy cannot escape). This leads unavoidably to the question: how have societies been able to emerge, after centuries of immobility, from a regime of stagnation? Through what means have countries finally been able to escape the Malthusian "trap"? What conditions made economic take-off possible? More specifically, what assumptions of the model in Chapter 3 need to be replaced in order to explain the exit from the stagnation regime, and the transition to the growth regime?

These are complex questions and this chapter will attempt to answer them in an incremental fashion. Section 4.1 suggests that, rather than accumulating at a constant rate (as in the previous chapter), knowledge grows at a rate that varies with population

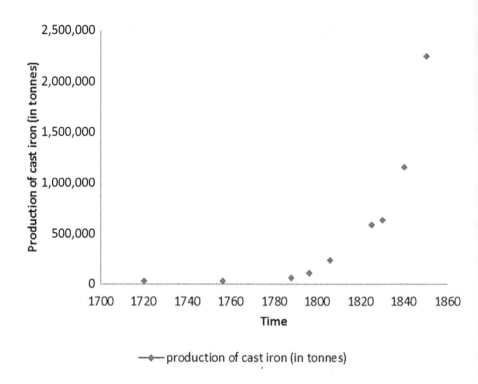

Figure 4.1 Production of cast iron in England, 1720–1850 (in tonnes). *(source:* Niveau 1976)

size, and is higher when the population exceeds a certain critical threshold. At the same time, we will relax hypothesis M2, which played a crucial role in the failure to achieve sustainable GDP per capita growth. Section 4.2 will then take up the model of Chapter 3 and incorporate these modifications. The modified model corresponds to a simplified, discrete-time variant of Kremer's (1993) model. Sustainable growth in output per capita is possible in this economy, despite the maintenance of the Malthusian hypothesis M1. In Section 4.3, we will show that this new model can explain why economies first experienced a long period of stagnation in output per capita and then a transition to a growth regime. Our modified model thus accounts for the transition from a stagnation regime to a growth regime without requiring an exogenous shock on a structural parameter. Finally, while Section 4.4 will return to the differences between this model and the previous chapter, Sections 4.5 and 4.6 will use our modified model to analyse differences between countries in the timing of their economic take-offs.

4.1   Technical Progress and Population

4.1.1   Scale Effects

Contrary to what Malthus believed in assuming that technical progress was independent from demographic variables, knowledge accumulation and change in technologies are not impervious to population size. The number of humans does influence change in techniques and knowledge through several mechanisms.

To put it another way, *the scale of the society* influences the process of knowledge accumulation and the improvement of production techniques. In contemporary economic theory, we have to consider what are called "scale effects". Scale effects refer to the idea of the non-neutrality of the size of an economy on the way it functions, whether at the local level (scale effects in a particular company) or at the global level (scale effects in society as a whole).

Let us first return to the model discussed in Chapter 3. In this economy, where the size of the land is fixed at L, one cannot speak of "economies of scale" in the classical sense of the term (Marshall 1890), a term that refers to the variation in output induced by a change in the size of *all* the factors of production. Let us look at what happens when only the population size is changed (the other variables are assumed to be constant). In this model, we had *negative* scale effects, in the sense that an increase in population size had the effect of reducing output per capita (through decreasing marginal returns to labour input). Indeed, the increase in the number of workers increased total output *less than proportionally* to the growth in labour, resulting in a decrease in output per capita.

It should be noted that the addition of workers was the *only* effect of population size on our model; there were no other channels for population size to influence the level of production.

This is where the major simplification of this model lies, by overlooking the important influence that population size can have on the accumulation of knowledge and on technical progress and thus on the productivity of workers.

Although the study of scale effects is today a central component of economic theory (in particular in studying the organisation of industry and the location of production units), it is useful to take a small diversion through the history of economic ideas to account for the origins (and the age) of these scale effects.

4.1.2   Smith (1776) and the Division of Labour

One of the first authors to highlight the existence of scale effects was Adam Smith. In his treatise, *An Inquiry on the Nature and Causes of the Wealth of Nations* (1776), Smith, through his theory of the division of labour, indirectly highlighted the crucial influence of population size on the functioning of the economy.

Smith considered that the driving force in increasing the wealth of nations – what we would now call "economic growth" – was the division of labour, that is, a distribution of tasks among workers such that each worker performs as few separate (distinct) tasks as possible. This division of labour takes place both within each production unit and in society as a whole. The latter is referred to as the social division of labour.

According to Smith, the division of labour constitutes the main driving force in nations becoming wealthier, because it allows for considerable productivity gains. In other words, for a given number of workers, total output can substantially vary, depending on whether tasks have been well distributed or not, that is, depending on the degree of specialisation of the workers. Smith illustrates this point with the example of a pin factory.[1] The total number of pins produced in one day by a team of ten workers can vary between 200 and 48,000, depending on whether each worker participates in the eighteen tasks required in the manufacture of a pin, or, on the contrary, performs only one or two separate tasks.

Task specialisation induced by the division of labour leads, according to Smith, to substantial productivity gains, in the sense that the same number of workers will produce a greater quantity of product when tasks are divided more finely, which leads to greater specialisation. Task allocation is therefore not neutral with regard to output per worker. According to Smith, the mechanisms by which the division of labour leads to labour productivity gains are threefold. First, specialisation generates, through the repetition of tasks, gains in skill and dexterity. Second, task specialisation makes it possible to avoid time losses induced by switching from one task to another. Third, division of labour also allows a complex production process to be divided into a sum of simple tasks. This is a first step towards the mechanisation (and later automation) of production processes, which results in considerable productivity gains. Through these three mechanisms, the division of labour generates productivity gains and leads to the wealth of nations.

What is then the relationship between division of labour and scale effects? The link is as follows: according to Smith, the extent of the division of labour is necessarily limited by the size of the economy under consideration.[2]

As it is the power of exchanging that gives occasion to the division of labour, so the extent of this division must always be limited by the extent of that power, or, in other words, by the extent of the market. When the market is very small, no person can have any encouragement to dedicate himself entirely to one employment, for want of the power to exchange all the surplus part of the produce of his own labour, which is over and above his own consumption, for such parts of the produce of other men's labour as he has occasion for.

The smaller the population size, the more the opportunities for worker specialisation are reduced. On the other hand, the larger the population size, the greater the possibilities for division of labour, thus making substantial productivity gains possible. The population size plays a key role by determining the scope of both division of labour and specialisation and thus directly influences productivity gains and the development of production techniques.[3]

In short, Smith is already proposing the idea of the non-neutrality of population size for labour productivity, and thus for the economic expansion of nations. Using the lens of Smith's work, our assumption that technology A_t is independent of population size

---

[1] See Smith (1776), pp. 18–19.   [2] See Smith (1776), chapter III, p. 35.

[3] It is worth noting that the size of the economy is not the only determinant of the extent of the division of labour. As Smith (1776) has shown, the social division of labour requires a place of exchange – the market – that allows each worker to obtain, through the exchange of goods produced, the things necessary for life. The institutional framework therefore plays a crucial role, as the absence of markets prevents specialisation and therefore limits productivity gains and hinders the process of economic development. We shall return to the role of institutions – and of the market in particular – in Chapter 5.

and grows at a constant rate a appears questionable. The arguments put forward in the *Wealth of Nations* require making the rate of technological progress dependent on the population size, and higher when the number of workers is larger. Gains from specialisation mean that a large population accelerates the improvement of production techniques and thus the growth of labour productivity.

4.1.3   Weyland (1816) and the Force of Necessity

As discussed above, Weyland (1816) also expressed the view that technical progress is not independent of population size. The "force of necessity" argument implies a dependence of the rate of technical progress on the population size. The greater the demographic pressure, the greater the threat of a shortage, which encourages people to develop new production techniques in order to solve the problem posed by that demographic pressure.[4]

This argument does not rely on division of labour, but rather on what drives technological progress and the productivity gains that go with it. According to Weyland, demographic pressure constitutes the *stimulus* that plays a key role in driving the wealth of nations. Weyland considered that demographic pressure is the origin of an acceleration in technical progress and also the source of institutional improvement. He thus described demographic pressure not as an obstacle but as one of the major driving forces behind the enrichment of nations.

In Weyland's opinion, it is the absence of demographic pressure that leads societies to remain unchanged; remaining forever in their initial stage of a small local economy of isolated producer–consumers, a simple subsistence economy, without experiencing any transformation over time. In the absence of the stimulus provided by the fear of food scarcity, societies would have experienced little technical or institutional progress and would have remained in a kind of *status quo*. Weyland considered that it was demographic pressure that brought societies into history.

4.1.4   Knowledge and Population Size: From Engels (1844) to Kremer (1993)

Another argument discussed earlier also deserves mentioning, that developed by Engels (1844). Engels put forward the idea that knowledge is produced by humans. Therefore, a larger population leads to greater knowledge production and faster technical progress. Engels's argument is not based on the division of labour, nor on what can motivate progress in knowledge: it is an argument based on purely technical considerations related to knowledge production. Since humans are the ones who produce knowledge, it is difficult to imagine through which mechanisms "human accumulation" might overtake knowledge accumulation.

Similar considerations are present in Kremer's (1993) more recent theory. According to Kremer, in every worker lies a potential inventor, who can discover a

---

[4] According to Weyland (1816), the effect of the "force of necessity" on production techniques depends on the quality of the institutional environment, a point we will further examine in Chapter 5.

new production technique, new solutions to old problems. Therefore, the higher the number of workers, the faster the technical progress will be. Kremer's (1993) argument is formulated as follows.

According to Kremer, the probability, for each single person, of discovering a new production technique is fixed and does not depend on the total number of humans. Consequently, when calculating the probability, at an aggregate level, of a technological discovery, this probability increases with the population size. It follows, according to Kremer, that the rate of technological progress is not independent of population size, but rather increases with population size. This law would explain the acceleration of major technical discoveries in the nineteenth and twentieth centuries. According to Kremer, this acceleration is not due to chance, but is linked to growth in the population size.

4.1.5   Revisiting the Accumulation of Knowledge

To summarise, many mechanisms link the accumulation of knowledge and the improvement of production techniques to population size. To account for these effects, this chapter will abandon the assumption of a constant knowledge growth factor and replace it with the following assumption: the knowledge growth factor is lower when the population size is below a critical threshold $\overline{N}$, and is higher when the population size is above that threshold. This hypothesis is a simplified version of the hypothesis formulated in Kremer (1993):

[Hypothesis K1]

$$\frac{A_{t+1}}{A_t} = \underline{a} > 1 \quad \text{when } N_t < \overline{N}$$

$$\frac{A_{t+1}}{A_t} = \overline{a} > 1 \quad \text{when } N_t \geq \overline{N}$$

with $\overline{a} > \underline{a}$.

Hypothesis K1 accounts for the existence of scale effects in the accumulation of knowledge. Depending on whether the population size is below or above a certain critical threshold, knowledge accumulation will either be slower or faster. It should be noted that this hypothesis posits only two levels for the knowledge growth factor, whereas we could make this factor a multi-value function, depending on the population size. We shall limit ourselves here to a two-valued function, in order to simplify the explanation.

Hypothesis K1 reflects the crucial role of population size in the production of knowledge. It should be noted that this hypothesis, by stating the existence of different knowledge growth rates according to population size, forces us de facto to abandon hypothesis M2 stated in Chapter 3, which was based on a single knowledge growth rate. The following sections will explore the consequences of these changes for our model and the possibility or impossibility of sustainable growth of the output per capita.

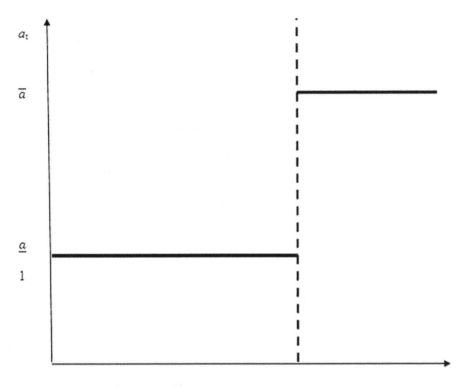

Figure 4.2 Hypothesis K1

4.2   A Modified Model

4.2.1   The Conditions for Growth

As in Chapter 3, the production function is:

$$Y_t = A_t(L)^\beta (N_t)^\alpha.$$

Furthermore, output per capita equals:

$$y_t = \frac{Y_t}{N_t} = \frac{A_t(L)^\beta}{(N_t)^{1-\alpha}}.$$

However, the output per capita growth rate equals:

$$g_{t+1} = \frac{a_t}{(n_t)^{1-\alpha}} - 1.$$

There is only one difference with what we saw in Chapter 3, but it is a crucial difference: the numerator of the first term on the right-hand side of the equation, the knowledge growth factor, is no longer constant but rather is time-dependent.

From hypothesis K1, we know that the knowledge growth factor is equal to $\underline{a}$ when the population size N_t is below the threshold $\overline{N}$ and equals $\overline{a} > \underline{a}$ when the population size N_t is above the threshold $\overline{N}$. This difference may seem trivial, but, as we shall see, it considerably modifies the properties of the long-run dynamics of the output per capita in our economy.

Indeed, regarding output per capita growth, three cases can now arise:

- if $a_t > (n_t)^{1-\alpha}$, output per capita grows at a positive rate, that is to say, $g_{t+1} > 0$;
- if $a_t = (n_t)^{1-\alpha}$, output per capita is constant, that is to say, $g_{t+1} = 0$;
- if $a_t < (n_t)^{1-\alpha}$, output per capita grows at a negative rate, that is to say, $g_{t+1} < 0$.

Once again, whether output per capita grows or not depends on whether knowledge accumulates faster than humans or not (with declining marginal returns to labour being taken into account as in Chapter 3). As previously, output per capita growth will occur when knowledge accumulation "wins its race" against human accumulation.

Regarding the population growth factor n_t, we will, as in Chapter 3, use hypothesis M1, which links population growth to the level of output per capita: when output per capita is below a threshold $\hat{y}$, the population growth factor equals $\underline{n} > 1$, whereas, when output per capita is above threshold $\hat{y}$, the population growth factor equals $\overline{n} > \underline{n}$.[5]

In Chapter 3, resolving the model depended on hypotheses relating to the speed of knowledge accumulation relative to human accumulation: that is hypothesis M2, which we discussed at length. As pointed out above, we can no longer maintain this hypothesis that is based on a single factor of knowledge growth. Instead of the hypothesis M2, we will posit hypothesis K2.

[Hypothesis K2]

$$\underline{a} = (\underline{n})^{1-\alpha} < (\overline{n})^{1-\alpha} < \overline{a}.$$

Hypothesis K2 amounts to assuming that the two values taken by the knowledge growth factor $\underline{a}$ and $\overline{a}$ are such that the lower value $\underline{a}$ is smaller than the high population growth factor brought to the power $1 - \alpha$, $(\overline{n})^{1-\alpha}$, while the upper value of the knowledge growth factor $\overline{a}$ is greater than $(\overline{n})^{1-\alpha}$.

In other words, when economies are small, they do not benefit much from scale effects and are more vulnerable to demographic pressure, which prevents output per capita growth. On the contrary, when economies are large, they benefit from powerful scale effects, which allow the accumulation of knowledge to dominate population growth, which then becomes a "second-order" determinant of the economic dynamics.

---

[5] Here again, we deliberately ignore cases of sustainable decline in population size.

4.2.2 Four Cases

Hypothesis K2 has immediate consequences for the increase or decrease in output per capita. Depending on the levels of output per capita and population size relative to the critical thresholds $\hat{y}$ and $\overline{N}$, four cases can arise. These four cases, denoted by the letters I, II, III and IV, are shown in Table 4.1.

Table 4.1 Conditions for output per capita growth

	Population size	
Output per capita	$N_t <$ **threshold, $\overline{N}$**	$N_t \geq$ **threshold, $\overline{N}$**
$y_t <$ threshold, $\overline{N}$	CASE I: $g_{t+1} = 0$	CASE III: $g_{t+1} > 0$
$y_t \geq$ threshold, $\overline{N}$	CASE II: $g_{t+1} < 0$	CASE IV: $g_{t+1} > 0$

As shown in Table 4.1, under hypothesis K2, the size of the economy plays a crucial role regarding the potential growth in output per capita. When the economy is small (cases I and II), output per capita tends to either stagnate (case I) or decrease (case II). Conversely, when the economy is larger than the critical size (cases III and IV), output per capita experiences growth due to scale effects made possible by a large enough economy.

Table 4.1 shows how important the size of the economy is under hypothesis K2. However, this table is not enough to tell us what the long-term dynamics of the output per capita will be; it only shows us four cases that are theoretically possible, but does not allow us to know what path an economy will take, how it will move from one case to another. This question is precisely the subject of the following section.

4.3 The Regime Shift

It is now possible to study the dynamics of the output per capita over the long period. This will enable us to show the extent to which the model studied in this chapter – specifically hypotheses K1 and K2 – can explain or rationalise the observed take-off of the output per capita during the nineteenth century and hence the transition from a pre-industrial stagnation regime to a modern growth regime, in spite of the presence of the Malthus-inspired hypothesis M1.

Let us consider the case of an economy with an initial low output per capita and small population size. We are therefore initially dealing with case I from Table 4.1. In that situation, we know that output per capita is stagnant because, following hypothesis K2, the knowledge growth factor is exactly equal to the population growth factor. An increase in the output per capita is impossible. We are dealing with a stagnation regime. The stagnation of the output per capita derives from the fact that the growth in population completely neutralises the productivity gains associated with the accumulation of knowledge.

Will the economy remain stagnant?

No, because the population in case I continues to grow. Admittedly, due to hypothesis M1, it grows by a small factor $\underline{n}$. However, it is still growing, and this slow growth will sooner or later cause the population size to exceed the critical threshold $\overline{N}$.

At the exact moment that the critical threshold $\overline{N}$ is reached, the economy enters case III, in which the size of the economy is large enough to allow the existence of powerful scale effects, effects that will contribute to the acceleration of the accumulation of knowledge and thus make it possible for knowledge to win its "race" against population. As a result, output per capita begins to increase. The economy then leaves the regime of stagnation and enters a regime of growth.

This configuration therefore explains why an economy that has known centuries, or even millennia, of stagnation in output per capita will, at some point, take off and see output per capita increase significantly and sustainably.

The ultimate transition of the economy to the third regime (case IV), which takes place when output per capita exceeds the threshold $\hat{y}$, is almost anecdotal, since population growth remains a second-order determinant alongside the rapid accumulation of knowledge made possible by scale effects. Indeed, in case IV, population growth is reinforced, but this does not prevent the growth of output per capita from continuing, since the power of scale effects induced by the large size of the economy continues to be the dominant force. It should be noted, however, that the output per capita growth rate, while still positive, is in case IV smaller than in case III, due to the higher growth in the population. Thus, we witness a slowdown in output per capita growth induced by higher population growth, without calling into question the sustainability of the latter. This slowdown in output per capita growth does not, in itself, constitute a distinct economic regime: in case III as in case IV, output per capita grows and the economy definitively leaves its initial stagnation regime (case I).[6]

To summarise, our economy goes through two distinct regimes: at first, a regime of stagnation of the output per capita; then, a regime of growth of the output per capita (with a reduced growth rate after the transition from case III to case IV).

In the first regime (case I), the population size is too small to allow scale effects to be achieved and the economy experiences stagnation in output per capita. This period of stagnation occurs despite the accumulation of knowledge, because the accumulation of knowledge is too slow in relation to the increase in population size. During this period of stagnation in output per capita, the population size continues to grow and will sooner or later cross the critical threshold beyond which scale effects become fully effective. The economy then leaves the stagnation regime to enter the output per capita growth regime (case III). This output per capita growth takes place despite population growth, because scale effects tend to accelerate the accumulation of knowledge and technical progress in such a way that population growth becomes a second-order determinant of output per capita growth.

For illustrative purposes, Figure 4.3 presents the dynamics of output per capita, population and knowledge over time, focusing on the transition between stagnation and growth regimes.

---

[6] It is worth noting, to further simplify our point, that we could have even assumed that the economy initially starts with an output per capita higher than $\hat{y}$, so as to focus only on the transition from case II (decrease in output per capita) to case IV (increase in output per capita), which is the most interesting transition.

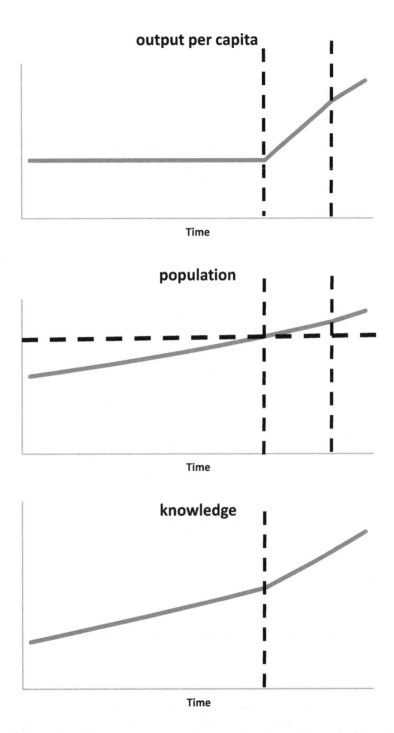

Figure 4.3 Dynamics of the output per capita, the population size and the stock of knowledge

Figure 4.3 first shows the stagnation in output per capita. This stagnation (top graph) is due to the fact that population growth (middle graph) cancels out the growth of knowledge (bottom graph). However, when population size reaches a certain critical threshold, the accumulation of knowledge accelerates (hypothesis K1), as can be seen in the lower graph in Figure 4.3.

Thanks to this acceleration in knowledge accumulation, the output per capita can "take off", as can be seen in the graph at the top of Figure 4.3. The economy is then in a growth regime. During this period, the population size continues to grow and knowledge continues to accumulate – as in the stagnation regime – but the difference is that scale effects have reinforced knowledge accumulation. This acceleration of technical progress allows the economy to take off.

It should be noted that once the output per capita reaches a certain threshold, population growth accelerates (see middle graph) and thus slows down the growth of output per capita (top graph). The economy then remains in the growth regime, but experiences a slowdown in output per capita growth compared to when it took off.

Figure 4.3 illustrates what we referred to above as a *regime shift*. The economy undergoes quantitative changes throughout its existence (population growth, growth in the stock of knowledge) but at a certain point – when the population size reaches the threshold $\overline{N}$ – we witness a major qualitative change: while the growth of N_t and A_t was associated with a *stagnation* of the output per capita y_t for a size below the threshold, these same growths are now associated not with stagnation but with a *growth* of output per capita. Here we are in the presence of a profound qualitative change, a change in the shape of the relationships between the variables. It is important to note that, in both regimes, total product, population and knowledge increase over time: however, a major qualitative difference concerns the relationship between these variables and output per capita product. In the stagnation regime, growth in the stock of variables is associated with stagnation in output per capita, while in the growth regime it is associated with growth in output per capita.

Our model thus makes it possible to explain or "rationalise" the transition, after centuries of immobility, from an economy where the output per capita is stagnating (despite the accumulation of knowledge) to an economy where the output per capita is growing (despite population growth).

4.4   Comparison with the Chapter 3 Stagnation Model

Let us now compare the dynamics of our economy with those of the previous chapter. The long-run dynamics of output per capita here are very different from those associated with the model in Chapter 3. As a reminder, in that theoretical framework, output per capita growth could not be sustained in the long term and was only a temporary or transitory phenomenon: sooner or later it caused an increase in population growth that, because of its magnitude in relation to the accumulation of knowledge, led to a fall in output per capita. In Chapter 3, the trend is therefore towards long-term stagnation in output per capita (more precisely, fluctuations around the critical threshold $\hat{y}$).

Things are quite different in the model explored in this chapter. In this model, the economy necessarily ends up, after a period (which can be quite long) of stagnation in output per capita, experiencing sustainable growth in output per capita. It is true that an increase in population growth beyond a certain threshold of output per capita slows down economic growth, but this is not enough to reverse the trend. Thus, in this second model, the economy necessarily ends up leaving a situation of stagnation in output per capita, in order to "take off". This take-off is not followed by a crash, but leads the economy on a path of long-term sustainable growth.

Where does this difference come from in terms of the possibility or impossibility of sustainable growth in GDP per capita? The fundamental difference between the two models lies in hypothesis K1, which makes technical progress dependent on the population size. This dependence on population size has a crucial impact here because it allows the economy, once it has reached a sufficiently large population size, to leave behind the state of poverty once and for all.

Indeed, in this second model, the population size is the variable that carries, as it were, the *latent dynamics* of the economy: this variable experiences a slow growth over time, a growth that may seem insignificant and without great effects, until the day when the population size exceeds a certain critical threshold, a threshold beyond which the qualitative properties of the economy fundamentally change.

This is referred to as "latent dynamics" because, at first glance, the population size does not seem to play a big role. However, it is this variable whose evolution will, at some point in time, precipitate the regime shift. Whereas the small economy was trapped by population growth and was condemned to stagnating standards of living, this is no longer the case at all for the large economy that has, in some ways, freed itself from this constraint thanks to the scale effects induced by the large population size, and now experiences a sustainable growth in output per capita.

This transition between the two regimes was made possible by the slow and gradual growth of the population over time. At first glance, this population growth seems benign, almost neutral in terms of the historical process. But this is not the case: at a certain point, the population reaches a critical threshold, which leads to the regime shift and the transition from a regime of stagnation to one of growth.

In this economy, what can be seen is the paradoxical role of demographic growth: although it is initially an obstacle to output per capita growth (as in a purely Malthusian economy), it nevertheless enables the economy to reach a critical size at a given moment, a size that will enable it to achieve sustainable growth of output per capita.

In conclusion, the model discussed in this chapter explains how an economy can, after centuries of stagnation in output per capita, suddenly "take off" and find itself on a path to sustainable growth. The essential ingredient in this model is that the rate of technical progress is dependent on population size and tends to grow with it. The population size plays a crucial role: once it has reached a certain threshold, the economy can benefit from powerful scale effects, allowing it to move from a regime of stagnation to one of growth.

4.5   International Comparisons: The Timing of Take-off

As shown by Rostow (1960) in *The Stages of Economic Growth*, take-off did not occur at the same time in all countries (see Chapter 1). Whereas the United Kingdom took off around 1783–1802, France only took off around 1830–1860, as did Belgium, while the United States followed around 1843–1860. Japan's take-off, according to Rostow, did not occur until 1878–1900. Chinese and South American economies, for their part, had a later take-off (in the 1950s).[7]

When examining such differences in the timing of take-off, a first question regarding our model is to ascertain the means through which it could explain differences from country to country as to when the take-off occurred.

To answer this question, let us use our model to compare several hypothetical economies that differ only in some dimensions, but are otherwise equal. Of course, many comparisons could be made. We will assume that the parameters present in hypotheses K1, K2 and M1 are the same in all the economies being compared, and focus on differences in initial conditions for the three factors of production: land, labour and knowledge. Is it possible, in our model, to explain differences in take-off timing by differences in initial conditions in terms of land, labour or knowledge?

4.5.1   Initial Conditions: Land

Let us first look at land. Consider two economies A and B that differ only in the amount of land available, which is greater in B than in A. On the other hand, the two economies A and B are identical in every other respect (same structural parameters), including the initial levels of population size N_0 and of knowledge stock A_0. What is the effect of the difference in surface area L on the timing of take-off?

In order to answer this question, it should be noted that the economy B's larger land area allows that country to initially have a higher output per capita than in country A. Two scenarios must be distinguished, depending on whether the difference in land area allows economy B to have an initial output per capita below or above the critical threshold $\hat{y}$. These two cases are represented in Figure 4.4.

Let us begin by considering the first case, in which the differential in available land area is relatively small, so that, despite a larger land area, economy B initially has an output per capita below the threshold $\hat{y}$. In this case, both countries are initially subject to the same demographic growth factor, and both experience stagnation. The only difference concerns the level of output per capita, which is higher in economy B. But as the demographic dynamics are the same in both countries, the population sizes of the two countries are equal in each period and will reach the critical threshold $\overline{N}$ at the same time. Both economies A and B will experience take-off at the same point in time, the only difference being the level of output per capita, which is higher in economy B. It should nonetheless be noted that, since country B has a higher output per capita in each

---

[7] See Rostow (1960), p. 81.

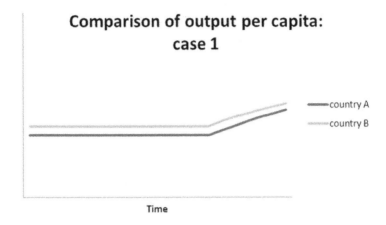

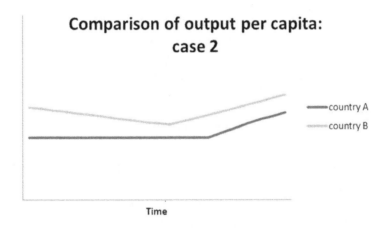

Figure 4.4 Comparisons of two countries differing in land area $(L_A < L_B)$

period, it will reach threshold $\hat{y}$ sooner, which will generate an earlier slowdown in growth in this country compared with that in country A.

Let us now consider the second case, in which the differential in land area is greater, so that economy B initially has an output per capita greater than the threshold $\hat{y}$. In that case, country B is subject from the outset to a different demographic dynamic than country A. Since the output per capita in country B is higher than the threshold $\hat{y}$, country B has a faster population growth, with two consequences. First of all, country B initially experiences a period of declining output per capita because population growth is too high relative to the accumulation of knowledge. Second, because the population size is growing faster in country B, it reaches the critical size needed for take-off more rapidly. Country B therefore experiences take-off faster than country A.

This can be summarised in the following manner: differences between countries in the amount of land available have varying effects on the timing of take-off, depending on whether these differences are of high magnitude or not. When differences in land

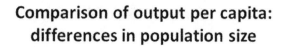

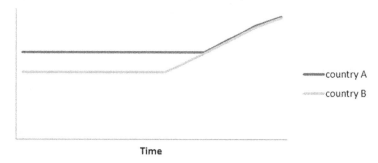

Figure 4.5 Comparison of countries differing in initial population size ($N_{0A} < N_{0B}$)

area are small, countries experience take-off at the same point in time. On the other hand, when these differences are large, population dynamics vary between countries, such that countries experience differences in the timing of take-off.

4.5.2   Initial Conditions: Population Size

Let us now examine the consequences of differences in the initial population size N_0, everything else being assumed to remain unchanged. As shown in Figure 4.5, differences in the size of the initial population lead to differences in the timing of take-off, with the country with the largest population initially experiencing a faster take-off. This is the case for country B in Figure 4.5. Country B has a larger population, resulting in an output per capita that is initially smaller than in country A. But the larger population size will allow it to take off more rapidly. The intuition behind this early take-off is as follows. Take-off occurs when scale effects accelerate the accumulation of knowledge and technical progress. However, these scale effects only occur when the economy reaches a large enough size. Since Economy B starts out with a larger population size, it reaches this critical size more rapidly, which explains its early take-off.

4.5.3   Initial Conditions: Stock of Knowledge

To conclude, let us compare two countries that are equal in all respects except for the initial stock of knowledge. Suppose that economy B initially enjoys a technological lead over economy A. Two scenarios must be distinguished here, depending on whether the difference in the stock of knowledge allows economy B to initially have an output per capita either below or above the critical threshold $\hat{y}$. Both cases are represented in Figure 4.6.

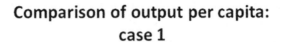

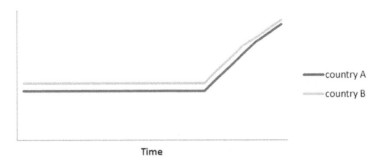

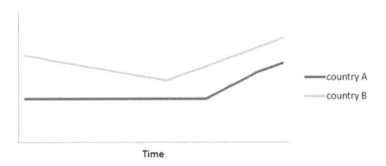

Figure 4.6 Comparison of two countries differing in terms of initial stock of knowledge $(A_{0A} < A_{0B})$

In the first case, the technological advance of country B is minimal, so that the output per capita initially remains below the threshold $\hat{y}$. In this case, the two countries have the same demographic dynamics, the only difference being that country B has a slightly higher output per capita than country A. However, since the two countries have the same demographic dynamics, they both reach the critical threshold at the same time, which leads to substantial scale effects and, therefore, these two economies take off at the same time. Note that country B will experience an earlier slowdown in growth than country A because it will reach the critical threshold $\hat{y}$ earlier.

In the second case, the technological advance of country B is such that it has, from the outset, an output per capita above the threshold $\hat{y}$. This country therefore experiences stronger demographic growth, with two consequences. The first is that country B initially faces a deterioration in material living conditions due to a drop in output per capita. But the second consequence is that the take-off will take place earlier in country B, because the strong demographic growth enables this country to reach more rapidly the critical size needed to see scale effects emerge and technical progress accelerate.

In conclusion, while initial differences in the population size necessarily lead to differentials in the timing of take-off, things are more complex when it comes to differences in the amount of land available or the stock of knowledge: these differences will only result in a different timing of take-off if they affect demographic dynamics.

4.6   The Industrial Revolution

Now that we have clarified the effects in our model of the initial differences in land quantity, population size and stock of knowledge, let us return to the data and the differences between countries in the timing of their take-off. From this perspective, an important question is why did the United Kingdom take off earlier than France, the United States or even India and China?

The United Kingdom's early take-off is all the more surprising given that, for centuries, it lagged behind other European economies. As Allen (2011) reminds us, around the year 1500 the most advanced economies were Italy and Spain. Those two countries had the largest cities and the most developed manufacturing. They were followed by what we now call Belgium and the Netherlands. But unlike Italy and Spain, Britain was still, around 1500, "little more than a sheep walk".[8] How did this "sheep walk" become, three centuries later, the economy that took off first?

Historians disagree on how to answer that question.[9]

- Allen (2011) emphasises that Britain had much higher income levels in the eighteenth century than elsewhere, and that these income gaps (vis-à-vis France and other countries) are likely to explain differences in worker health, labour productivity and investment, leading to the earlier take-off of the economy. He also highlights two other dimensions: access to cheap energy (thanks to coal deposits) and the development of a large trading empire around the world.
- Clark (2007) offers an evolutionary explanation. According to him, the advantage of Britain appears when one studies the strength of the link between wealth and the number of descendants who survive to adulthood in different countries. In every country, in the pre-industrial period, the wealthiest individuals left more descendants than the least wealthy. But this link was stronger in Britain than elsewhere and it contributed to the greater diffusion of skills and knowledge across *all* levels of English society (the elites, with a greater evolutionary advantage, were more evenly distributed across all occupations than in other countries, where the relatively smaller numbers of members of the elites occupied only certain occupations). This wider distribution of elites across all jobs is, in Clark's view, what favoured an early take-off of the British economy.

---

[8] See Allen (2011), p. 23.

[9] It should be noted that these arguments are based on empirical material relating to Great Britain (rather than the United Kingdom as a whole). But since Great Britain is the largest component of the United Kingdom, these arguments are relevant to the issue at hand.

- Acemoglu and Robinson (2013) consider that if Britain experienced an early economic take-off compared to other economies, it is above all thanks to its leadership when it comes to the institutional framework. According to these authors, the Glorious Revolution (1688), by establishing a parliamentary monarchy, helped establish a better balance of power in Britain compared to other countries. This more balanced and more open institutional framework was more favourable to innovation, technological advances and, ultimately, economic take-off. Indeed, this institutional framework would have given individuals stronger incentives to innovate and be entrepreneurial, incentives that led the economy to take off earlier.

What can the model studied in this chapter tell us about these three hypotheses?

Let us start with Allen's (2011) hypothesis. In our model, can a higher initial output per capita be associated with an earlier take-off? As we saw in the previous section, the answer is mixed. If the difference in initial output per capita is small, then there will be no difference in the timing of take-off, all other things being equal. This is true when the differences in land quantity or technological advance are too small to allow the country to reach the threshold $\hat{y}$. On the other hand, if these differences are sufficient to reach the $\hat{y}$ threshold early, then the resulting higher population growth favours an early take-off, *ceteris paribus*.

The United Kingdom did not have an advantage in terms of available land area compared to France or China, but it is possible that, in the eighteenth century, the United Kingdom had a certain technological edge, leading to a higher output per capita. The higher population growth would then have allowed the country to reach the critical size threshold more rapidly, leading to an early take-off.

But this explanation hits a substantial snag. In the eighteenth century, other countries, such as France, India or China, already had larger populations than the United Kingdom. As a result, those economies should have reached critical size long before the United Kingdom. Therefore, while the initial output per capita may have played a role, it could not have been due to the effect of population size. One piece seems to be missing from the puzzle to explain the United Kingdom's early take-off.

Let us move on to the explanation proposed by Clark (2007). This explanation mobilises elements that are absent from our model (heterogeneity within the cohort), but if this hypothesis is correct, it should result in a higher average level of knowledge and skills in the United Kingdom than elsewhere at the dawn of the industrial revolution (due to the greater dispersion of elites in that country).

In our model, such an advance in skills may, in some cases, explain an earlier take-off. But, as we showed in the previous section, this technological advance must be large enough to accelerate population growth, allowing the country in question to reach the critical size leading to positive scale effects sooner. We come back to the same problem as mentioned above: in our model, a technological advance only translates into an early take-off if this advance leads to the critical population size being reached sooner. At the dawn of the industrial revolution, the United Kingdom had a smaller population size than France, China or India. Our model therefore does not account for all the elements that may explain the early take-off of the United Kingdom compared to other economies.

Let us now consider the explanation of Acemoglu and Robinson (2013), based on the institutional framework. According to these authors, the United Kingdom's early take-off is mainly explained by the fact that, in the eighteenth century, it had better political and economic institutions than the rest of the world.

This "institutional" dimension is absent from our model. It should be noted, however, that the British advance at the institutional level only resulted in a greater stock of knowledge, so that we are left with the same problem. Indeed, technological advance alone cannot, in our model, explain an early take-off relative to larger economies such as France, China or India. Therefore, if we want to further explore the "institutional" angle, we must introduce this dimension explicitly into the model.

In short, these negative results lead us to take a critical look at the modelling studied in this chapter. This model leads to satisfactory results for the study of take-off in a single economy, but is less successful in explaining the differences in the timing of take-off between countries. According to our model, it is the population size that plays a crucial role in the timing of take-off. If this assumption were true, we should have seen early take-off not in the United Kingdom, but in France, China or India.[10] Therefore, there must have been other critical elements in the early take-off in the United Kingdom, and these elements need to be incorporated into our modelling. This is the task we will pursue in the next chapters.

4.7   Conclusion

This chapter has offered a model to explain or "rationalise" the transition from the stagnation regime of the pre-industrial era to the modern growth regime that has prevailed since the industrial revolution. This is a first attempt to theoretically rationalise the "structural break" observed in the GDP per capita historical date presented in Chapter 2.

This model does not require an exogenous shock to a variable or parameter to explain the economic "take-off". *It is the slow but continuous growth in population size that constitutes the latent dynamic leading the economy from a regime of stagnation to a regime of growth.* This transition is based on the crossing of a critical threshold concerning the population size, a transition that allows the economy to benefit from powerful positive scale effects that, by accelerating technical progress, help to counterbalance the negative effects of population growth on output per capita (through decreasing marginal returns to labour input).

---

[10] One way to make the model more compatible with historical facts would be to re-qualify what is meant by the relevant "population" for latent dynamics and threshold effects, for example by focusing only on the *urban* population (and leaving out the rural population). We will not develop this approach here, but introducing a distinction between these two sub-populations would make it possible to include in the analysis of take-off the crucial role played by the phenomenon of urbanisation, a phenomenon that happened well before the Industrial Revolution, and that nourished it (see Wrigley 1969).

It is important, at this stage, to recall the crucial role played by population growth in our explanation. It is true that demographic growth initially curbs economic expansion, by diluting the meagre productivity gains over a larger number of people. However, population growth also allows the economy to reach a sufficiently large size at a certain point to take advantage of beneficial scale effects leading to sustainable growth in output per capita.

Our modelling, which is a simplified version of Kremer's (1993), makes it possible to somehow combine the ideas of Malthus and Weyland in the same model. From Malthus, we retain the dependence of population growth on material conditions; from Weyland, flows the idea that population size can have a positive influence on the accumulation of knowledge and, more fundamentally, can be the driving force of historical change, the engine of transition from one economic regime to another.

This model explains the regime shift without resorting to external artifices. However, like all models, it is subject to limitations. We have emphasised the difficulties of our model in explaining the differences in the timing of take-off between countries. Allen (2011), Clark (2007) and Acemoglu and Robinson (2013) explain the early take-off of the English economy either through a higher initial level of income per capita, a higher average skill stock or institutions that are more open. Our model excludes these possibilities and favours a demographic size effect, an effect that should have led countries such as India or China to experience earlier take-offs. In the remainder of this book, we will modify this modelling of the economic take-off process to make it more compatible with international differences in the timing of take-off.

Appendix 4A.1 Further Reading

This chapter is based on a simplified, discrete-time version of Kremer's (1993) model. This article, which has highlighted the fundamental role of scale effects for economic take-off, is an essential reference.

In the same vein, chapter 2 of Galor (2011) is another reference. In it, Galor develops a more complex model – including microeconomic foundations – of the transition from a stagnation regime to a growth regime. This chapter can be seen as a simplified form of the theoretical framework studied by Galor (2011).

On the differentiated timing of economic take-off across countries, the classic reference is Rostow (1960), already discussed in Chapter 1. Rostow does not explain take-off solely by scale effects (although building a large market is one of the preconditions for take-off). Rostow's explanations of take-off are, in part, different from those proposed by Kremer (1993), for whom size effects are the only factor in take-off, as in this chapter.

Contemporary debates on the occurrence of the Industrial Revolution in Britain and on the early take-off in that economy are far from settled. The references cited above, Allen (2011), Clark (2007) and Acemoglu and Robinson (2013), are essential albeit contradictory references.

Appendix 4A.2 Exercises

1. According to North (2005, p. 19):

> An ergodic stochastic process simply means that averages calculated from past observations cannot be persistently different from the time average of future outcomes.

a. Let us take the time series of output per capita associated with the model in Chapter 3. Does this series satisfy the ergodicity criterion? Justify your answer. [Hint: Calculate the average of this variable over several successive periods and then compare these averages to study their (in)variance over time.]

b. Repeat for the time series of output per capita associated with the model in Chapter 4.

2. Consider an economy with the following time series for knowledge A_t and population size N_t.

Periods	$t = 0$	$t = 1$	$t = 2$	$t = 3$	$t = 4$	$t = 5$
N_t	10	20	40	80	160	320
A_t	1	1.5	3	6	9	18

a. Are these time series compatible with hypothesis K1? Justify your answer.

3. Returning to hypothesis K2:

$$\underline{a} = (\underline{n})^{1-\alpha} < (\bar{n})^{1-\alpha} < \bar{a}.$$

a. Is hypothesis K2 compatible with the Malthusian doctrine of population, as presented in *An Essay on the Principle of Population* (Malthus 1798)? Justify your answer.

b. Use your answer for a. to revisit the conditions necessary for the existence of a take-off of output per capita.

4. Consider the case of the island of Inferno, a heap of rocks lost somewhere in the Pacific Ocean. Supposing that at time t, the island of Inferno comes out of the stagnation regime and experiences an output per capita take-off. Unfortunately, at time $t + 10$, this economy is hit by a high magnitude earthquake. This earthquake leads to large-scale human losses: about 1/3 of the population is decimated. However, the other dimensions of the economy are not affected by the earthquake: neither the stock of knowledge, nor the surface area of cultivated land, nor the parameters of knowledge accumulation and population growth. Hypotheses K1 and K2 also remain valid.

a. According to the model studied in this chapter, what is the immediate impact of this earthquake on the level of output per capita on the island of Inferno?

b. Following this earthquake, does the economy of the island of Inferno fall back into the stagnation regime, or does it remain in the growth regime? Justify your answer.

c. Repeat b. but now consider a longer time horizon.

d. Repeat a., b. and c. if the earthquake has caused a long-term reduction in the area of cultivated land.

5   Institutions and Distribution

The model developed in the previous chapter rationalises the transition from a stagnation regime to a growth regime. This model was inspired by Malthus, in so far as population size is the key variable for economic change in this analytical framework. Although population growth is at first an obstacle to economic growth, it eventually makes it possible for the economy to reach a certain critical size, which allows it to benefit from scale effects. These powerful scale effects will lead the economy to "take off", thus enabling the economy to shift from a stagnation regime to a sustainable growth regime.

Admittedly, in his work, Malthus concentrated on explaining stagnation by demographic pressure and did not consider that the economy could transition to another regime. But the fact remains that, in spite of its conclusions regarding take-off, the model in Chapter 4 remains Malthusian in spirit, in the sense that it makes population size the key variable in the historical process, the one that governs the future of societies.

This view of history can be challenged in many ways. Even in the days of Malthus, many authors considered the question of population to be a secondary aspect, of little interest in understanding the mechanisms of progress in societies. The socialist Godwin (1793) considered that the misery that afflicted a large part of Britain in the eighteenth century was not due to excessive population growth, but rather had its origins in a poor distribution of resources. Godwin's utilitarian view was that property rights, as an institution, were justifiable *only* insofar as they led to the highest social utility, but not otherwise. Godwin advocated a redistribution of wealth and called for extending the system of the Poor Laws. On the other side of the Channel, Condorcet (1795) argued that human reason had formed very slowly over centuries, thanks to the progress of civilisations. For Condorcet, the main obstacles to the progress of the human mind were the corruption and ignorance of governments. These were the scourges that had slowed the progress of reason. Condorcet was very optimistic regarding the ability of humans to free themselves from these chains in order to build a prosperous and free society through the crafting of constitutions.

This "institutionalist" vision of history was quite widespread in the eighteenth century, and it was against this very vision that Malthus built his reasoning. It is no coincidence that the full original title of his *Essay* is *An Essay on the Principle of Population, as it Affects the Future Improvement of Society, with Remarks on the Speculations of Mr. Godwin, Mr. Condorcet and Other Writers*. Malthus argued that institutional change would not provide a solution, as the universal prevalence of the principle of population would prevent sustainable progress in societies, regardless of the institutions in place.[1]

The debate between these different visions of history continues today, in the twenty-first century. Some historians, such as North (1981, 2005), have insisted on the fundamental role played by institutions in the process of economic development. North (2005) compares these institutions to "scaffolds humans erect":[2]

All organized activity by humans entails a structure to define the "way the game is played", whether it is a sporting activity or the working of an economy. That structure is made up of institutions – formal rules, informal norms, and their enforcement characteristics.

These scaffolds have a fundamental influence on the course of history. Changing the "way the game is played" leads to a modification in the way the economy functions. Institutional changes have a determinant role, because they modify both the incentives that individuals face when making decisions, but also the, often unexpected, outcomes that occur as a result of those decisions.

The concept of "institution" is very broad: North (1981) includes all the factors affecting the "way the game is played", including all the elements that influence the costs of acquiring information in an uncertain economic environment, as well as, more generally speaking, all the factors determining what are known as transaction costs. For given quantities of production factors and of production techniques, these transaction costs create an obstacle to exchanges and thus hinder the development of economic activity in general.[3] Since the role of institutions is so important to the process of economic development, North (1981) concludes that:[4]

Explaining economic performance in history requires a theory of demographic change, a theory of the growth in the stock of knowledge, and a theory of institutions [. . .].

Contemporary advocates of an "institutionalist" approach include Acemoglu and Robinson. In their book, *Why Nations Fail* (2013), the authors use numerous historical comparisons to demonstrate that the determining factor in a nation's economic progress or failure lies not in demographic factors, geographical location or cultural differences, but in the quality of the institutional environment. For the authors, institutions are of good quality when they provide incentives for individuals to innovate and improve production techniques. Such incentives exist when, under the prevailing "way the game is played", individuals can benefit from the fruits of their labour.

---

[1] According to Malthus, institutional changes will only have a temporary effect on standards of living, but no lasting effect, because the additional population growth induced by improved living conditions will automatically drive living conditions downwards.

[2] See North (2005), p. 48.

[3] Excessive transaction costs can even lead to the absence of transactions between individuals, i.e. the absence of a market.

[4] See North (1981), chapter 1, p. 7.

Acemoglu and Robinson consider that the quality of institutions is the key variable in understanding long-run economic dynamics.[5]

The model developed in Chapter 4 did not explicitly include this institutional dimension and therefore could not do justice to the visions of North (1981, 2005) and Acemoglu and Robinson (2013). In order to include this dimension in the economic analysis of the long period, this chapter aims to present an "institutional" variant of the regime shift model discussed above. This variant includes the quality of institutions as a key variable. In this new model, the "driving force" of history will no longer be the population size, but the quality of the institutional framework. We will proceed in three stages.

In the first stage (Section 5.1), we return to the arguments put forward by Acemoglu and Robinson (2013), trying to understand what constitutes the quality of institutions and what are the links between the quality of institutions prevailing in a society and any technological innovations. This will lead us to reformulate some of the assumptions of the model studied previously, so as to include this institutional dimension.

Section 5.2 presents a variant of the model studied above, but where the driving variable, the one that carries the latent dynamics of the economy, is the quality of institutions. We will show the ways in which poor institutional quality can keep economies in the stagnation regime. We will study how successive improvements in the institutional framework can strengthen the capacity of societies to innovate, enabling them to leave the stagnation regime and take off towards the growth regime. This model will also allow us to return to the question of the United Kingdom's early take-off, in the light of the more balanced institutional framework established by the Glorious Revolution (Section 5.3) and in the light of the establishment of a trading area of unparalleled size: the British Empire (Section 5.4).

Finally, in a third stage (Section 5.5), we will examine the causes governing institutional change. As such change is often linked to revolutions (which introduce a discontinuity in history), this will lead us to reflect on the causes of revolutions and, in particular, their links with inequality in the distribution of resources. This last part will sketch a variant of the Section 5.2 model, in which institutional quality is affected by the level of inequality, that, when it surpasses a certain threshold, can lead to revolutions and "leaps" in the quality of institutions.

5.1   Institutions and Innovations

5.1.1   The Failure and Success of Nations: Acemoglu and Robinson (2013)

In *Why Nations Fail*, Acemoglu and Robinson (2013) have drawn on much of their scientific work to defend the following hypothesis: the real driving force of history, the key variable that explains why some societies stagnate while others enjoy

---

[5] This perspective is developed in numerous works, such as Acemoglu et al. (2002, 2005), Acemoglu (2008), or Acemoglu et al. (2008).

sustainable growth, lies in the quality of the institutions that prevail in the economies in question.

Acemoglu and Robinson define "institutions" quite broadly: political institutions include the written constitutions of states and how democratic (or non-democratic) they are, but go far beyond that. They also include the power and capacity of a state to regulate and govern, as well as the factors determining the more or less unequal distribution of power in society.[6] Alongside these political institutions, there are also economic institutions: markets, patent systems, the education system, etc. These economic institutions play a crucial role in converting (or not converting) the efforts and talents of individuals into higher remuneration. "Institutions" thus constitute a general environment in which individuals are led to make decisions. This institutional environment affects individuals in their multiple choices (labour supply, education, investment, research, etc.) with ultimate consequences for these individuals and for society as a whole.

Acemoglu and Robinson consider that the quality of this institutional environment is the determining variable explaining why an economy can take off or, on the contrary, remain in a stagnation regime. For the authors, a "good quality" institutional environment is one that provides the right incentives, that is, it encourages individuals to make the decisions that will have the best consequences for society. On the contrary, a poor institutional environment does not give individuals the right incentives, so that the resulting individual decisions will not be optimal for society as a whole.

An example of a bad institutional environment is the extreme example of a dictatorial society where a single individual, let us call him the "sovereign", concentrates all the powers (legislative, executive, judicial) in one person and can thus arbitrarily confiscate the income of citizens or companies. In this institutional context, individuals have little incentive to produce more or to seek improvements in production techniques. Indeed, the income gains from such changes could be arbitrarily confiscated by the sovereign. Individuals have little incentive to try to increase their income. As a result, they remain in subsistence activities, without seeking to go beyond them, which would be useless as it would imply additional efforts without any impact on their living conditions.

Another case studied by Acemoglu and Robinson is that of a society whose leaders prevent the realisation and dissemination of technological innovations. Acemoglu and Robinson give numerous historical examples of situations where the discovery of new technologies has not led to their implementation.[7] For fear of conflicts, the sovereigns preferred to "bury" these innovations and, by doing so, buried all the positive effects they would have had on the economy. In the past, it was not uncommon for individuals who had discovered new production techniques to see their lives put in danger

---

[6] See Acemoglu and Robinson (2013), pp. 42–43.

[7] An example given by Acemoglu and Robinson (2013, p. 171) is that of the inventor of flexible (unbreakable) glass, who tried to convince the Roman Emperor Tiberius of his invention's appeal. Once the invention had been demonstrated, Tiberius asked the inventor if he had told others about his invention and then had him executed.

once their discoveries were revealed, because the institutional framework would not only not allow them to benefit from the fruits of their discovery, but, worse still, would lead to their neutralisation in order to maintain the interests involved. It is easy to understand that, in such an institutional context, the incentives for innovation were, to say the least, reduced.

Beyond local historical examples of innovations that were buried or delayed in their implementation, Acemoglu and Robinson defend their vision of history in a broader way, by comparing countries which have similar conditions at all levels (e.g. in terms of land quality, climate or culture), except at the institutional level, and by showing that it is the countries benefiting from better quality institutional environments that have been able to emerge earlier from stagnation, and thus take advantage of earlier economic growth.

In particular, Acemoglu and Robinson argue that if the Industrial Revolution took place at the end of the eighteenth century in Britain rather than in France or the Netherlands, it was due to the better institutional quality that Britain enjoyed at that time compared to its neighbours. Acemoglu and Robinson specifically highlight the crucial role played by the Glorious Revolution of 1688, which, by establishing the parliamentary monarchy in Britain and relocating power to the parliamentary level, created a more balanced society, which in turn provided a more favourable institutional framework for entrepreneurial initiative and innovation.[8] According to Acemoglu and Robinson, the Industrial Revolution first took place in Britain because it had a more favourable institutional environment compared to neighbouring economies. This thesis has been the subject of much debate among historians, and is far from settled at the present time.[9]

Alongside the extremely interesting, but widely debated, case of the Industrial Revolution, Acemoglu and Robinson propose a number of other comparisons between countries, in Europe, South America, Africa and Asia, that are very close on many dimensions – often neighbouring countries with similar cultures and climates – but which differ significantly at the institutional level. They show that these institutional differences between close countries on all other dimensions are likely to be the cause of varied economic trajectories, with countries with better institutional frameworks experiencing more favourable trajectories.

5.1.2   Modelling the Quality of Institutions

One way of formalising these considerations in our model is to define a new variable, which we can call "institutional quality", denoted by Q_t. This variable is, of course, subject to change over time.

---

[8] See Acemoglu and Robinson (2013), pp. 102–103.
[9] The "institutional" thesis defended by Acemoglu and Robinson is opposed by many historians, such as Clark (2007) and Allen (2011), who point to other factors (see above). In particular, Allen (2011, chapter 3) is very critical of Britain's so-called institutional "edge" (only 3–5% of the English population could actually vote) and prefers to emphasise that wage levels were 60% higher in Britain than on the continent, while Britain had the cheapest energy in the world, thanks to the coal deposits in the north of England and the Midlands.

The "institutional quality" Q_t offers a theoretical shortcut which makes it possible to model in a single variable the quality of all economic and political institutions: the quality of all institutional factors. This variable is supposed to account for the institutional dimension of development, which North (1981, 2005), notably, holds dear. A low Q_t value corresponds to an economy in which transaction costs are high, which is detrimental to the smooth functioning of the market. Conversely, a high Q_t value refers to an economy with low transaction costs.

Reducing the quality of economic and political institutions to a single variable, Q_t, may be a non-negligible theoretical shortcut, but it proves to be a useful shortcut because it allows us to "re-embed" the production activity into the wider framework of the society in which that activity takes place. The models in Chapters 3 and 4 could give the impression that economic activity takes place "outside of everything", whereas, as North (1981, 2005) and Acemoglu and Robinson (2013) point out, it is located within a specific institutional framework, that influences the prospects for economic expansion.

5.1.3   Accumulation of Knowledge and Institutions

According to Acemoglu and Robinson (2013), one of the major means through which the institutional framework influences the prosperity of nations lies in the effect of these institutions on innovation, on the discovery and dissemination of new production techniques. With this in mind, we will assume throughout this chapter that the quality of institutions influences the innovation process and the accumulation of knowledge.

To do so, we will assume that there exists a threshold of institutional quality $\overline{Q}$ such that, if the economy benefits from institutional quality below this threshold, knowledge A_t grows at a lower rate, while if institutional quality exceeds this threshold, knowledge accumulates at a higher rate. This hypothesis is as follows:

[Hypothesis AR1]

$$\frac{A_{t+1}}{A_t} = \underline{a} > 1 \quad \text{when } Q_t < \overline{Q}$$

$$\frac{A_{t+1}}{A_t} = \overline{a} > 1 \quad \text{when } Q_t \geq \overline{Q}$$

with $\overline{a} > \underline{a}$.

The intuition behind hypothesis AR1 is very simple. The quality of the institutional framework determines the magnitude of the incentives offered to individuals, that is to say to potential innovators. AR1 tells us that if the quality of institutions is above a certain critical threshold, then the greater incentives associated with this institutional framework will encourage more innovation with a faster accumulation of knowledge and higher technological progress as a consequence.

Hypothesis AR1 is the equivalent, in institutional terms, of hypothesis K1 that we posited in Chapter 4. This hypothesis, like K1, posits that the accumulation of

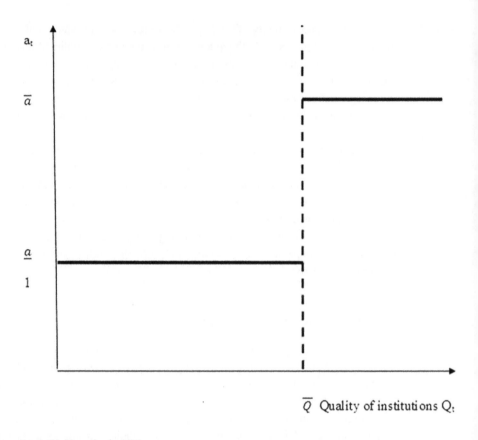

Figure 5.1 Hypothesis AR1

knowledge and, more generally, the improvement of production techniques, depends on the state of the economy in relation to a certain threshold. The only but fundamental difference concerns the nature of this threshold. Under hypothesis K1, the threshold relates to the population size, while under hypothesis AR1 it relates to another variable, the quality of the institutional environment.

Hypothesis AR1 is a way of bringing our model closer to the "institutionalist" work of Acemoglu and Robinson. In the next section, we will examine the consequences of this hypothesis for long-run economic dynamics.

5.2   A First Institutional Variant of the Model

5.2.1   Hypotheses

This section explores an institutional variant of the model in Chapter 4 in which hypothesis K1 is replaced by hypothesis AR1, which makes the process of knowledge accumulation dependent on the level of quality of the institutional framework, Q_t.

To put it simply, and as a first approximation, we are going to assume that the quality of the institutional framework of an economy improves over time according to the following law:

$$Q_{t+1} = qQ_t,$$

where q denotes the factor of increase in the quality of the institutional framework. We will assume that $q > 1$, so that, as time passes, people develop institutional improvements. If the parameter q is close to 1, the quality of the institutional environment increases extremely slowly over the course of many centuries.

This hypothesis is obviously an approximation of reality. It reflects, in a rather crude way, the idea of a slow improvement in the quality of institutions over time. This hypothesis formalises the idea that our contemporary democratic societies, which benefit from the division of powers and a whole series of institutional guarantees given by written constitutions, are in fact the product of a long process of institutional improvement that has taken place over several centuries.

This assumption may be grounded in common sense, but it is nonetheless debatable, because it assumes a kind of continuity in the process of improving the institutional framework, whereas the historical dynamics of the institutional framework are in fact much more complex. The institutional framework does not evolve "mechanically" towards improved institutions: history has not often experienced a continuous evolution, but rather revolutions, which have in turn led to discontinuous variations in the institutional framework. We shall return to this point later in Section 5.5 and will keep this hypothesis as a first approximation in the meantime.

For purposes of explanation, we will simplify the demographic component of our model and assume that the population grows at a constant rate, which is not dependent on material conditions. We thus replace the Malthusian hypothesis M1 with the following hypothesis:

$$N_{t+1} = nN_t,$$

where n is the population growth factor, here assumed to be constant in order to simplify the analysis. Here again we will assume that there is population growth, hence $n > 1$.

As before, completing the model requires making assumptions about the relative speed of human accumulation (captured by n) and knowledge accumulation (captured by $\underline{a}$ and $\bar{a}$). Let us make the following hypothesis:

[Hypothesis AR2]

$$\underline{a} = (n)^{1-\alpha} < \bar{a}.$$

According to this hypothesis, when the economy benefits from an institutional quality below the threshold $\bar{Q}$, knowledge accumulates according to a factor that just manages to compensate for population growth, whereas when the economy benefits from an institutional quality above the threshold $\bar{Q}$, then the accumulation of knowledge, reinforced by the presence of institutions that are more favourable to the development of new ideas and new production processes, dominates population growth.

5.2.2   The Conditions for Growth

In this variant of our initial model, the production function remains the same as previously:

$$Y_t = A_t(L)^\beta (N_t)^\alpha$$

so that the output per capita is still given by the following expression:

$$y_t = \frac{Y_t}{N_t} = \frac{A_t(L)^\beta}{(N_t)^{1-\alpha}}.$$

The growth rate of the output per capita is now equal to:

$$g_{t+1} = \frac{a_t}{(n)^{1-\alpha}} - 1,$$

where a_t takes on a higher or lower value depending on the quality of the institutional framework.

According to hypothesis AR2, the question of whether the growth rate of the output per capita will be positive or not depends on the level of the quality of the institutions, that is, the value of the variable Q_t. Two cases are possible:

- either Q_t is below the critical threshold $\overline{Q}$, in which case a_t takes on its lower value and there is no growth in output per capita;
- or Q_t is above (or equal to) the critical threshold $\overline{Q}$, in which case a_t takes on its higher value and the growth in output per capita is positive.

5.2.3   Dynamics over the Long Period

In light of these considerations, we are now able to describe the dynamics of output per capita and other variables over the long period.

Let us assume that the quality of institutions is initially low, so that Q_0 is below the critical threshold $\overline{Q}$. In this case, according to hypothesis AR1, knowledge accumulates according to a growth factor $\underline{a}$. Since this factor is, by hypothesis AR2, exactly equal to $(n)^{1-\alpha}$, the output per capita y_t remains constant. The economy is in a stagnation regime. The output per capita is not growing because the productivity gains associated with improved production techniques are completely absorbed by population growth.

Will the economy remain forever in this stagnation regime? The answer to this question is obtained by considering the key variable of this model, the quality of institutions Q_t. This quality is assumed to grow over time. This growth can be extremely slow so that Q_t changes very little from one period to the next. The economy then remains in its stagnation regime.

Here we are in the presence of a sort of latent institutional dynamic: changes are slow and, for a very long time, the variable Q_t remains below the threshold $\overline{Q}$, keeping the economy in a stagnation regime. However, the growth of Q_t continues and, sooner or later, the variable Q_t will reach the threshold $\overline{Q}$. At that point, the sufficiently high quality of the institutional framework will give innovators and entrepreneurs more incentives to produce new knowledge and techniques. These increased incentives will strengthen knowledge accumulation, which is now based on the accumulation factor $\bar{a}$. Under hypothesis AR2, this knowledge accumulation factor is higher than $(n)^{1-\alpha}$, so the economy takes off. The economy thus finally shifts from a stagnation regime to a growth regime.

Figure 5.2 illustrates the dynamics of the output per capita, knowledge stock and institutional quality variables over the long period. This figure shows two important things.

First of all, the role played here by the quality of institutions as a *latent variable*. When this variable reaches a critical threshold, there will be a regime shift which will allow the economy to take off. Knowledge accumulation and innovations take place within a given institutional environment. Depending on whether or not this institutional framework is conducive to knowledge accumulation, technical progress happens more or less rapidly. As long as the quality of the institutions remains below the critical threshold $\bar{Q}$, knowledge accumulates slowly. However, once the critical threshold $\bar{Q}$ has been reached, the institutional environment becomes sufficiently favourable to accelerate the accumulation of knowledge. The resulting higher rate of technical progress will allow the economy to take off, despite the demographic growth that has hitherto prevented growth in output per capita.

The second observation that appears here is the presence of a crucial *qualitative change* during the regime shift. Certainly, throughout history, the quality of institutions has, as a global trend, been increasing and improvements have been made to human organisations. However, in the first regime, these improvements do not translate into an increase in output per capita, which stagnates, whereas in the second regime they are associated with an increase in output per capita. We are therefore in the presence of a major qualitative change and this change is driven here by the dynamics of institutions.

In short, this section has proposed an institutional variant of the model from Chapter 4. Both models are capable of explaining or rationalising the existence of a long period of stagnation spanning several centuries, and the transition from the stagnation regime to the growth regime. It should be noted, however, that these two analytical frameworks differ with regard to the key variable, the variable whose latent dynamics will generate the economic regime shift. In the context of Chapter 4, this variable was of a demographic nature, and consisted of the population size; in the context of this chapter, the key variable is of an institutional nature: it is the quality of the political and economic institutions that regulate human activities at a given time.

What we have here are two distinct theoretical frameworks to explain the same phenomenon: the transition from a stagnation regime, in which output per capita does not vary, to a growth regime, in which output per capita grows. We are not going to try to favour one model over another: probably *both* mechanisms are present in the transitions, and the relevance of each of them varies according to the economy under study.[10] However, it is important to underline what these two frameworks share: in

---

[10] The two mechanisms are also potentially linked to each other. According to Weyland (1816), demographic pressure is not only the cause of an acceleration of technical progress but also the root of institutional innovations. In particular, Weyland links the emergence of markets – and the price signals associated with them – to demographic pressure.

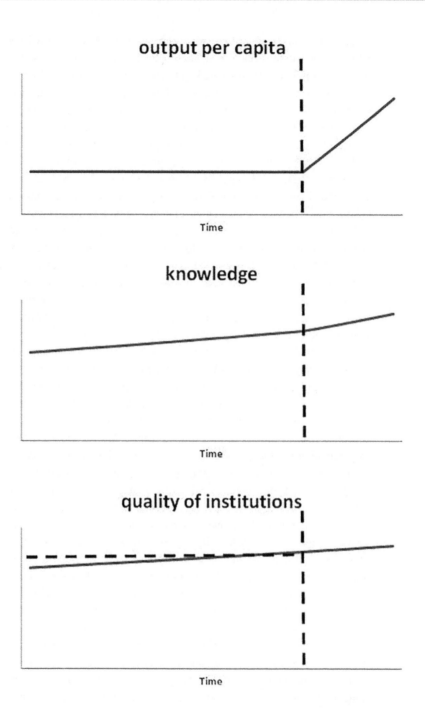

Figure 5.2 Dynamics of the output per capita, stock of knowledge and quality of institutions

both cases, a latent dynamic is at work and, in each case, at some point the latent variable under consideration – either population size or quality of institutions – crosses a critical threshold, thus generating a qualitative change, a regime shift.

Finally, it should be noted that there may be certain connections between these two analytical frameworks, as the dynamics of institutional change are linked to the population size. For example, Acemoglu and Robinson (2013), when referring to the existence of slavery, point out that it is probably more difficult to enslave men when the population density is low (because in that case it is easy for individuals to leave and free themselves from the sovereign). Conversely, a higher population density could make enslavement and slavery easier. This type of consideration suggests possible crossovers between the two analytical frameworks studied above, since demographic and institutional dynamics are not independent of each other.

5.3   The Early British Take-off (1): The Glorious Revolution (1688)

In the previous chapter, we tried to link our theoretical modelling to the work of historians on the Industrial Revolution, returning to the question of why this techno-logical revolution first took place in the United Kingdom, and not in France, China or India.

Our analyses had convinced us that the model in Chapter 4 did not offer a satisfactory explanation for the early take-off of the British economy. In that model, take-off was based on the condition that the population size reached a certain critical threshold, a size providing the scale effects needed for take-off. However, the United Kingdom did not have the largest population at the dawn of the industrial revolution: the populations of France and, above all, of India and China were larger. According to a theory based on the size threshold effect, those countries should therefore have experienced take-off *before* the United Kingdom, which was not the case.

Does the institutional variant developed in this chapter provide a better fit with the data? Can it explain the United Kingdom's early take-off?

There are several reasons to believe that England – the largest component of the United Kingdom – had a substantial lead in the quality of its institutional framework in the mid-eighteenth century. This advantage could explain the early economic take-off of that country compared to other economies.

Britain's advantage at the institutional level is twofold. On the one hand, thanks to the Glorious Revolution, the country benefited from a more balanced sharing of power, which favoured entrepreneurial initiative and innovation; on the other hand, the country was at the centre of a huge commercial empire, which favoured its take-off.

Let us look at the first part of this institutional advantage, and leave the British trading empire to the next section.

According to Acemoglu and Robinson (2013), the Glorious Revolution of 1688 contributed to a profound change in the institutional framework in Britain, contributing to a more balanced sharing of power, which was more conducive to economic development. This revolution followed a long period of economic stagna-tion and social unrest. During the seventeenth century, the English economy had suffered from heavy taxation, imposed in an authoritarian manner by the sovereigns

(James I and Charles I) against the wishes of Parliament.[11] Tensions between the Crown and Parliament led to civil war. Charles I was condemned and beheaded in 1649, and these conflicts led to the Glorious Revolution of 1688, which brought an end to absolute monarchy and marked the beginning of parliamentary monarchy. Parliament became the supreme authority, and the sovereign's power was limited.

Acemoglu and Robinson (2013) believe that the Glorious Revolution gave Britain a decisive advantage, which explains the early take-off of the economy. According to the authors, the British institutional framework, which gave more powers to Parliament vis-à-vis the monarch, was more favourable to the discovery and dissemination of new production processes because it offered inventors and entrepreneurs the legal guarantee of being able to benefit from the fruits of their discoveries and ideas:[12]

It is not a coincidence that the Industrial Revolution started in England a few decades following the Glorious Revolution. The great inventors such as James Watt (perfecter of the steam engine), Richard Trevithick (the builder of the first steam locomotive), Richard Arkwright (the inventor of the spinning frame), and Isambard Kingdom Brunel (the creator of several revolutionary steamships) were able to take up the economic opportunities generated by their ideas, were confident that their property rights would be respected, and had access to markets where their innovations could be profitably sold and used.

By putting an end to absolute monarchy and opening up a legal era of greater power sharing, the Glorious Revolution of 1688 would have had the effect of giving entrepreneurs and innovators a whole series of legal guarantees, guarantees that would have enabled them to take advantage of the opportunities offered by their discoveries. This balanced legal framework, referred to by Acemoglu and Robinson (2013) as "inclusive institutions", would have given entrepreneurs an incentive structure to drive innovation. Acemoglu and Robinson's thesis is that such an incentive framework only existed in Britain, and that this explains the emergence of a large number of innovations in that country, resulting in the early take-off of that economy. The English Industrial Revolution would thus have been a child of the Glorious Revolution of 1688.

Is it possible to account for Acemoglu and Robinson's thesis using the model developed in this chapter?

Absolutely. In fact, within our model, giving Britain an institutional advantage would be tantamount to assuming that the initial level of quality of the institutional environment in Britain, Q_0, was higher than elsewhere. This difference is sufficient to explain the early take-off of that country, despite the fact that its economy was smaller than competing economies.

This point is illustrated in Figure 5.3, which compares two economies, A and B, at the level of output per capita and institutional quality. Economy A benefits from a better quality institutional framework than economy B, while country B benefits from a larger population size. Economy B, which has a larger population size, has a smaller output per capita than economy A. Above all, the more favourable institutional framework in economy A will enable economy A to reach the critical threshold $\overline{Q}$ more rapidly, which will lead it to take off earlier.

---

[11] See Allen (2011), chapter 2.   [12] See Acemoglu and Robinson (2013), pp. 103–104.

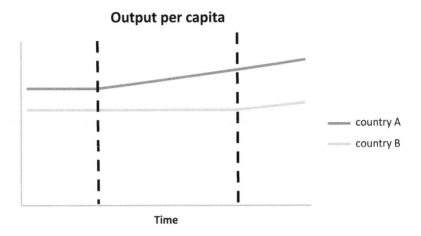

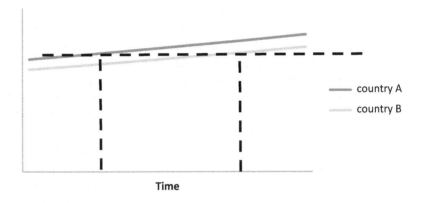

Figure 5.3 Comparison of two economies that differ in the size of the initial population and the initial quality of institutions

Economy B, on the other hand, will not be able to reach that threshold as rapidly. Several periods will elapse, in which economy B remains in a stagnation regime, while economy A is in a growth regime. During that time, the gaps between the two countries increase in terms of output per capita. Finally, the quality of the institutional environment in economy B will reach the critical threshold, allowing it to take off.

Figure 5.3 illustrates how differences in the quality of the institutional framework can explain differences in the timing of economic take-off. Economies characterised by better institutions may experience an earlier take-off because those better institutions allow, once a certain threshold is reached, an acceleration of knowledge accumulation and innovation, leading to take-off.

In summary, our model accounts not only for a long phase of stagnation of output per capita followed by a take-off towards the growth regime, but also for the fact that the take-off took place first in economies initially benefiting from a more favourable institutional framework (such as the United Kingdom).

5.4   The Early British Take-off (2): A Commercial Empire

While the introduction of legal guarantees may have encouraged entrepreneurs and innovators to invest more and therefore contribute to the early take-off of the English economy, this was not that economy's only institutional advantage.

At the dawn of the Industrial Revolution, Britain's institutional advantage was also at another level: that of trade relations. Britain was at the centre of a vast trading empire, a huge trading area spanning all five continents, offering large outlets for all its goods. This second aspect of Britain's institutional advantage – the fact that it lay at the heart of a large market – complements the first aspect. What is the point of benefiting from significant legal guarantees if the company's outlets are limited to (small) local markets?

Several historians, such as Braudel (1985) and Allen (2011), consider that the Industrial Revolution is the distant result of the "first globalisation", a process of opening up trade at the world level that began around 1500. From the fifteenth century onwards, Europeans had ships at their disposal that allowed them to travel on the high seas. The era of coastal navigation was over and the voyages of explorers led to the Age of Discovery, which opened up new trading areas. In the sixteenth century, the Spanish and Portuguese were the ones to establish trading posts all over the world. It was only in the seventeenth century that the countries of northern Europe – especially Britain and the Netherlands – became great imperialist powers.[13] As Allen (2011) points out, Britain and the Netherlands took advantage of their trade with their colonies to develop their economies. The development of these economies was based on the export of the industrial production of the cities (especially the cotton industries). This contributed to making these two countries the most advanced economies at the dawn of the Industrial Revolution. In the second half of the seventeenth century, Britain further expanded its empire, at the expense of the Dutch, and thus became the largest colonial power.

According to Braudel (1985), the question as to why the Industrial Revolution first took place in Britain cannot be answered satisfactorily if one ignores the substantial advantage that that country derived from its vast trading empire:[14]

However, the English Revolution would certainly not have been what it was without the circumstances that made England, practically, the undisputed ruler of the wide world. The French Revolution and the Napoleonic Wars, as is well known, contributed greatly to this. And if the cotton boom remained widely in place, for a long time, it is because it was constantly fuelled by the opening of new markets: Portuguese America, Spanish America, the Turkish Empire, the Indies... The world was the effective, if unwitting, accomplice of the English Revolution.

So that the acrimonious debate between those who only accept an internal explanation of capitalism and the Industrial Revolution by a (local) transformation of socio-economic structures, and those who only want to see an external explanation (in reality, the imperialist exploitation of the world) seems to me to be irrelevant. Exploiting the world is not given to just anyone. One needs a slowly matured pre-existing power.

---

[13] The situation of local populations under imperialist domination is examined in Chapter 8, which is dedicated to the emergence of democratic institutions around the world.

[14] See Braudel (1985), p. 101 [translated by Colette J. Windish].

Braudel stresses the great role played by the establishment of the English trading empire in the early take-off and sustained growth of that economy. Britain benefited from important outlets for the sale of its industrial production, thanks to the construction of an immense commercial space extending over the five continents. The early take-off and sustained growth of the English economy are difficult to separate from the country's geopolitical domination.

In the light of these analyses, Britain's advantage cannot be reduced to purely internal considerations, such as its more balanced legal framework resulting from the Glorious Revolution. Other factors played a major role and these factors are external in nature, as they relate to Britain's relationships with the rest of the world. But these external factors are also institutional: we are talking here about trade rules, and therefore the "way the game is played" between Britain and the other countries.

Returning to our model, the institutional advantage of Britain – of an external rather than internal nature – can be formalised as a higher level of the variable Q_0 in Britain. This higher level of Q_0 reflects the privileged access of the British Empire to the world market at the dawn of the Industrial Revolution. Using this formalisation, it is possible to repurpose the results of Figure 5.3. With an initial institutional advantage – access to a vast trading space to sell its industrial products – Britain experienced an early acceleration of technical progress, which led it to "take off" several decades before the other countries. The reasoning developed in the previous section, which pertained an internal institutional advantage, also works in the case of an external institutional advantage.

5.5   Inequality and Institutional Progress

5.5.1   Discontinuities in Institutional Dynamics

The theoretical framework studied so far suffers from a major limitation, regarding the dynamics of institutional change. Indeed, the model is based on the assumption that the institutional framework continuously improves over time. Such a hypothesis is only defensible as a first approximation, as we have pointed out above.

History is made up of conflicts, insurrections and revolutions that have led to sudden and discontinuous changes in both economic and political institutions: the English Glorious Revolution (1688), the French Revolution (1789), the October Revolution in Russia (1917) are all examples of major institutional transformations that testify to a *discontinuous* dynamic of institutional change. In these examples, institutions did not evolve in a progressive and continuous manner, but rather in fits and starts and a discontinuous manner. To use the terms of our model, the institutional quality variable Q_t did not grow continuously over centuries, but rather has tended to evolve in stages, with long periods of stagnation interrupted by revolutions which cause "leaps" in the institutional dynamic.

The institutional dynamic is not a smooth dynamic, but is closer to a jerky dynamic through "leaps", which is driven by the singular events that are revolutions. It is therefore necessary, in order to offer a realistic representation of the dynamics of institutional change, to take into account revolutions, those moments of discontinuity that are at the origin of major institutional changes.[15]

5.5.2   Institutional Changes and Inequality

Studying the origin and characteristics of revolutions and uprisings goes far beyond the scope of this book. We will not attempt to go into the details of these singular moments in history, but merely enhance the theoretical framework studied above in order to incorporate revolutions. In order to do so, it is important to examine the circumstances that encourage the occurrence of such uprisings.

Let us make a very plausible assumption as to the origin of revolutions: revolutions are not linked to the general level of economic activity – as history is punctuated by revolutions in societies with diverse and varied levels of economic development – but, rather, they occur when *inequality* exceeds a certain threshold. The origin of uprisings should thus be sought not in the average product or output per capita, but in the distribution of the product within the population.

This assumption supposes that it is the dynamics of resource allocation that govern institutional change. In making this assumption, we are simply following the first proposition made by North (2005), according to which "The continuous interaction between institutions and organizations in the economic setting of scarcity and hence competition is the key to institutional change."[16]

Until now, the models studied in this book have focused on the dynamics of the total product, without addressing the question of the distribution of this product within the population.[17] This was an important simplification: subsequent to Ricardo (1817) and Marx (1867), it has been known that long-run dynamics is intrinsically linked to the question of the distribution of resources and the struggles between social groups for the appropriation of the product.

In his *Principles of Political Economy and Taxation*, Ricardo (1817) highlighted the influence of income distribution on the wealth of nations. When an economy develops, its population grows and new land is cultivated, land that is of lower average quality than the land already under cultivation. The result is an increase in the share of total income paying rents to landowners and a decrease in the share of total income devoted to the profits received by capitalists. This decline in the share of profits undermines capital accumulation, the driving force of the economy according to Ricardo. The economy is condemned to long-term stagnation (the stationary state).

---

[15] Considering that revolutions are local phenomena, this section focuses on the *internal* institutional aspects of economies, in contrast to the previous section.

[16] See North (2005), p. 59.

[17] If we assumed that labour and land factors were paid at their marginal productivity, then our model would give us a key to understanding the distribution of income between labour wages and land rents. However, this is one assumption among others, and since our model does not specify how land is distributed, this distribution key would not be sufficient to fully characterise the distribution of income.

In *Das Kapital*, Marx (1867) further formalised his theory of history – historical materialism – in order to study the links between historical change and the distribution of income.[18] Among the "contradictions" of the capitalist mode of production – the very contradictions Marx believes will lead to the end of capitalism – Marx put forward two phenomena which are linked to income distribution: on the one hand, the impoverishment of labour, which will aggravate the class struggle; on the other hand, the law of the falling rate of profit (as the organic composition of capital progressively increases due to the mechanisation of the economy).[19] This historical dynamic is inseparable from income distribution.[20]

There are several mathematical formalisations of Ricardo and Marx's theories (see Sraffa, 1960; Eltis, 1984; Morishima, 1973, 1989; Foley and Michl, 1999). We will not attempt to formalise these two systems of thought. More modestly, this section will simply amend our model to examine income distribution and, in particular, the links between income inequality, institutional change and long-run dynamics. To this end, we will proceed in two stages.

First of all, it is important to understand what determines the extent of income inequality in an economy at a given point in time. Let us denote the level of inequality prevailing at time t by I_t. In the following pages, we will assume that inequality has two main determinants: total output and the quality of the institutional framework.

Let us consider the first determinant of income inequality: the level of total product Y_t. As highlighted by Milanovic et al. (2011) and Milanovic (2016), the level of total product delimits the maximum level of income inequality that can be achieved. Let us take a population of workers of a given size N_t to which we add a small elite, tiny in size relative to N_t. If this economy is not very productive, the average income should be just above the subsistence level. There is therefore little surplus left for the elite to capture, so income inequality cannot be very high. The intuition is that everyone but the elite then has an income close to the subsistence level, and the elite does not have a large surplus to seize. But when productivity increases, the economy produces a large amount of resources, and as the average income is now well above the subsistence level, it is possible for the elite to collect a higher surplus. The total level of income therefore delimits the maximum level of inequality that can be achieved in an economy. The higher the Y_t, the higher the inequality *ceteris paribus*, that is, with a given institutional framework.[21]

Let us now turn to the second determinant of income inequality: the quality of the institutional environment Q_t. As Acemoglu and Robinson (2013) have pointed out,

---

[18] See the section in Chapter 1 on historical materialism.

[19] The "organic composition of capital" was, for Marx, the ratio of constant capital (machines and tools) to variable capital (wage bill).

[20] The third contradiction in the capitalist mode of production relates to the overproduction of goods (Marx, 1867).

[21] See Milanovic (2016), p. 63.

there is a link between the quality of a country's institutions – their "inclusiveness" – and the level of income inequality. The concentration of political power in the hands of a few favours the concentration of income (and also of accumulated wealth).[22] Therefore, the building of more balanced institutions, by generating power sharing, leads to a more egalitarian distribution of income. It follows that the higher the quality of the institutional framework Q_t, the lower, *ceteris paribus*, is the income inequality.

Two forces are therefore present in the dynamics of income inequality. Within a given institutional framework, income inequality increases with total product (because the opportunities of capturing income expand when total income increases), but when the institutional framework improves, then income inequality declines. In light of this, we will, in the following pages, adopt the following formulation for the level of inequality as a function of time:

[Hypothesis I1]

$$I_t = \Xi \frac{(Y_t)^\kappa}{Q_t}$$

where $\kappa, \Xi > 0$.

This expression accounts for the effect of the total product and the institutional framework on income inequality. The parameter Ξ is a normalisation parameter. The parameter κ is positive and takes a value higher (or lower) than one when the degree of inequality is convex (or concave) in the total income to be distributed.[23]

Hypothesis I1 is a theoretical shortcut that makes it possible to study the dynamics of income inequality as a function of the total product and the quality of the institutional framework, without having to take other elements into account. In particular, Hypothesis I1 allows us to account for the dynamics of inequality without having to explicitly model the rules of remuneration of the labour and land factors of production, the structure of property rights on these factors and the rules of intergenerational transmission of land.[24]

We also need to model the effect of inequality on the occurrence of revolutions and, thus, on institutional dynamics. As pointed out above, institutional dynamics are rather erratic, and proceed in "fits and starts". Let us therefore replace hypothesis $Q_{t+1} = qQ_t$ by the hypothesis that institutional quality remains unchanged in the

---

[22] Acemoglu and Robinson (2013) highlighted in particular the predation and spoliation that occur under dictatorial regimes, in which a small ruling elite confiscates the income earned by the majority of the population in a totally arbitrary manner.

[23] The concavity or convexity of this relationship depends on the inequality indicator taken into account. For example, Milanovic (2016) proposes a concave relationship regarding the impact of income on the Gini indicator. Other choices of indicators are obviously possible, leading to other forms of relationships.

[24] Hypothesis I1 is a general way of representing the dynamics of inequality. According to the precise assumptions concerning distribution (rules of product sharing, structure of property rights, rules of transmission), the dynamics of income inequality would take a singular form, and would present a particular dependence on the variables Y_t and Q_t. The parameters κ and Ξ would then have to take specific values in order to come as close as possible to the dynamics of inequality under these hypotheses.

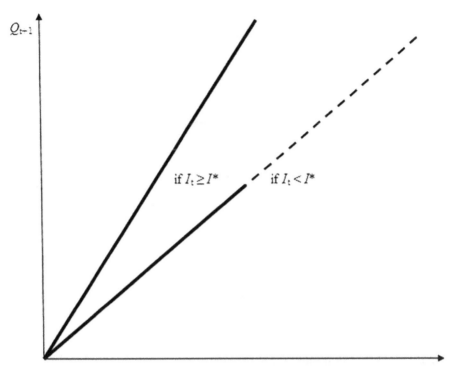

Q_{t-1}

if $I_t \geq I^*$ if $I_t < I^*$

Quality of institutions Q_t

Figure 5.4 Hypothesis I2

absence of revolution but then increases when a revolution occurs. This occurs only when the level of income inequality exceeds a certain threshold I^*:

[Hypothesis I2]

$$Q_{t+1} = Q_t \quad \text{if } I_t < I^*$$

$$Q_{t+1} = qQ_t \quad \text{if } I_t \geq I^*$$

with $q > 1$.

According to hypothesis I2, the dependence of institutional dynamics on income distribution takes a particular form. When inequality is below a certain critical threshold I^*, institutions reproduce themselves unchanged from one period to the next. On the other hand, when inequality is above a certain critical threshold I^*, then an institutional change takes place and the quality of institutions experiences a leap forward.

Figure 5.4 presents hypothesis I2, as a graphic in space (Q_t, Q_{t+1}). As long as inequality remains below the critical threshold I^*, the quality of institutions in $t + 1$ is equal to the quality of institutions in t. We therefore remain on the 45° diagonal line connecting the pairs (Q_t, Q_{t+1}) such that institutional quality is constant over time. On the other hand, when the level of inequality reaches the threshold I^*, a revolution takes place and this is reflected in an increase in the quality of institutions which becomes a multiple $q > 1$ of the quality of institutions in the previous period. This change is graphically represented by a line with a slope greater than one, located above the line at $45°$.

The dynamics created by hypotheses I1 and I2 are far from being simple. In fact, a situation characterised by low institutional quality is likely to lead to major inequalities (hypothesis I1) which may themselves bring about a revolution ultimately resulting in an improvement in institutional quality and a reduction in inequality (hypothesis I2). Moreover, institutional quality also influences the speed of the process of knowledge accumulation and thus the total product, which determines the degree of inequality. The next section examines the implications of Hypotheses I1 and I2 for the analysis of long-run dynamics, focusing on output per capita and inequality.

5.6   A Second Institutional Variant of the Model

This section follows the model developed in Section 5.3, replacing the hypothesis relating to the dynamics of institutional change with hypotheses I1 and I2.

5.6.1   From Institutions to Inequality

Given that the key latent variable is the quality of the institutional framework, and that this quality changes as revolutions take place, it is important first to understand the dynamics of income inequality since it is the level of income inequality that determines the occurrence of revolutions. To this end, let us rewrite the ratio of the level of inequality over two successive periods. We have:

$$\frac{I_{t+1}}{I_t} = \frac{\Xi(Y_{t+1})^\kappa (Q_{t+1})^{-1}}{\Xi(Y_t)^\kappa (Q_t)^{-1}}.$$

In the absence of a revolution in $t+1$, we have $Q_{t+1} = Q_t$, so that inequality necessarily increases from one period to the next, since the total product tends to grow over time as a result of population growth and the accumulation of knowledge. Therefore, in the absence of a revolution, we have a growth in inequality.

In the presence of a revolution in $t+1$, we have $Q_{t+1} = qQ_t$ with $q > 1$. In this case, inequality is likely to decrease. This holds true in our economy when the following condition is met:

$$\frac{I_{t+1}}{I_t} = \frac{(Y_{t+1})^\kappa}{(Y_t)^\kappa q} < 1.$$

This inequality holds when:

$$\frac{(a_t n^\alpha)^\kappa}{q} < 1.$$

When this condition is true, the occurrence of a revolution decreases the level of inequality, because the institutional change that has taken place counterbalances the "natural" increase in inequality induced by the increase in the total product to be shared. It should be noted that the plausibility of this condition depends on the values of the population growth parameters and the value of the knowledge accumulation parameter a_t, which depends on the quality of the institutions in period t.

Let us assume that this condition is true for the two possible values of knowledge accumulation factors, such that:

[Hypothesis I3]

$$\frac{(\overline{a}n^a)^{\kappa}}{q} < 1.$$

Under this hypothesis, a revolution necessarily leads to an instant decrease in inequality.

5.6.2   Revisiting the Dynamics over the Long Period

We are now able to explore the economic dynamics over the long period in our economy under hypotheses I1, I2 and I3, while retaining hypotheses AR1 and AR2 from the previous section.

Consider an economy with a low institutional quality at the outset, that is, an economy where Q_0 is below the critical threshold $\overline{Q}$. Knowledge accumulates with a multiplicative factor $\underline{a}$. The population grows by a factor n. Under hypothesis AR2, the output per capita is constant. The economy is in a stagnation regime. On the other hand, as the population grows and knowledge accumulates, the total product Y_t increases.

Let us assume that income inequality I_t is initially below the threshold I^*. There is therefore no revolution, Q_{t+1} is equal to Q_t and remains below the critical threshold $\overline{Q}$. The knowledge accumulation factor will remain equal to the factor $\underline{a}$.

Regarding the evolution of inequality, we know that when the product grows, inequality increases. We will therefore have $I_{t+1} > I_t$. This increase in inequality can have two possible consequences.

Either the new level of inequality I_{t+1} remains below threshold I^*, in which case there is no revolution. In this case, the economy remains in the stagnation regime and the level of institutional quality will, in the following period, remain equal to $Q_{t+2} = Q_{t+1} = Q_t$.

Or the new level of inequality I_{t+1} reaches threshold I^* and in this case a revolution takes place. The new level of institutional quality will be $Q_{t+2} = qQ_{t+1}$. It follows from hypothesis I3 that inequality then decreases: $I_{t+2} < I_{t+1}$.

As in the model described in Section 5.3, growth in the quality of institutions can have two possible impacts on knowledge accumulation, depending on whether the new level Q_{t+2} exceeds or not the threshold $\overline{Q}$. If the threshold is not exceeded, the economy remains stagnant. If, on the contrary, the threshold is exceeded, knowledge will accumulate in the future depending on the factor $\bar{a} > n$, so that the economy will exit the stagnation regime.

The dynamics of output per capita exhibits the following path: a long period of stagnation precedes a transition to a growth regime. The only difference with respect to Section 5.3 is that the improvement in the quality of institutions is now no longer continuous, but irregular, as the revolutions occur. Several revolutionary episodes are likely to be necessary to finally allow the variable Q_t to exceed the critical threshold $\overline{Q}$ and thus lead the economy to take off.

But the main contribution of this variant of the model studied in Section 5.3 does not lie so much in the dynamics of the output per capita that it generates as in the dynamics of inequality. In fact, in this model, inequality increases in the absence of institutional change, due to the continuous increase in total product Y_t, but decreases as a result of these changes. Here we are in the presence of a pattern that resembles the "Kuznets waves" or "Kuznets cycles" studied by Milanovic (2016).[25]

According to Milanovic, income inequality is *cyclical* over time, with periods of increasing inequality ("rising waves") followed by periods of decreasing inequality ("falling waves"). This theory of inequality cycles is a generalisation which aims to include the stylised facts documented earlier, notably by Kuznets (1955) and Piketty (2013), as particular moments in the inequality cycle.

From the perspective of this theory of inequality cycles, the famous Kuznets (1955) curve – an inverted U-shaped curve – linking the level of inequality to the level of income is only one part of a long-run cyclical process, just as the rise in inequality since the 1980s documented by Piketty (2013) is only a new "rising wave" of this cyclical process.

Our model replicates these long cycles in the prevalence of inequality. For illustrative purposes, Figure 5.5 shows the dynamics, over the long period, of the main variables: output per capita, the quality of institutions and the level of inequality. At the beginning of the period under study, the economy is in a situation of stagnation, in the sense that the output per capita is constant (top graph). This stagnation results from the fact that improvements in production techniques are completely offset by population growth.

But, behind this stagnation, there actually exists a latent dynamic. Admittedly, inequality is initially below the critical threshold leading to revolutions, but it tends to grow over time as the total product increases, which contributes to the expansion of inequality (bottom graph). But as long as inequality remains below threshold I^*, there is no revolution, and the quality of institutions (middle graph) remains constant.

The growth of inequality with the level of total product will lead to the inequality reaching the critical threshold I^* sooner or later. The result is a revolution or social upheaval, which suddenly increases the quality of institutions. However, the new institutions, although better than the previous ones, are not good enough to lead to take-off. The economy therefore remains in the stagnation regime.

---

[25] See Milanovic (2016), chapter 2.

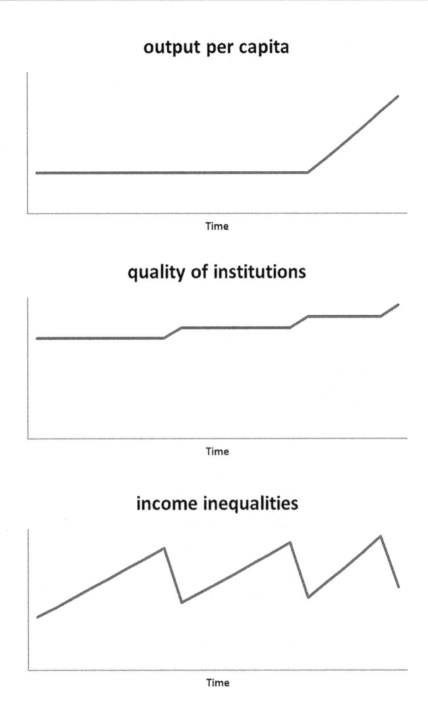

Figure 5.5 Dynamics of output per capita, quality of institutions and inequality

It should be noted that the first revolution brought only a very *temporary* decrease in inequality. Indeed, as the total product continues to grow, inequality inevitably starts to rise again after the first revolution.

A second revolution will then take place when inequality once again reaches the critical threshold I^*. At this point, the quality of institutions will "jump" and then reach the threshold $\overline{Q}$. Thanks to this leap in the quality of institutions, the economy can now benefit from an accelerated accumulation of knowledge and innovation. The acceleration of technical progress thus enables the economy to take off.

This take-off will not prevent inequality from rising again and it will rise again all the more rapidly as total output is now growing faster, thanks to the acceleration of technical progress. We can therefore expect, in the future, other revolutions, which will give rise to new institutional leaps.

This model explains why a certain number of revolutions can take place without directly generating a take-off in the economy: indeed, a revolution leads to institutional improvement, but there is no guarantee that this will be sufficient to cross the required quality threshold beyond which, and only once it has been crossed, individuals will benefit from better incentives for innovation and improved production processes. It is therefore sometimes necessary to have a number of revolutions before the threshold $\overline{Q}$ is crossed, the threshold beyond which the economy leaves the stagnation regime and really takes off, with output per capita finally experiencing sustainable growth.

Another important observation is that our analysis shows that inequality plays a crucial role in the process of economic development, because only inequality can generate the upheavals and revolutions that are necessary for institutional improvement, which is itself a prerequisite for take-off. It thus appears that once the institutional dimension of economic development is seriously taken into account, the question of distribution becomes central.

Despite the economy entering the growth regime, inequality will continue to increase in the absence of a revolution. Revolutions will take place, bringing inequality down to a (temporarily) lower level, before product growth increases inequality again. We see that the cyclical dynamics of inequality, as well as the occurrence of revolutions, apply as much to the stagnation regime as to the growth regime. The advent of output per capita growth will not prevent the rise of inequality, nor the occurrence of revolutions aimed at "correcting" inequality. On the contrary, by reinforcing technological progress, the advent of the growth regime reinforces the growth of total product and the growth of inequality, which increases the frequency of revolutions.

5.7   Conclusion

This chapter has focused on an essential dimension of the historical process, a dimension that we have deliberately set aside until now: political and economic institutions. We have shown that it is quite possible to construct an "institutional" variant of Kremer's (1993) model, one that would take institutions into account and demonstrate the mechanisms by which the quality of institutions has played a key role in the development process over the long period.

A reasonable assumption is that the quality of institutions influences the incentives for individuals to innovate and thus determines the rate of technological progress. It follows that *economies with low-quality institutions were initially in a stagnation regime, before entering, thanks to an improvement of the institutional framework, a transition phase towards the modern regime of economic growth.*

In this variant of the model, the key variable, whose latent dynamics governs the transition from one economic regime to another, is not the population size but the quality of the institutional framework. This does not, of course, imply that population has become a detail in the historical dynamic – it is population growth that prevents the take-off during the stagnation regime, by counterbalancing the accumulation of knowledge – but nevertheless this variable no longer plays the role of a key variable "driving" the development process and contributing to an economy shifting from one regime to another.

We have also tried to further expand our analysis, by introducing the notion of discontinuity into the institutional dynamic, and by linking these discontinuities (revolutions and upheavals) to the broad question of distribution. This second institutional variant of our model allowed us to show that inequality plays a fundamental role in the development process, by being at the origin of revolutions and institutional changes. By provoking upheavals and revolutions, inequality contributes to the replacement of old and arbitrary institutions by better institutions, institutions that will provide stronger incentives for innovation and economic activity in general, allowing the economy to take off and exit the stagnation regime. It should be noted, however, that the advent of the growth regime is not sufficient to eliminate inequality, and even tends to reinforce it.

Appendix 5A.1 Further Reading

The institutional variant of our model remains, for the most part, based on Kremer (1993), with the central assumption replaced here, so that it is no longer the population size, but the quality of the institutions, which "drives" the take-off process by allowing the economy to benefit from an acceleration of technical progress.

The role of institutions in economic take-off was first studied by Rostow (1960). Rostow emphasises the role of economic and political institutions when he refers to the "preconditions for take-off" (his "second stage of growth").[26] According to Rostow, the development of quality institutions is a necessary precondition for the process of economic take-off. In terms of economic institutions, banks need to be established in order to mobilise the capital needed for take-off. On the political side, it

---

[26] See Chapter 1.

is necessary to build a centralised and efficient national state, without which take-off cannot take place. We can interpret the critical threshold $\overline{Q}$ of our model as formalising, in a single parameter, the idea of "preconditions for take-off".

The importance of institutions in the process of economic development was also highlighted by North (1981, 2005). In particular, North examined the many and varied different mechanisms through which institutions influence individuals and thus can determine long-run economic dynamics. Institutions define the constraints that individuals face in their decisions, including the bargaining power they have in their interactions. But the effect of institutions does not stop there: institutions also influence the perception that individuals have regarding the situations in which they find themselves. In addition to his work on the effects of institutions, North (1981, 2005) has also analysed the dynamics of long-run institutional change, including the links between slow institutional change, gridlock and the resulting revolutions.

The question of the links between growth and distribution is a long-standing one. In the twentieth century, this question was revisited by Kuznets (1955), who showed that the process of economic development leads, first, to an increase in income inequality and, second, to a decrease in this inequality. These analyses were challenged by Piketty (2013) using longer time series. In particular, Piketty demonstrated that the decline in inequality over the period 1920–1980, which is largely linked to the two world wars, was followed by a period of rising inequality.

The section on inequality is largely based on Milanovic (2016), in particular on his theory about Kuznets's waves. He has shown that the extent of inequality in an economy is not independent of the general level of production in that country. The higher the level of production, the higher the maximum level of inequality achievable in the economy (see chapter 3 of Milanovic 2016). Indeed, in a very poor economy, it is difficult for an oligarch to confiscate much of the low output. On the other hand, in economies where production is higher, an oligarch can appropriate a greater portion of that production.

Appendix 5A.2 Exercises

1. North (1981) wrote about the advent of agriculture (around 8500 BCE):[27]

    The First Economic Revolution was not a revolution because it shifted man's major economic activity from hunting and gathering to settled agriculture. It was a revolution because the transition created for mankind an incentive change of fundamental proportions. [...] When common property rights over resources exist, there is little incentive for the acquisition of superior technology and learning. In contrast, exclusive property rights which reward the owners provide a direct incentive to improve efficiency and productivity, or, in more fundamental terms, to acquire more knowledge and new techniques. It is this change in incentive that explains the rapid progress made by mankind in the last 10,000 years in contrast to his slow development during the long era of primitive hunting/gathering.

---

[27] See North (1981), chapter 7, p. 89.

a. Explain how this quote disproves the stagnation model studied in Chapter 3.
b. Explain how this quote also disproves the take-off model studied in Chapter 4.
c. Is it possible to use the first institutional variant studied in this chapter to account for North's analysis? Justify your answer.

2. Returning to hypothesis I1:

$$I_t = \Xi \frac{(Y_t)^\kappa}{Q_t}.$$

Consider two countries A and B which have the same institutional quality at time t. Supposing that countries A and B have the same land area, but that country A's population is larger than country B's.

a. Is inequality at time t higher in country A or in country B? Justify your answer.
b. Supposing now that both countries have the same initial conditions and the same structural parameters, the only exception being country A's larger population. Which country will experience a revolution first?
c. Which country will experience a take-off in output per capita first?

3. Looking at Bairoch (1993), p. 224:

If I had to summarise the essence of what economic history can bring to economic science, I would say that there are no "laws" or rules in economics that are valid for all periods of history or for each of the various economic systems.[28]

a. Generally speaking, is the model developed in this chapter compatible with this statement by Bairoch?
b. Can this model explain how different economic systems may be characterised by different "economic laws"?

---

[28] Translated by Colette J. Windish.

6 The Natural Environment

Up until now and for the sake of simplicity, our analyses of the long period have not taken into account an essential dimension of the long-run dynamics: *the natural environment*. The human species, like all others species, faces constraints imposed by the ecosystem in which it evolves and the possibilities for improving its living conditions depend not only on the level of its knowledge but also on the state of the natural environment.

This dimension appeared in the models we studied only in an extremely restricted form: it was in the land L – available in fixed quantities – that is part of the production process in the same way as labour and knowledge. The "land area" variable played some role in our economy, but had no influence on the transition from the stagnation regime to the growth regime.

So, let us take a brief look at the role of land in our models. The land area L determines the total product, since the more land, the greater the total product, all other things being equal. Similarly, L also influences the level of output per capita: *ceteris paribus*, a larger land area increases the output per capita. Furthermore, recalling Malthus's hypotheses on population growth (M1), we see that a larger land area, by leading to a higher output per capita, is likely to generate a higher population growth rate.

This last point was in fact widely debated in Malthus's time. Well before Malthus, Cantillon, in his *Essay on the Nature of Trade in General* (1755), explained that the amount of arable land is one of the major determinants of population size. Our model, which makes the population growth rate dependent on output per capita and thus on the amount of land, is in line with this.

However, it is important to recall here that despite this influence, the land area does not affect the transition from the stagnation regime to the growth regime in the models in Chapters 4 and 5. Indeed, as long as output per capita stagnates, the population growth rate must also stagnate. The transition from the stagnation regime to the growth regime in Chapter 4 is only due to the fact that the population size exceeds a certain critical threshold at a given point in time, beyond which scale effects come into play and lead to an acceleration of technical progress and hence to the take-off of output per capita. The amount of land available played no role in this regime shift: its influence was limited to the path taken by the output per capita, but had no effect on the precise shape of this path, its slope and its evolution over time.[1]

---

[1] Similarly, the amount of land had no direct impact on the transition from stagnation to growth in Chapter 5.

The most striking evidence of the weak role played by the natural environment in Chapter 4 was the result that, in the long term, the population size would continue to grow, indefinitely, without any limits, despite the fixed land areas available. Is it realistic to imagine a population of infinite size on a finite planet? The plausibility of such a situation is doubtful. Certainly, the number of humans has undoubtedly had a favourable effect on the accumulation of knowledge and the development of technology, but to imagine a population growing indefinitely seems frankly unrealistic. The Earth being of finite size, sooner or later this population growth will lead to a situation of crowding. The model in Chapter 4 needs to be modified to take this problem into account.

But the failure to take congestion into account is not the only difficulty posed by the very limited impact of the natural environment in Chapters 4 and 5. Scientific research in recent decades has shown that economic activity has caused significant damage to the planet and has led to global warming. Climate change calls into question the sustainability of economic growth. Even more fundamentally, global warming poses a threat to all living species, including humans.

The models developed in Chapters 4 and 5 offer very little information about this threat. In these models, knowledge accumulation was used to "drive" output per capita growth despite population growth, but there was no mention of the environmental damage associated with growth. In particular, the amount of available land L was assumed to be constant over time, regardless of economic activity. This implicitly assumed that the natural environment was *100% renewable* from one period to the next, regardless of the extent of human activity. This was a major simplification. It is therefore important to amend our model once again to include the adverse effects of economic activity on the natural environment and their consequences for long-run dynamics.

The purpose of this chapter is to introduce the environmental dimension into our baseline model of long-run development studied in Chapter 4. For the sake of clarity, we will leave aside the issues regarding institutions and distribution covered in Chapter 5 and return to a simpler theoretical framework that will allow us to incorporate the problems of congestion and environmental pollution and, more generally, the damage to the planet.

To this end, Section 6.1 introduces the notion of congestion and examines its implications for long-run economic dynamics. In particular, this section examines how the finite nature of planet Earth may – or may not – be an obstacle to the long-term growth of output per capita. Comparing the effects of congestion on population growth and on technical progress will provide an answer to this question.

Section 6.3 will then introduce the notion of environmental damage that results in a change in the nature of the variable L, the quantity of land, at the modelling level. The quantity of land was previously assumed to be a parameter (constant over time). The introduction of environmental damage will lead us to treat the quantity of land no longer as a *parameter*, but as a *variable L_t* whose dynamics depend on the pressure that human activities exert on the planet. This modelling will allow us to address the consequences of environmental damage not only on the prospects for growth or decline in output per capita but also on the question of the possible extinction of humanity in the long term.

6.1   Finite Land and Congestion

6.1.1   Land Congestion as a Limit to Population Growth: Marshall

In his *Principles of Economics*, Marshall (1890) offers a re-evaluation of the Malthusian population doctrine.[2] He acknowledges that Malthus was probably too pessimistic about the potential for technological progress and the ability of technical progress to counteract population growth. Marshall was also aware of the opportunities provided by scale effects: he did not see a large population as an obstacle to the further enrichment of nations.

However, Marshall identifies *a limit to population growth*: congestion. The land surface is fixed, and technological progress will, he believes, be able to compensate, in terms of production, for this fixed nature of cultivable land. But this compensation by technical progress does not solve every problem. Marshall thought that the question of overpopulation could not be reduced to the sole problem of the production of means of subsistence, as Malthus did. In particular, a major difficulty posed by the finiteness of the Earth concerns how humans live in a crowded world (irrespective of their diet).[3] Even well-fed humans, if overcrowded, may run out of space and experience a "growing difficulty of finding solitude and quiet and even fresh air".[4] In a crowded world, where population density exceeds a certain threshold, humans will eventually suffer from congestion – the phenomenon of Earth's overcrowding. It is therefore not conceivable in the long term to have a population that grows without limit.

Marshall's reasoning leads us to modify our assumptions about population dynamics. In this chapter, we will replace hypothesis M1 with hypothesis C1.

[Hypothesis C1]
There exists a population size threshold $N^c > 0$ such that:

$$n_t = n > 1 \quad \text{if } N_t < N^c$$

$$n_t = 1 \qquad \text{if } N_t \geq N^c.$$

Hypothesis C1 offers a simple way of introducing the concept of congestion.[5] It states that once the population size reaches or exceeds the critical threshold N^c, it will stabilise and the population growth rate will become equal to 0.

This threshold effect can be justified as follows. Recall that the size of the available land L is fixed. The area of land per person is, in period t, equal to L / N_t. Hypothesis

---

[2] See Marshall (1890), pp. 148–149.   [3] See Marshall (1890), pp. 267–268.
[4] See Marshall (1890), p. 267.
[5] There are other ways to take congestion into account in our model. Instead of having only one threshold N^c, we could introduce several thresholds or even model the population growth rate n_t as a continuous function of space per capita. In comparison to these approaches, hypothesis C1 has the merit of being simple.

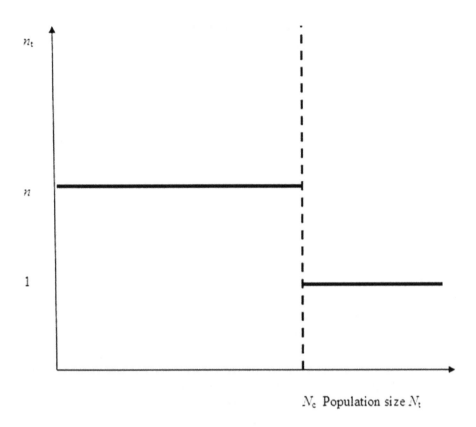

Figure 6.1 Hypothesis C1

C1 amounts to assuming that there exists a critical threshold in terms of available space per person L/N^c, a threshold below which demographic growth is not possible.[6] Hypothesis C1 accounts for *the capacity constraint* imposed by the finiteness of the Earth. This capacity constraint does not depend on the output per capita or the knowledge stock. Whatever the values of these variables, the finiteness of the Earth imposes a capacity constraint or maximum population size. Once this critical size N^c is reached, the population growth rate falls to zero and the population is simply "replaced" from one period to the next.

Hypothesis C1 seems at first sight very strong, but it is in fact extremely weak as the level of the threshold N^c can take on a potentially very high value, much higher than the current size of the world population, which exceeds 7.5 billion individuals. Without making any risky predictions about the level of this critical threshold, assuming its existence seems relatively reasonable.[7]

---

[6] Another option would be to define a critical threshold of population density N^c/L, beyond which the population can no longer grow.

[7] See Heilig (1994) on the various projections of the Earth's maximum capacity for human beings. Depending on the time and the author, the predictions have ranged from a few million to 1 trillion.

6.1.2   Congestion and Labour Productivity

While it seems plausible to assume that the size of the human population will have to stabilise in the long run due to congestion, thereby imposing a limit on the amount of labour available, it is legitimate to ask whether this is the only effect of congestion on economic activity. What about the effects of congestion on labour productivity, represented by the variable A_t?

The model in Chapter 4 relies on the existence of positive scale effects, whereby a larger economy leads to high productivity gains through accelerated technical progress and knowledge accumulation. We have studied the different mechanisms behind these positive scale effects: a greater division of labour within production units and within society as a whole (Smith), a stimulus for the search for new technologies and institutions (Weyland), and a higher aggregate probability of making discoveries when the population is larger (Kremer).

These positive mechanisms have certainly been at work in recent centuries and are likely to continue to remain prevalent in the future. But assuming the persistence of these positive scale effects does not exclude, a priori, the appearance of other scale effects that would be *negative* (i.e. leading to a slowdown in technological progress) for higher population sizes. These effects would be brought about by the congestion phenomenon and would slow down the growth of labour productivity. These negative scale effects would appear for large population sizes and would partly counterbalance the positive scale effects studied in Chapter 4.

Assuming the emergence of negative scale effects beyond a certain population size seems pessimistic, especially when considering the significant productivity gains achieved in recent centuries through positive scale effects. However, by looking at the question from a distance, one realises that assuming the possibility of negative scale effects is simply assuming the existence of an "interior optimal size" of the population regarding knowledge accumulation. In concrete terms, negative scale effects could take several forms. Congestion could slow down the accumulation and transmission of knowledge, by making it more difficult for information to circulate and be evaluated. On the other hand, an excessive division of labour could increase the fragility of the production chain, create heavy organisational costs, lead to major dysfunctions and thus reduce the labour productivity gains associated with a larger population size.

The prospect of negative scale effects that may, in part, counterbalance positive scale effects above a certain population size leads us to replace hypothesis K1 with the following hypothesis.

[Hypothesis C2]

$$\frac{A_{t+1}}{A_t} = \underline{a} > 1 \quad \text{when } N_t < \bar{N}$$

$$\frac{A_{t+1}}{A_t} = \bar{a} > 1 \quad \text{when } \bar{N} \leq N_t < N^c$$

$$\frac{A_{t+1}}{A_t} = \check{a} > 1 \quad \text{when } N_t \geq N^c$$

with $\bar{a} > \check{a} \geq \underline{a}$.

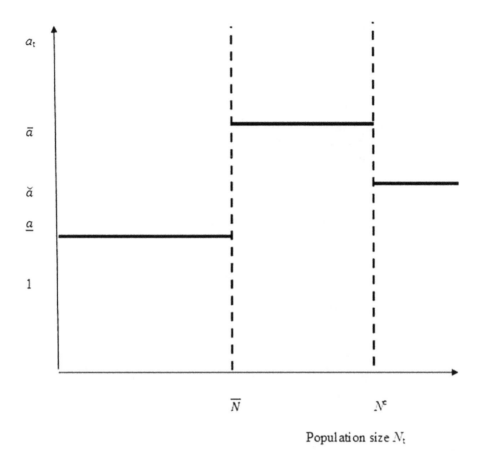

Population size N_t

Figure 6.2 Hypothesis C2

Hypothesis C2 means assuming that there exist not one, but *two* population size thresholds relevant for the dynamics of knowledge accumulation. As under hypothesis K1, an economy that reaches size $\overline{N}$ will benefit from positive scale effects and will thus experience an acceleration of technical progress. However, once the population size reaches the second threshold N^c, negative scale effects related to congestion appear and slow down knowledge accumulation and productivity gains.[8]

In order to complete the model, we will supplement hypotheses C1 and C2 with hypothesis C3, which concerns the relative size of the technological growth factor in relation to the demographic growth factor.

---

[8] To simplify the presentation, we assume that the population size threshold at which congestion occurs is unique, and is therefore the same for both demographic dynamics (C1) and knowledge dynamics (C2).

[Hypothesis C3]

$$1 < \underline{a} = (n)^{1-\alpha} \leq \check{a} < \bar{a}$$

$$\text{and} \quad \bar{a} > (n)^{1-\alpha}\check{a}.$$

The first part of hypothesis C3 places the knowledge accumulation factor in the case of congestion at an intermediate level between the levels that prevail for a low population size or a high population size, which leads to congestion. The second part of hypothesis C3 states that congestion has had the effect of significantly slowing down the accumulation of knowledge.

6.2   Revisiting the Dynamics over the Long Period

Let us now study the consequences of congestion on economic dynamics over the long period. This can be done by simply studying the effects of hypotheses C1, C2 and C3 on the output per capita and on the conditions for its growth.

As a reminder, the growth rate of y_t is determined by:

$$g_{t+1} = \frac{a_t}{(n_t)^{1-\alpha}} - 1.$$

Considering an initially small economy, below the threshold $\bar{N}$, we then have $a_t = \underline{a} = n_t = n$ (hypothesis C3), so that output per capita remains constant ($g_{t+1} = 0$). At the beginning, that economy is in the stagnation regime.

However, the population size grows over time and eventually N_t will reach the critical threshold $\bar{N}$: positive scale effects appear and allow the economy to experience an acceleration of the accumulation of knowledge. Thanks to this acceleration, knowledge increases by a factor $\bar{a}$, so that, under hypothesis C3, output per capita is growing: the economy has reached a growth regime.

In this regime, the economy experiences a continuous increase in output per capita (despite population growth), as well as an improvement in material living conditions. The population will continue to increase during this growth regime until it eventually reaches the threshold N^c. The economy is now entering a *congestion regime*: the very large population size will generate new constraints because of the fixed nature of the planet (L being fixed). Congestion will have two consequences: on the one hand, a forced stabilisation of the population size (hypothesis C1), so we will have $n_t = 1$; on the other hand, a slowdown in the accumulation of knowledge (hypothesis C2).

The consequences of this double slowdown on the growth rate of output per capita are as follows. Given that $\check{a} > 1$, in the congestion regime, the economy experiences output per capita growth. However, as $\bar{a} > (n)^{1-\alpha}\check{a}$ (hypothesis C3), the slowdown in knowledge accumulation leads to a weakening of the growth of output per capita compared to the previous growth regime. Indeed, we have:

$$\frac{\check{a}}{1} < \frac{\bar{a}}{(n)^{1-\alpha}}.$$

The congestion regime is characterised by output per capita growth, but a smaller growth than in the growth regime.

For illustrative purposes, Figure 6.3 presents the dynamics, over the long period, of the main variables, output per capita, population size and knowledge, for the three regimes considered. Figure 6.3 shows that the introduction of the congestion phenomenon has important qualitative and quantitative effects for long-run dynamics. The first regime, the stagnation regime, is associated with constant output per capita, as well as growth in population and knowledge stock. The second regime, the growth regime, is associated with a growth in output per capita, while the population and the knowledge stock continue to grow. Finally, the third regime, the congestion regime, is characterised by an accumulation of knowledge and a growth in output per capita, while the population size stagnates.

It should also be noted that, at the quantitative level, the congestion regime is also characterised by a slowdown in the growth of output per capita compared with its growth during the second regime. This slowdown is not easily visible to the naked eye, because congestion introduces two forces that work in opposite directions: on the one hand, the disappearance of demographic growth tends mechanically to push up the growth of output per capita; but on the other hand, the slowdown in knowledge accumulation slows down the growth of output per capita.

In other words, the introduction of congestion is by no means a negligible factor for economic dynamics over the long period. Allowing for the finiteness of the Earth does not lead to catastrophic predictions for the future in this simple model. Nevertheless, in the long term, this phenomenon implies the emergence of a new regime – the congestion regime – characterised by demographic stagnation and by a slowdown in the growth of output per capita, to a level lower than that which prevailed during the growth regime (in the absence of congestion). It should, however, be noted that the emergence of this congestion regime only affects economies that have reached extreme overpopulation. This regime thus probably only applies to what could be called the "very long term".

6.3   Pollution and Environmental Damage

6.3.1   Beyond Congestion: Pollution

The previous section showed that taking into account the finiteness of the Earth could influence growth prospects in the very long term and lead to the existence of a congestion regime characterised by lower growth in output per capita and stagnation in population size. This section has thus taken a first step towards taking the natural environment into account in our theory of the long-run.

An important aspect overlooked in the previous section is the *damage* to the natural environment resulting from economic activity: air pollution, water pollution, soil pollution, global warming, the extinction of certain species, etc. This damage is likely to seriously affect the shape of life on our planet and also influence the level of economic activity and it must be taken into account in the construction of a theory of long-term economic development.

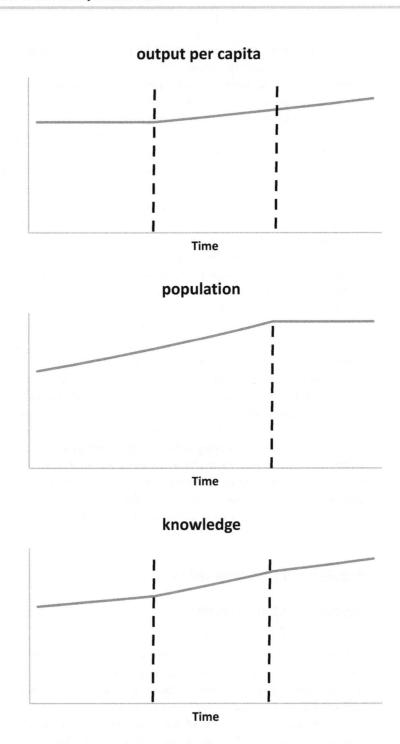

Figure 6.3 Dynamics of output per capita, population size and knowledge stock

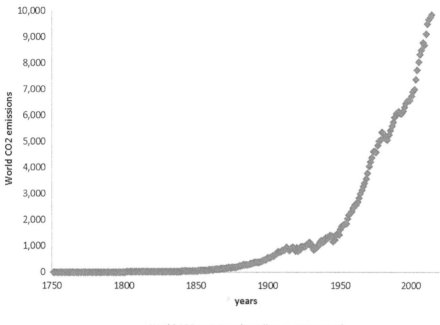

Figure 6.4 Global carbon dioxide emissions (million metric tonnes of carbon)
(*source*: Carbon Dioxide Information Analysis Center)

For illustrative purposes, Figure 6.4 shows the evolution of global carbon dioxide emissions over the last 250 years. We can see that the level of emissions, which remained relatively stable until about 1870, started a slow growth at that time, which accelerated after 1950. It is now widely accepted by the scientific community that these emissions are largely responsible for global warming and the resulting environmental damage.

6.3.2   Modelling Pollution

In order to take into account environmental damage, we will make two major changes to the model studied in the previous section.

First, we will introduce a new variable, P_t that symbolises the extent of environmental damage caused by economic activity. This variable broadly represents the global phenomenon of environmental pollution, whose determinants are multiple. We will also assume that global pollution is proportional to the population size.

[Hypothesis P1]

$$P_t = \gamma N_t$$

in which $\gamma > 0$.

Hypothesis P1 accounts for a simple dependency relationship between population size and the extent of environmental damage. The larger the population size, the greater the damage. Parameter γ reflects the strength or intensity of this link. A low value of this parameter reflects a weak connection between population and pollution; on the contrary, a high value of γ reflects a strong dependence between the magnitude of pollution and the extent of environmental damage. This relationship formalises the idea that when the size of the human population was smaller, the magnitude of environmental damage was smaller, while population growth contributed to an increase in the amount of damage.

It should be noted that hypothesis P1 is a first approximation of the pollution phenomenon, for at least two reasons. First, it establishes a linear relationship between population size and pollution, whereas non-linear relationships are conceivable. Second, hypothesis P1 excludes other potential determinants of pollution, such as lifestyles. These could be taken into account by assuming, as an alternative hypothesis, that pollution is an increasing function not of the population alone N_t, but of the total output $Y_t = N_t y_t$. Such a hypothesis would make it possible to include more effects but would complicate the analyses. We retain hypothesis P1 for the sake of simplicity, even if it only holds true as a first approximation.[9]

Let us now turn to the modelling of the effects of environmental damage on economic activity and on the dynamics of development in general. To do this, we will distinguish two types of effects.

6.3.3   Non-reproduction of the Natural Environment

A first effect of environmental damage affects the amount of land available for production. We will assume that once the level of pollution exceeds a certain critical threshold P^L, the stock of available land cannot be renewed from one period to the next and so declines over time.

Two factors are at the origin of this decrease in the amount of available land: on the one hand, the phenomenon of desertification linked to global warming; on the other hand, the phenomenon of flooding of many coastal lands as a result of global warming, through the melting of ice at the Earth's poles. These two factors have led to a decrease in the surface area of available land over the centuries. The variable L thus becomes time-dependent, and will be designated L_t.

[Hypothesis P2]
There exists a pollution threshold P^L such that:

$$L_{t+1} = L_t \quad \text{if } P_t < P^L$$

$$L_{t+1} = x L_t \quad \text{if } P_t \geq P^L$$

with $0 < x < 1$.

---

[9] We will revisit lifestyles and their influence on the quality of the environment in Chapter 9.

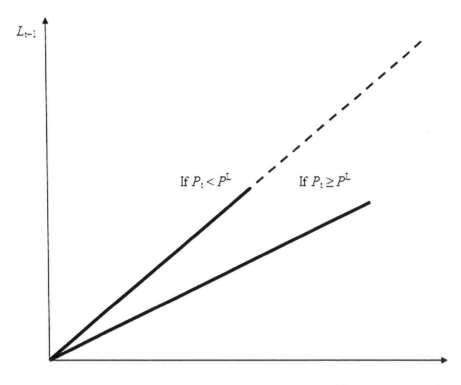

Figure 6.5 Hypothesis P2

Hypothesis P2 formalises the phenomena of desertification and land flooding, which are consequences of man-made global warming. This hypothesis accounts for one of the major influences of environmental damage: it reduces the space available for humans and, as a result, transforms a previously self-renewing resource into one that is only partially renewable.

Figure 6.5 is a representation of hypothesis P2 in the (L_t, L_{t+1}) space. The 45° line connects all (L_t, L_{t+1}) pairs, such that the natural resource stock L_t is constant over time. We see that as long as the environmental damage is below the P^L threshold, the natural environment regenerates completely from one period to the next. On the other hand, when the level of pollution is higher than the P^L threshold, nature can no longer regenerate from one period to the next. The level of the natural resource in $t + 1$ then becomes a fraction of its level in period t. This is represented by the straight line with a slope of less than 1, which in Figure 6.5 lies below the 45° line.

Hypothesis P2 introduces a kind of change into our model that we have not yet encountered in this book: a change that is *irreversible* by nature.[10] In the field of

---

[10] It should be noted, to be accurate, that our modelling of knowledge accumulation also takes the form of an irreversible accumulation, as we do not model the possible erosion/depreciation of knowledge.

economic analysis, Kondratiev (1924) was the first to propose a distinction between reversible and irreversible change (see Chapter 1).

To understand how P2 introduces an irreversible change, it should be noted that when environmental damage exceeds the critical threshold P^L, the natural environment can no longer fully regenerate and will be a fraction of its initial level in the next period. Let us now assume that the pollution falls below the critical threshold P^L again. What will happen then? Quite simply, a stabilisation of the natural environment that will reproduce itself identically in the following period. But the problem is that this perfect regeneration will no longer involve the whole of the natural environment but only the part that had previously regenerated. In other words, hypothesis P2 specifies that any part of the natural environment that is not regenerated is lost forever, because, in the best-case scenario, only what has been preserved so far will be preserved in the future.

6.3.4   Environmental Damage and the Reproduction of Humans

The second effect of environmental damage that we are going to consider is even more dramatic and deals with demography. In addition to the phenomena of desertification and land flooding, it is possible to imagine that, beyond an even higher pollution threshold, the survival of the human species could be threatened. The impact of the deterioration of the natural environment would now impact population: the reproduction of populations would be threatened by the poor quality of the natural environment. The economy would then experience a population growth factor n smaller than 1. This second more dramatic effect is presented in hypothesis P3.

[Hypothesis P3]
There exists a second pollution threshold, $P^N > P^L$, such that:

$$N_{t+1} = nN_t \quad \text{for } P_t < P^N$$

$$N_{t+1} = rN_t \quad \text{for } P_t \geq P^N$$

with $0 < r < 1 < n$.

Hypothesis P3 accounts for the possibility, in the case of extreme environmental damage, of an effect of pollution on population dynamics. According to P3, once an extreme pollution threshold is reached, the human population would no longer be able to reproduce over time, but would inexorably decline.

It should be noted that hypothesis P3 does not predict an extinction of the human species: the parameter r is assumed to be positive. An extreme level of pollution leads to a reduction in the population size, which nevertheless remains strictly positive. This reduction, by hypothesis P1, leads to a decrease in pollution. We can then hope to see pollution drop back below the threshold P^N.

However, this hypothesis was formulated for simplification purposes. Hypothesis P2, on the other hand, accounts for irreversible environmental damage not for the sake of simplification, but for the sake of realism.

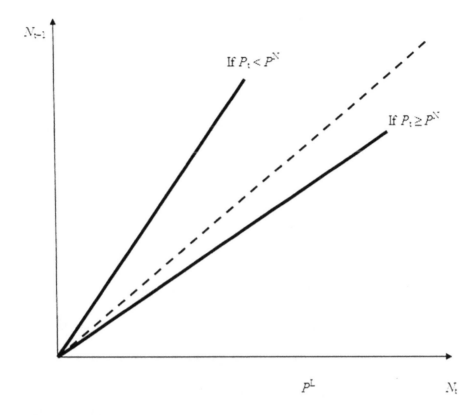

Figure 6.6 Hypothesis P3

Figure 6.6 is a representation of hypothesis P3 in the (N_t, N_{t+1}) space, with the 45° line. This figure shows that when the pollution level is below the threshold P^N, the population increases, and the ratio of N_{t+1} to N_t is a constant n greater than one. N_{t+1} is a linear function of N_t, a function that constitutes a straight line passing through the origin and with a slope greater than 1. This line is therefore above the 45° line, along which the population size is constant. On the contrary, when the pollution level is greater than or equal to the threshold P^N, the ratio of N_{t+1} to N_t is a constant r smaller than one. In this case, N_{t+1} is a linear function of N_t that, in the (N_t, N_{t+1}) space, takes the form of a straight line passing through the origin and with a slope of less than 1. This line lies below the 45° line; in this case, the population size will therefore decrease over time.

6.4   Environmental Damage and the Dynamics over the Long Period

6.4.1   Economic Dynamics over the Long Period

With three hypotheses representing environmental damage and its consequences on the population and the economy, we are now in a position to analyse the effects of including this damage on economic dynamics over the long period.

To do this, let us first rewrite the output per capita y_t:

$$y_t = \frac{Y_t}{N_t} = \frac{A_t(L_t)^\beta}{(N_t)^{1-\alpha}}.$$

It should be noted here that the output per capita growth rate takes a form that depends on the level of environmental damage:

$$g_{t+1} = \frac{a_t}{(n)^{1-\alpha}} - 1 \quad \text{when } P < P^L$$

$$g_{t+1} = \frac{a_t x^\beta}{(n)^{1-\alpha}} - 1 \quad \text{when } P^L \le P < P^N.$$

This dependence on the level of environmental damage stems from the fact that, for pollution above the P^L threshold, the natural environment becomes a variable that declines over time, as the Earth is no longer able to renew itself perfectly from one period to the next due to the extent of the pollution.

Let us now consider long-run dynamics. For this purpose, we will assume that knowledge accumulation follows the K1 rule. In doing so, we ignore here the adverse effects of congestion.[11]

N^L is the population level such that $P_t = P^L = \gamma N^L$ and N^N the population level such that $P_t = P^N = \gamma N^N$.

Let us suppose that $N^C > N^N > N^L > \overline{N} > N_0$.

As the economy starts with a population size N_0 below the critical threshold $\overline{N}$, knowledge accumulates according to a growth factor $\underline{a}$. This factor is barely large enough to compensate for the population growth. Consequently, the economy initially experiences stagnation of its output per capita y_t. Moreover, as $N_0 < N^L$, pollution remains below the P^L threshold. The economy is in a stagnation regime similar to the one studied in the previous chapters.

As the population size increases over time, it eventually reaches the critical threshold $\overline{N}$, which is synonymous with the appearance of positive scale effects that accelerate the accumulation of knowledge. The economy then takes off: output per capita grows at a positive rate (because $\overline{a} > (n)^{1-\alpha}$). This is the end of stagnation.

If pollution (or congestion) were not taken into account, this growth would last forever. But, unfortunately, environmental damage increases with population size (hypothesis P1). Therefore, eventually, the P^L pollution threshold will be reached. Once this critical threshold is reached, the growth rate of output per capita falls, because of the non-regeneration of the natural environment (hypothesis P2). We are now entering a third regime, that of the non-regeneration of the Earth.

[11] However, this hypothesis has little impact on our results because, as we shall see, the economy will not, in general, reach the N^C threshold under our hypotheses.

There are several possible scenarios for the dynamics of output per capita in this third regime:

- if $\bar{a}x^\beta > (n)^{1-\alpha}$, the economy experiences output per capita growth but at a lower rate than during the growth regime (because $x^\beta < 1$);
- if $\bar{a}x^\beta = (n)^{1-\alpha}$, the economy experiences output per capita stagnation because the accumulation of knowledge only compensates for the non-regeneration of the Earth, without any surplus;
- if $\bar{a}x^\beta < (n)^{1-\alpha}$, the economy enters a phase of decreasing output per capita because the accumulation of knowledge is not sufficient to compensate for the non-regeneration of the Earth.

The third regime, that of non-regeneration of the land, is thus characterised by either a slowdown in the growth of output per capita, or by stagnation, or by a decrease in output per capita. The plausibility of each of these three scenarios depends on the extent of environmental damage.

It should be noted, however, that this regime does not represent the end of history. Indeed, the population size continues to grow in this regime until N_t reaches the critical threshold N^N that corresponds to the second pollution threshold (P^N), beyond which the environmental damage is such that demographic dynamics are impacted.

Assuming that the threshold P^N is reached. In that case, population starts decreasing, because $N_{t+1} = r\,N_t$ with $r < 1$. This is the depopulation regime.

Population contraction can have several different consequences:

- Either it brings us back to a value of N_t below the threshold $\overline{N}$, in which case the economy returns to the regime of output per capita stagnation ($g_{t+1} = 0$).
- Or it brings us back to a value of N_t between $\overline{N}$ and N^L, in which case the economy returns to the regime of output per capita growth. This regime is characterised by a growth rate equal to:

$$g_{t+1} = \frac{\bar{a}}{(n)^{1-\alpha}} - 1.$$

- Or it brings us back to a value of N_t such that $N^L < N_t < N^P$, in which case we are back to the non-regeneration regime, characterised by either growth, stagnation or decline in output per capita:

$$g_{t+1} = \frac{\bar{a}x^\beta}{(n)^{1-\alpha}} - 1.$$

- Or it maintains a value of $N_t > N^P$, in which case the population will contract again. In this case, we are in a depopulation regime and the growth rate is:

$$g_{t+1} = \frac{\bar{a}x^\beta}{(r)^{1-\alpha}} - 1.$$

These four scenarios are possible, depending on the extent of the population size correction. The population size correction may: (1) if it is very large, push the economy into the stagnation regime ($g_{t+1} = 0$); (2) if it is significant, bring it back into the growth regime ($g_{t+1} > 0$); (3) if it is small, lead the economy into the non-regeneration regime ($g_{t+1} >< 0$); (4) if it is very low, keep it in the depopulation regime ($g_{t+1} >< 0$).

It should be noted that, in all cases, the economy will return to the non-regeneration regime at some point. Indeed, in the first case, we know that the economy will eventually leave the stagnation regime for the growth regime, then reach the N^L threshold again and return to the non-regeneration regime. In the second case, the economy will also reach the N^L threshold in the future and thus return to the non-regeneration regime. Finally, in the fourth case, as the population size contracts, the population will at some point fall below the N^N threshold, so that pollution will again fall below the P^N threshold: once again the non-regeneration regime will prevail.

The economy will therefore eventually return to the regime of non-regeneration. Since this regime is characterised by population growth and, consequently, by an increase in pollution, it follows that the economy will necessarily return to the depopulation regime. This brings us back to the situation described above, with the four types of possible consequences of a downward correction of the population size.

In other words, the economy is, over the long period, caught up in a *cyclical dynamic*, characterised by long-term oscillations, oscillations that correspond to a succession of regime sequences. This dynamic can be described as "regime cycles".

6.4.2   Regime Cycles

Several types of regime cycles are possible, depending on the extent of the population correction (parameter r). Here are some examples of possible regime cycles:

- cycle A: stagnation regime → growth regime → non-regeneration regime → depopulation regime → stagnation regime.
- cycle B: growth regime → non-regeneration regime → depopulation regime → growth regime.
- cycle C: non-regeneration regime → depopulation regime → non-regeneration regime

We cannot a priori exclude the possibility of the existence of other types of regime cycles, where one would move from cycle A to cycle B or even C over time. Many trajectories are possible, depending on the parameterisations of the model, in particular the population contraction parameter r.

In every case, the economy experiences a cyclical dynamic that is reminiscent of the Malthusian dynamic model studied in Chapter 3: the economy exhibits long-run oscillations, without ever being able to stabilise. The reasons for these perpetual oscillations stem from the contradictory consequences of population growth, not unlike the Malthusian model studied earlier.

Once a critical size threshold has been crossed, demographic growth makes it possible to achieve scale effects and, consequently, growth in output per capita. However, it also leads to an increase in pollution and a deterioration in the quality of the natural environment that, beyond a certain threshold, calls into question the sustainability of this growth regime. The economy then enters a regime of non-regeneration, and then a regime of depopulation: the cause of all these dynamics is then reduced to a smaller size, thus paving the way for a new "turn" in the cycle and to other fluctuations.

In other words, under hypotheses P1, P2 and P3, the economy faces, over the long period, cycles of more or less long regimes, leading to a return to former regimes belonging to a more or less distant past. Once the depopulation regime is reached, the return to the pre-industrial stagnation regime (cycle A) constitutes an extreme case, resulting from a substantial downward correction of the population size. A return to the growth regime (cycle B) would also require a substantial reduction in population size. This is another unlikely case.

The most likely case is that, once the depopulation regime is reached, the economy goes through an oscillation between depopulation regime and non-regeneration regime (cycle C). The economy would have phases where the population size contracts, allowing for a reduction in environmental damage, which would pave the way for further population growth, bringing damage back above the critical P^N level, and the economy would then return to the depopulation regime.

For illustrative purposes, Figures 6.7, 6.8 and 6.9 depict three possible long-run dynamics that all fall under cycle C, where the economy, once the non-regeneration regime is reached, fluctuates between this regime and the depopulation regime. The examples in Figures 6.7, 6.8 and 6.9 have several things in common:

- the period begins in a regime of stagnation in which demographic growth exactly counterbalances technical progress,
- then, once a certain population size is reached, scale effects appear and the economy takes off (output per capita growth),
- once the P^L pollution threshold is reached, the economy enters the regime of non-regeneration in which the natural environment can no longer regenerate completely,
- and, finally, once a second P^N pollution threshold is reached, a cycle between the non-regeneration regime and the depopulation regime appears. (Cycle C)

The only difference, albeit a fundamental one, between these three cases relates to the extent of environmental damage and its effect on growth.

Figure 6.7 illustrates a situation in which the non-regeneration of the natural environment is not very important quantitatively, and simply leads, during the non-regeneration regime, to a slowdown in the growth of output per capita compared to the growth regime. In this case, reaching the P^L pollution threshold at a given moment only implies a slowdown in the growth of output per capita (because the natural environment cannot regenerate completely). It should be noted that once the P^N pollution threshold is reached, the population size is adjusted downwards, which tends, paradoxically enough, to boost the growth of output per capita, which then fluctuates along a growth path.

Figure 6.8 presents a different situation. In this case, once the pollution threshold P^L is reached, the damage is such that the non-regeneration of the natural environment

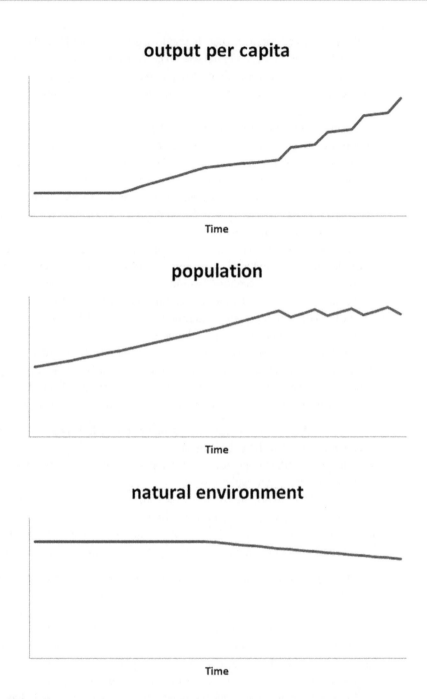

Figure 6.7 Dynamics of output per capita, population size and natural environment in a C cycle: case of slow economic growth in a non-regeneration regime

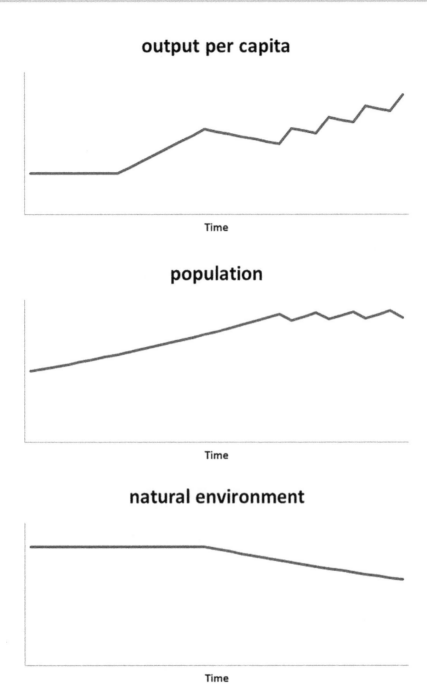

Figure 6.8 Dynamics of output per capita, population size and natural environment in a C cycle: case of temporary negative economic growth

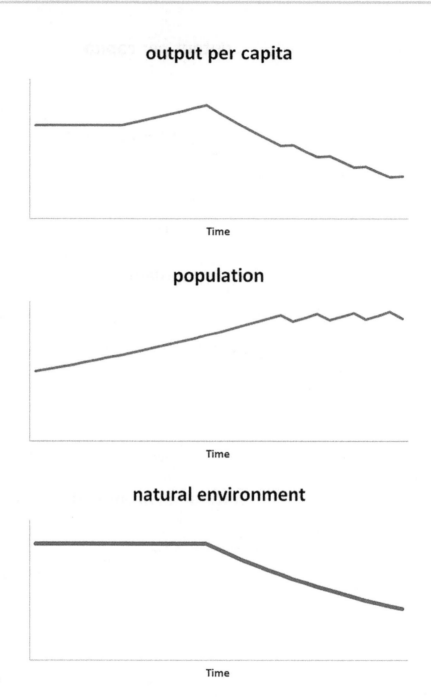

Figure 6.9 Dynamics of output per capita, population size and natural environment in a C cycle: case of sustainable negative economic growth

is more substantial, and this plunges the economy into a period of decreasing output per capita. Unlike the case in Figure 6.7, the regime of non-regeneration is here a regime of decreasing output per capita. However, this decrease in output per capita is temporary because once the second pollution threshold P^N is reached, the decrease in the population size will allow output per capita to take off again, but only temporarily: once the economy has entered the type C cycle, between the non-regeneration regime and the depopulation regime, output per capita will fluctuate around a growth path.

Finally, Figure 6.9 illustrates the worst-case scenario. In this case, not only is the non-regeneration regime characterised by a decrease in output per capita, but the environmental damage is so high that even downward adjustments in population size in the depopulation regime do not restore the growth of output per capita. In the latter case, the decline is a sustainable phenomenon.

Taken together, Figures 6.7, 6.8 and 6.9 present several possible future scenarios. They are all of a type C cycle, in which the adjustment of the population size in the depopulation regime is small, leading the economy back to the non-regeneration regime, without returning to the previous regimes of growth or stagnation. We are therefore in cases of "short regime cycles", in the sense that the economy experiences fluctuations over the long period, but just between two regimes, and not between three or four regimes as occurs with types A and B cycles.

In all these cases, the very long term will be characterised by cycles in population size and in the extent of environmental damage. Knowledge would certainly continue to accumulate, but this would not prevent the non-regeneration of the natural environment or downward population corrections. Periods of high pollution and high population would be followed by periods of lower pollution and lower population, which in turn would precede new periods of high pollution and high population, and so on.

The reason for this cyclicality is that the population size can never stabilise under our hypotheses. Given the hypothesis $N^L < N^N < N^C$, the congestion threshold at which the population stabilises is never reached during the non-regeneration regime. Therefore, a decrease in population and in the accompanying pollution will only be temporary and, eventually, the economy will return to the depopulation regime.

One way for the economy to escape these long-run fluctuations would be to relax the hypothesis $N^L < N^N < N^C$, by imposing, alternatively, $N^L < N^C < N^P$. In this case, the population could stabilise during the non-regeneration regime. This would lead to a stabilisation of pollution that would prevent the emergence of the depopulation regime. The economy could then escape the depopulation/repopulation regime cycles. In the long run, it would remain in the non-regeneration regime.

Although this situation seems less unfavourable on the surface, it would not be ideal: in the non-regeneration regime, it is possible for output per capita to grow slowly, stagnate or even decrease. The latter case would occur if the accumulation of knowledge could not compensate for the non-regeneration of the natural environment. The end of history would then be characterised by a stagnation of a population facing perpetual impoverishment. Even under the hypothesis $N^L < N^C < N^P$, the future does not look much rosier.

In other words, the best possible outcome would arise in another case, that of: $N^C < N^L < N^P$. In this case, the population size would stabilise well before environmental damage exceeds the critical threshold beyond which the non-regeneration regime occurs. In this case, the economy could remain in the growth regime in the long run. This seems to be the best case scenario, but unfortunately the phenomena of desertification, species extinction and global warming suggest that this very favourable case is not the one in which our societies will find themselves. It seems that our societies have probably already entered the regime of non-regeneration.

6.5   Conclusion

This chapter has attempted to include the natural environment in our economic analysis of the long period. To do so, we first introduced the notion of congestion. Taking into account the finiteness of our planet and its effects leads us to anticipate the emergence of a third regime: the congestion regime, which comes after the stagnation and growth regimes. In this regime, the population size stabilises, while the growth of output per capita slows down.

Such a scenario remains too optimistic, as it ignores the environmental damage caused by human activities and the consequences of this damage on living conditions and population. Once this damage has been taken into account, it appears that the economy will, after the growth regime, enter the regime of non-regeneration of the natural environment. This regime of non-regeneration is characterised either by weaker growth, stagnation or a decrease in output per capita, depending on the capacity of technological progress to compensate – or not – the non-regeneration of the natural environment.

This regime of non-regeneration is, unfortunately, not the end of history. Unless the population stabilises during this regime, it is likely that environmental damage will eventually reach a second, even more dramatic, critical threshold, where the deterioration of living conditions is such that the population will no longer be able to reproduce. In this case, the economy would enter a regime of depopulation with population contractions. These corrections, not unlike the corrections posited by Malthus (although from quite different causes), would plunge the economy into "regime cycles". In this scenario, humanity would escape extinction but our societies would evolve in a cyclical infernal dynamic made of oscillations between the regime of non-regeneration and the regime of depopulation.

6.6   First Lessons: Relativity of Economic Laws and Latent Dynamics

Stagnation regime, growth regime, congestion regime, non-regeneration regime, depopulation regime: more so than previous chapters, this chapter has illustrated Unified Growth Theory's potential to help us think about the long period. Within this theory, the long period is modelled as a succession of regimes, each regime being characterised by its own relationships between the variables under study.

Starting from a few hypotheses on the initial conditions of the economy and on the rates of accumulation of factors of production and other variables, it is possible, as we have done, to deduce the existence of several economic regimes and to describe these regimes, as well as the mechanism of transition from one regime to the next. This pattern of analysis can be reproduced whichever "latent" variable governs the development process, the transition from one regime to another depending on that variable's value.

Each economic regime is characterised by its own "laws", by its own qualitative relationships between the variables. This result was already apparent in Chapter 4: in the stagnation regime, population growth is associated with a constant output per capita, whereas in the growth regime it is associated with an increase in output per capita. We are therefore in the presence of a change in the shape of the relations between the variables, the "qualitative" change studied by Kondratiev (1924).

The qualitative changes associated with regime shift are also evident in this chapter. Figures 6.7, 6.8 and 6.9 show that population growth can be associated with either stagnation of output per capita, growth of output per capita or a decline in output per capita, depending on the regime studied. Everything depends on the regime in which the economy finds itself. Moreover, depending on the regime, population growth may coexist either with the conservation of the natural environment or with its deterioration. The relationship between the population and the natural environment is therefore also relative to a given regime.

One of the first major lessons of Unified Growth Theory is that there exists no "law" or "absolute" regularity in economics, as in a "law" that holds across all regimes, throughout history. *An economic "law" is relative to a particular regime.* The regime shift can make one "law" disappear and replace it by another. This relativity of laws in economics does not imply the absence of regularities; these laws exist, but they are relative, conditioned to a particular regime. These laws have validity, but only within a given regime.[12]

Unified Growth Theory also provides us with a second lesson that is not about regimes, but about regime shifts. As we have seen, regime shift in Unified Growth Theory is always based on a given variable crossing a critical threshold, a threshold beyond which the relationships between variables change. We have called these variables, which are the driving force of historical change, "latent variables". They govern a latent process, a kind of "latent dynamic", which is (almost) neutral or benign in the short term, but which will at some point lead to a regime shift.

Several variables were used throughout the chapters to drive this "latent dynamic": population size (Chapters 4 and 6), the quality of institutions (Chapter 5) and environmental pollution (Chapter 6). In each of these cases, the latent variable under study had its own pace of accumulation, which could be extremely slow: a quasi-stagnant population, institutions that evolve very slowly, pollution whose magnitude seems initially not to change very much. But at some point, this slow accumulation process

---

[12] One cannot fail to see similarities here with Marx's conclusions on the relativism of population laws, each mode of production being characterised by its own population laws (see Chapters 1 and 4).

will lead the latent variable to cross a critical threshold, resulting in major qualitative changes in the economy.[13]

This brings us to the second lesson we can draw from these first chapters: *the variables that govern historical change are not always those that experience the most significant developments or show the strongest growth.* On the contrary, Unified Growth Theory emphasises the role played by slow latent processes with little apparent impact. This is a second lesson to be drawn from our analysis.

Appendix 6A.1 Further Reading

The economist who probably has put the most emphasis on the issue of Earth's congestion and finite nature is Boulding (1966), who coined the vivid expression of "Earth as a Spaceship". Foley and Michl (1999) devote chapter 11 of their treatise to the limitations imposed on growth by Earth's finiteness.

The issue of congestion has also been addressed in the demographic literature. Heilig (1994) reviews attempts to define the maximum population size that could live on Earth. This review shows the extent of the difficulties in setting a value for the critical threshold N^C. However, the difficulties in setting this threshold cannot be taken as evidence that the threshold does not exist or that the world's population can grow indefinitely.

A classic reference on the economic theory of natural resources is the work of Dasgupta and Heal (1979), which examines the different types of natural resources: fully renewable, partially renewable and non-renewable. It also looks at the interactions between these natural resources and the economic growth process.

Theories of economic growth have progressively taken the environmental dimension into account. The links between growth and non-renewable natural resources are discussed in chapter 12 of Foley and Michl (1999) and chapter 10 of Hritonenko and Yatsenko (2013).

John and Pecchenino (1994), Michel and Rotillon (1995) and Withagen (1995) published groundbreaking papers on the interactions between the growth process and environmental damage (modelled as the result of pollution). A synthesis of articles studying the relationship between growth and the environment is presented by Xepapadeas (2005).

The last few decades have seen the emergence of "integrated assessment models", which are unique in that they include the effect of human activities on the environment, particularly on temperature change, in much greater detail. The literature on integrated assessment models was initiated by Nordhaus (1993a, 1993b, 2010). These models have a number of "building blocks" and are used for exclusively numerical analyses. They are generally not intended to study the past; they are most often used

---

[13] Once again, a parallel can be drawn with Marx's ideas, since for Marx, the change in the mode of production is associated with a latent process: the development of the productive forces (see Chapter 1).

for forecasting purposes. Chapter 12 of Hritonenko and Yatsenko (2013) provides a detailed overview of recent developments in integrated assessment models.

Appendix 6A.2 Exercises

1. Consider hypothesis C1:
   There exists a population threshold $N^c > 0$ such that:

$$n_t = n > 1 \quad \text{if } N_t < N^c$$

$$n_t = 1 \quad \text{if } N_t \geq N^c.$$

   Let us assume that the initial population size is $N_0 > 1$.

   a. What does hypothesis C1 imply for the long-term population size?
   b. Let us now replace hypothesis C1 by the following hypothesis:

$$n_t = n > 1 \quad \text{if } N_t > 0.$$

   What will the long-term population size be now?
   c. Let us assume a third hypothesis for the population dynamics: There exists a population threshold $N^c > 0$ such that:

$$n_t = n > 1 \quad \text{if } N_t < N^c$$

$$n_t = \breve{n} < 1 \quad \text{if } N_t \geq N^c.$$

   What will the long-term population dynamics look like?

2. Reading Forrester (1973), in *World Dynamics*, regarding the limits to growth:[14]

   Overemphasis of the physical limits [to growth] occurs for several reasons. Physical characteristics of the world – resource shortage, pollution, and inadequate food – are more tangible and evident than social limits. [...] Social limits arise as population density increases and as urbanization spreads. With industrialization comes more specialization of work and a greater need for coordination, management, and political compromise. As more time is devoted to negotiation, frustration increases. [...] Now, pushing back the physical limits means not more space but higher population densities. Technology [...] now is directed to higher buildings, more concentrated transportation systems, and a more complex infra-structure. But these new directions of technology raise rather than relieve social stresses.

   a. Is this excerpt compatible with Rostow's "stages of growth"? [Hint: review the mass consumption stage.]
   b. Can we link the issue of "social limits" to growth with the models studied in this chapter? If the answer is yes, through which mechanisms?

---

[14] See Forrester (1973), pp. 129–130.

Part III

Unified Growth Theory
Microeconomics of Regime Shift

7 Economic Growth and Education

Although they are useful for understanding economic dynamics over the long period, the models in Part II suffer from some imperfections. First, these formalisations do not include all the dimensions relevant to explain how societies evolve over the long term. We have focused on demography, technology and knowledge accumulation (Chapters 3 and 4), then on institutions (Chapter 5) and finally on the natural environment (Chapter 6), but other dimensions could be added: cultural and religious dimensions, geographical dimensions, etc.

At a more fundamental level, one of the main limitations of these models is that they present the process of development of societies in a rather "mechanistic" way: given initial conditions and hypotheses on the processes of factor accumulation, the existence of economic regimes and their succession over time occur almost mechanically. In other words, these theoretical frameworks propose a formalisation of an economic history "without individual agency": in these models, men and women do not make any decisions. The long period is reduced to a succession of regimes dictated by processes of accumulation that respond to certain laws, laws that are imposed on human beings and over which they have no control.

Although such a view of history can be developed as a first approximation, it is not entirely satisfactory, as it is based on a simplification of the historical process. Over the centuries, humans have changed their ways of life, and the process of historical change is inherently linked to these developments. The lives of people who inhabited the Earth in 1500 differ in many dimensions from those of people born in, say, 1850, just as generations born in the twenty-second century are likely to have very different lifestyles from ours. A study of the process of historical change cannot afford to ignore the analysis of lifestyles and individual behaviours and their evolution over time.

Unified Growth Theory, which was developed in the twenty-first century by Galor and his co-authors (Galor and Weil 1999, 2000; Galor 2005, 2010, 2011; Galor and Moav 2002, 2005), based the study of economic regimes and regime shifts on individual decisions about lifestyles and behaviour. This theory analyses the historical process as a succession of regimes, with the transition between them resulting from changes in lifestyles and behaviours studied using microeconomic analysis. For pedagogical purposes, Part II of this book temporarily leaves out the microeconomic analysis of individual behaviour. It is now necessary, in order to give readers a comprehensive presentation of Unified Growth Theory, to introduce these microeconomic foundations into our analyses.

The third part of this book will, once again, study the existence of economic regimes, their properties and the processes of transition from one regime to another.

However, we will introduce microeconomic foundations into the models and *analyse how an economic regime exists as a result of decisions taken at the individual level*. The key concepts introduced in Part II (economic regimes, quantitative and qualitative changes, critical thresholds, latent dynamics, etc.) will be revisited, but within a broader theoretical framework: the macroeconomic analysis of regimes and regime shifts will here be based on microeconomic foundations. This third part will thus propose a formalisation of history as a succession of distinct regimes, in which human beings are now full actors in the historical process through their lifestyles and behaviour.

In terms of human lives, a major development that has taken place over the centuries is the growth in the level of *cognitive abilities* of individuals. A fundamental difference between our contemporaries and their ancestors is their ability to learn, which is now called "level of education". To give an idea of the extent of the overall change, based on statistics from Allen (2011, p. 35), Figure 7.1 compares literacy levels in 1500 and 1800 in several countries. Literacy levels are measured by the percentage of the adult population able to sign their name.[1]

Figure 7.1 illustrates a major development in our societies. In 1500, only a very small proportion of the population was literate – at most 10% in some areas – whereas three centuries later, in 1800, literacy rates were much higher: England reached 53% and the Netherlands were even higher at 68%.

This change in the literacy rate – and, more generally, in the level of education – is fundamental from a long-run perspective. As we saw in Part II, one of the major factors in the long-term dynamics is the process of knowledge accumulation. It is the accumulation of knowledge that makes it possible to improve production techniques, opening up the prospect of a rise in material living standards. The more literate the population, the faster the accumulation of knowledge. The higher the level of literacy, the greater the accumulation of knowledge and the greater the productivity gains.

For a very long time, only a very small part of the population, an "elite", was literate. The stagnation regime of the pre-industrial era was thus a regime in which a very large majority of the population was poorly educated. The emergence from the stagnation regime can be seen as deeply linked to the spread of literacy – and education in general – to a large part of the population, which accelerated technical progress and thereby led to economic take-off.

This chapter seeks to revisit the issue of take-off by explicitly introducing the variable "education" into the analysis. Since education requires effort on the part of individuals, much of the success of learning depends on the willingness to learn.[2] To account for this dimension and for the role of education in economic take-off, this chapter develops a microeconomic model of choosing to invest in education and revisits the issue of regime shift from this perspective.

---

[1] We could use other indicators of the level of education, such as the average number of years of schooling per cohort (see Jones and Romer 2011). It should nonetheless be noted that these indicators are usually only available for more recent and much shorter time periods (basically since the end of the nineteenth century). This is why we prefer to use a less "refined" indicator of the level of education here, but one that is available over a long time period.

[2] We are dealing here with the "demand" side of education; we will be studying the "supply" side in Chapter 8, which centres on the dynamics of the general institutional framework (including the education system).

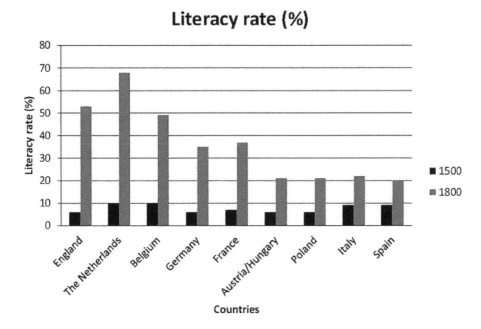

Figure 7.1 Literacy levels (proportion of the adult population able to sign their name) in Europe, in 1500 and 1800
(*source*: Allen 2011)

To this end, Section 7.1 will first provide a brief introduction to the microeconomic analysis of individual choices, through a short digression on what economists call the Marginalist Revolution. Then, in Sections 7.2, 7.3 and 7.4, we will study a microeconomic model in which individuals decide to invest – or not – in education. In the process, we will study how it is possible to explain first the existence of a stagnation regime (where education is non-existent or, more precisely, reserved for a small elite) and, second, the possibility of a transition to the growth regime (where education is widespread), based on decisions regarding education. In light of these results, Sections 7.5 and 7.6 will then return to international comparisons in terms of the timing of economic take-off. As such, this chapter offers a microeconomic complement, so to speak, to Chapter 4 dedicated to the determinants of the economic take-off.

7.1   The Marginalist Revolution and the Study of Individual Decisions

The importance given to the individual as an autonomous decision-making unit in classical and even pre-classical economic thought (mercantilism, physiocracy) is not easily determined. Several interpretations are possible.

On the surface, it seems that Classical political economy was essentially based on an aggregate understanding of the economy, a perspective based on a partition of society into social classes: workers, landowners, capitalists. Classical political economy paid little attention to individuals or to the decisions they made. For example, in his *Essay on the Principle of Population*, Malthus (1798) criticised Godwin's (1793) conception of the rational man. According to Malthus, man is not a rational being, but rather a "compound subject" governed by his passions and desires, which are completely beyond his control.[3] Human beings cannot be expected to change their behaviour in order to achieve this or that goal. They behave as mechanically as any other species. Malthus has very little to say about individual decisions.

This first assessment is reinforced by the fact that, before and during the classical era, the notion of "individual decision" had little empirical relevance for most people. According to the Classics (from Smith to Marx), the hourly wage was fixed at its so-called "natural", that is, subsistence level, so that for the vast majority of the population there was little relevance in talking about "savings decisions" or "trade-offs" between work and leisure. Moreover, in the absence of modern means of contraception, the number of children depended on social rules regarding the age at which people married, the length of time women breastfed and the survival rates of mothers, so that there was little room for real "fertility decisions" (see Wrigley 1969). In this context, it is not surprising that individual choices and decisions were not theorised by early economists.

This initial judgement must be qualified, however, because even if the Classics and their predecessors often reasoned by adopting an aggregate understanding of the economy, a careful reading of their works reveals, here and there, considerations relating to individual behaviour. For example, in his *Essay on the Nature of Trade in General*, Cantillon (1755) develops an analysis of how the market works and how prices are formed based on two examples – the meat market and the green pea market – and studies the behaviour of sellers and its impact on how prices are determined. Starting with Smith (1776), the Classics provide extensive studies of the market, price determination and the relationship between market prices and natural prices (or production prices). It is therefore premature to conclude that the Classics shared only aggregate perspectives on the economy.

Although the importance given to individual decisions by the Classics is debatable, one thing is certain: following the work of the pioneers of marginalist analysis – mainly Cournot (1838) and Jevons (1871) – economic analysis took a microeconomic turn at the end of the nineteenth century and during the twentieth century. This is what historians of economic thought call the "Marginalist Revolution". The extent of this revolution and of the discontinuity it introduced into economic discourse is not independent of the considerations mentioned above. Depending on whether one considers that the study of individual decisions was, in a preliminary form, "already there" or not, this theoretical turn will appear as more or less revolutionary.[4]

---

[3] See Malthus (1798), chapter 13. This perception is a very long way from *homo economicus*.

[4] It should nonetheless be noted that, even though Classical political economy has sometimes examined individual decisions, we can see in later works a fundamental discontinuity in the *nature* of these studies: with Cournot (1838) and Jevons (1871), economic analysis took a decisive step towards the mathematisation of the discipline. Its language will no longer be exclusively natural language, but also, and increasingly so, mathematical language. This is a fundamental discontinuity in the nature

7.1.1   Cournot

Cournot is the founder of microeconomic analysis. In his *Researches on the Mathematical Principles of the Theory of Wealth*, Cournot (1838) introduced marginalist analysis into the field of production, in particular into the supply decisions of firms. His analyses are meant to show that the level of the equilibrium product in a market – as well as the equilibrium price – depends on the structure of the market, and in particular on the number of existing firms (which determines their market power).

To that end, Cournot models supply decisions in several types of markets (monopoly, duopoly, oligopoly). These supply decisions are all based on the same objective: profit maximisation, which is defined as the difference between sales revenues and production costs. Cournot shows that when profits are maximised by firms, there is an alignment or equalisation, at the margin, of what the firm would earn from one more unit of output (the marginal revenue) and what it would cost to produce that additional unit (the marginal cost).

The economic intuition behind this result is simple: in the absence of such equality, the firm could increase its profits either by reducing its output (if the marginal cost of the last unit produced is higher than the marginal revenue associated with that unit) or by increasing its output (if the marginal cost of the last unit produced is lower than the marginal revenue associated with that unit). Profit maximisation therefore inevitably implies this equality between variations, "at the margin", of revenues and costs, that is, between marginal revenue and marginal cost, hence the term "marginalist" analysis.

7.1.2   Jevons

While Cournot (1838) developed the marginalist analysis of individual decisions on the supply side (producers), Jevons laid the foundations for the microeconomic analysis of consumers.[5] In *The Theory of Political Economy* (1871), Jevons developed his theory of utility, defined not as an intrinsic quality of things, but rather as "*a circumstance of things* arising out of their relation to man's requirements".[6] This theory of utility allowed Jevons to later derive a theory of value based on the concept of marginal utility.

In order to introduce the concept of marginal utility, let us take the case of an individual who has to allocate resources between different uses, say, for simplicity's sake, two uses only. Jevons tells us that it is impossible for the economist to know the total level of utility attained by this individual, nor that associated with the consumption of a particular commodity. On the other hand, assuming that the individual allocates their resources in such a way as to maximise their utility, we

---

of economic discourse. Jevons (1871) is also responsible for the terminological shift from "political economy" to "economics" (following the model of "physics").

[5] An entire chapter is also devoted to the labour supply decision, giving rise to the famous "final equivalence of labour and utility": the optimal labour supply equals the marginal disutility of labour and the hourly wage times the marginal utility of consumption (see Jevons, 1871, p. 194).

[6] See Jevons (1871), p. 105.

can be certain that the chosen allocation equalises the variations in utility associated with the last units of the resource allocated in the two uses considered:[7]

Let s be the whole stock of some commodity, and let it be capable of two distinct uses. Then we may represent the two quantities appropriated to these uses by x_1 and y_1, it being a condition that $x_1 + y_1 = s$. [...] Now it is the inevitable tendency of human nature to choose that course which appears to offer the greatest advantage at the moment. Hence, when the person remains satisfied with the distribution he has made, it follows that no alteration would yield him more pleasure; which amounts to saying that an increment of commodity would yield exactly as much utility in one use as in another. Let Δu_1, Δu_2, be the increments of utility, which might arise respectively from consuming an increment of commodity in the two different ways. When the distribution is completed, we ought to have $\Delta u_1 = \Delta u_2$; or at the limit we have the equation $du_1/dx = du_2/dy$, which is true when x, y are respectively equal to x_1, y_1. We must, in other words, have the *final degrees of utility* in the two uses equal.

What Jevons called the "final degrees of utility" are what microeconomic textbooks call the "marginal utilities" of the last units allocated. The intuition behind Jevons's marginalist calculation is the same as the one Cournot (1838) applied in the area of production. If, for a given allocation, the equalisation of the marginal utilities is not associated with the last units allocated in the two uses, then it is possible to reallocate a unit from one use to another, thereby increasing the total utility. If, for example, we had $\Delta u_1 > \Delta u_2$, then the individual could increase their utility by reallocating units of the commodity from the second use to the first. In doing so, it would gain more on one side than it would lose on the other, and total utility would be increased. Only when $\Delta u_1 = \Delta u_2$ can no reallocation improve the individual's circumstances.

Jevons's reasoning is generalisable to the allocation of any resource. In the case of a budget expressed in monetary units (such as British pounds), the optimal basket of goods and services for the consumer is such that there is an equalisation of the marginal utilities associated with the different goods and services, these being divided by the price of the good or service in question (if the price of a commodity is p, spending an additional pound on this commodity gives the right to $1/p$ additional unit of the commodity). The consumer who maximises their utility chooses a basket such that the variations in utility resulting from the allocation of an additional pound to each of the goods are strictly equal. If this were not the case, it would be possible to allocate the amount of pounds differently so as to increase the total utility. After rewriting this equality of price-weighted marginal utilities, we get an equality of the price ratios to the marginal utility ratios of the last units of the consumed commodities. This is Jevons's theory of utility-value.[8]

In other words, the marginalist analysis attempts to describe human behaviour as the result of an optimisation strategy on the part of individuals, who seek the best possible use of the resources at their disposal, given all the constraints they face. This famous "optimisation principle" became standard in economics during the twentieth

---

[7] See Jevons (1871), pp. 115–116. Jevons considers an interior optimum (in which individuals avail themselves of both uses of resources).

[8] Jevons (1871, pp. 186–187) shows that his theory of value is more general than the labour-incorporated theory of value offered by Ricardo (1817).

century. *To give microeconomic foundations to a phenomenon – to "rationalise" it – is to explain how this phenomenon – rather than another – will arise, on the basis of decisions taken by individuals maximising their well-being or utility.*

Unified Growth Theory aims to provide microeconomic foundations for the existence of regimes and regime shifts. It starts from individual decisions and then deduces the existence of relationships between the variables under study. In this perspective, a major difficulty lies in the area of regime shift. Based on individual decisions, how can we explain that relationships between variables will change over time? How can we rationalise a qualitative change?

To answer this question, Galor (2011) analyses a model in which individuals make a number of decisions, whereby the existence of particular economic regimes can be inferred. Each regime shift originates in the "latent dynamics" discussed above: *by influencing individuals' decisions, it is the latent variable that will lead to the regime shift.* The remainder of this chapter provides a deliberately simplified study of the microeconomic foundations of regime shift, starting with the education decision.

7.2   Production and Knowledge Accumulation

Let us return to our study of long-run dynamics. In this chapter we will assume, as before, that the production of a composite good requires labour, land and knowledge. The production function is still given by:

$$Y_t = A_t(L)^\beta (N_t)^\alpha.$$

We will assume that the quantity and quality of land are constant. For the sake of simplicity, let us also assume that the population grows by a constant factor n.

$$N_{t+1} = nN_t.$$

Knowledge, for its part, accumulates according to the following law:

$$A_{t+1} = (a + \theta e_t)A_t,$$

where $a > 1$ is a factor in the accumulation of knowledge as seen earlier. This accumulation comes from what is known as "learning by doing": the mere activity of production automatically contributes to increasing knowledge.

The new element in the knowledge accumulation equation is the variable e_t, which represents the investment of individuals in education.[9] This investment has the effect of enhancing the process of knowledge accumulation, to an extent formalised by the parameter $\theta > 0$. This variable e_t reflects individual choice. Given the impacts of

---

[9] Given that we are in a representative agent model, the variable e_t represents the education of the mass of individuals, and not that of the elites, which represent a small minority of the population.

education on knowledge, this variable can also be interpreted as an investment in knowledge or in the improvement of production techniques.[10]

With the variable e_t, we introduce a kind of "behavioural component" in knowledge accumulation. The underlying idea is that knowledge accumulation requires effort or investment on the part of individuals. A higher level of investment in education will lead to a faster accumulation of knowledge.

The variable e_t could be interpreted as an "education" variable, but that definition would be too narrow. In fact, long before the birth and generalisation of formal education, people have always been able to ask themselves about possible improvements in production processes, all the while taking part in their routine production activities. The accumulation of knowledge is not only based on formal education, but also on informal efforts to understand production processes. These efforts are based on individual decisions and cannot be seen as simple learning by doing, which takes place by the mere fact of producing, without any additional effort.

7.3   Microeconomic Foundations: Objectives and Constraints

This section focuses on a microeconomic variant of the model presented in Chapter 4. As stated earlier, individuals live for only one period, during which they work. During this single period of life, they have n children, who will work in the next period.

The purpose of this section is to reflect on the microeconomic foundations of regime shift and the interactions between individual decisions and long-term economic dynamics. To this end, we assume that individuals can contribute to the accumulation of knowledge through their investment e_t. The level of investment in education e_t is chosen by individuals.

There are several microeconomic models for analysing this choice of education, which differ in terms of the objectives of individuals and the constraints affecting them.[11] For simplification purposes, this section considers a very streamlined model, where education e_t improves the future state of knowledge, but at the cost of a decrease in the individual's consumption. We will assume that this trade-off between the level of consumption on the one hand and the level of education on the other is the only trade-off that individuals face.[12]

This section presents a simple model of this trade-off. To this end, we use the basic concepts of microeconomic analysis: the individuals' objectives, represented by their utility function, and the constraints they face.

---

[10] In reality, education is not reducible to the mere "improvement of production techniques". Given that we are studying the production of a composite good, it is possible to include in this good all the things that humans value (beyond the mere consumption of material goods). From this point of view, the activity of education is an investment in the improvement of production techniques *in the broad sense*.

[11] See de la Croix and Michel (2002).

[12] The purpose of this hypothesis is to simplify the analysis as much as possible. Other decisions, regarding the choice of lifestyles, will be discussed in the next chapters.

7.3.1   Modelling Individual Objectives

Let us start with the objective. To keep things simple, we will assume that the representative individual at time t is interested in two things: on the one hand, their consumption (c_t) and, on the other, the accumulation of knowledge (A_{t+1}).[13] The individuals' interests are therefore divided between a short-term objective – what they consume – and another objective that extends beyond the horizon of their own life, but which is important to them: future knowledge. This trade-off between consumption c_t and future knowledge A_{t+1} is *intertemporal* in nature: it involves economic quantities located in different time periods, periods t and $t + 1$.[14]

Among a large number of possible formalisations, one simple way of representing the interests of the representative individual is to assume the utility function:[15]

$$U(c_t, A_{t+1}) = c_t + \delta\log(A_{t+1} + \varepsilon),$$

where parameters $\delta > 0$ and $\varepsilon > 0$ are preference parameters. The utility function presented above is described as "quasi-linear", because it is linear in its first term (while the second term here takes the form of a logarithm).

The preference parameter δ represents the (absolute) interest that the individual has in the accumulation of knowledge. The preference parameter ε captures the importance that individuals attach, at the margin, to additions to future knowledge. Since the logarithmic function is concave, we see that the higher ε is, the lower the value of the marginal gains in knowledge (for a given level of the parameter δ). The parameter ε is a simple way of varying the degree of concavity of the utility associated with future knowledge.

The representative individual chooses the variable e_t in such a way as to maximise their objective, which is given by the utility function $U(c_t, A_{t+1})$. The education variable e_t is not explicitly present in the formulation of the utility function, but it is nevertheless implicitly present, since it determines both consumption c_t (through the budget constraint) and the knowledge stock A_{t+1} (through the knowledge accumulation equation).

7.3.2   Modelling Constraints

There are two constraints in play here.

First of all, representative individuals cannot consume more than what they produce from their labour. Assuming that each worker receives a wage equal to the

---

[13] There is a cost associated with using a fictional "representative individual": this section does not consider inequalities.

[14] In keeping with Unified Growth Theory (Galor, 2011), this intertemporal trade-off takes a deliberately simplified form. The individual is interested in the state of knowledge at period $t + 1$, but is not interested in the state of knowledge at later periods $t + 2$, $t + 3$, etc. This modelling is refined compared to other intertemporal optimisation models, such as dynastic altruism models (Barro and Becker, 1989), in which individuals choose profiles for certain variables (consumption, etc.) by adopting an infinite planning horizon (see Barro and Sala-I-Martin, 1996).

[15] By using the fiction of the representative individual, we eliminate "free rider"-type coordination problems.

marginal productivity of labour, this wage is therefore equal to $\alpha A_t (L)^\beta (N_t)^{\alpha-1}$. In the absence of credit, this wage level represents the maximum level of consumption.[16]

Furthermore, investing in education has a cost. We will assume that the cost of investing in education is unitary, so that the cost of investing in one unit of education e_t is exactly equal to e_t. This cost reduces the individual's consumption.

Therefore, the budget constraint of the representative individual is the following:

$$c_t \leq \alpha A_t (L)^\beta (N_t)^{\alpha-1} - e_t.$$

This budget constraint accounts for the conflict between the individuals' two objectives: the amount that can be consumed decreases with the amount of investment in education. The more they invest in knowledge, the lower their consumption. Conversely, the more they consume, the less they can invest in education. The representative individual is therefore constrained and must make trade-offs between their two interests.

The representative individual faces a second constraint: the law of accumulation of knowledge. The representative individual's contribution to future knowledge through their educational efforts is made according to the law of accumulation stated above:

$$A_{t+1} = (a + \theta e_t) A_t.$$

In light of these two constraints, the problem of educational choice e_t for the representative individual can be written as the following utility maximisation problem:

$$\max_{e_t} c_t + \delta log(A_{t+1} + \varepsilon)$$

$$\text{under constraints } c_t \leq \alpha A_t (L)^\beta (N_t)^{\alpha-1} - e_t,$$

$$A_{t+1} = (a + \theta e_t) A_t.$$

7.3.3   The Problem of the Representative Individual

By substituting constraints in the objective function (which amounts to assuming that all disposable income is spent on either consumption or investment in education), the representative individual's problem can be re-written as follows:

$$\max_{e_t} \alpha A_t (L)^\beta (N_t)^{\alpha-1} - e_t + \delta log((a + \theta e_t) A_t + \varepsilon).$$

This utility maximisation programme is the standard way of modelling agents' decisions in microeconomic analysis. This representation of choices leaves room for individual freedom: it is the individual, through their preferences, who makes the

---

[16] It should be noted that if all factors (labour and land) are paid at their marginal productivity, the sum of all wages on N_t workers (i.e. the wage bill) and all rents on L land is equal to: $\alpha N_t A_t L^\beta (N_t)^{\alpha-1} + \beta L A_t L^{\beta-1} (N_t)^\alpha = (\alpha + \beta) A_t L^\beta (N_t)^\alpha$. In the presence of constant returns to scale ($\alpha + \beta = 1$), the sum of the compensations of all factors is therefore equal to the total product Y_t.

trade-offs between their different interests, in this case between consumption and education. However, this freedom is relative, as the individual is constrained, particularly in their budget. The individual has no other choice but to consume and invest in education in a manner that is consistent with their labour income. The following section studies the solution to this utility maximisation problem and analyses the determinants of the choice of the optimal level of investment in education.

7.4   The Choice of the Education Investment

When examining individual choices, microeconomic analysis most often uses a so-called "marginalist" approach, introduced by Cournot (1838) for production and by Jevons (1871) for consumption. As we have studied, the marginalist approach consists of characterising the individual's optimal choice, their "optimal basket", by comparing what individuals would gain by deviating a little from their optimal basket with what they would lose by such a marginal deviation.

The intuition behind the marginalist calculation developed by Jevons is simple: given an optimal basket, a small deviation should not raise the individual's utility. Indeed, if such a marginal change in the basket were to increase the individual's utility, it would mean that their initial basket was not optimal, with other baskets leading to a higher level of utility. This insight from the marginalist analysis is central to resolving decision problems such as the choice of education discussed below.

7.4.1   The First-Order Condition

The maximisation problem at hand can be solved by deriving a so-called first-order condition, which is a necessary condition for the existence of an interior optimal basket, in this case for the optimality of a strictly positive level of the investment in education e_t. This condition is obtained by deriving the objective function with respect to the choice variable e_t and setting it to 0. As a result:

$$-1 + \frac{\delta A_t \theta}{A_t(a + \theta e_t) + \varepsilon} = 0.$$

The first term of this condition is the marginal loss of utility incurred by the fall in consumption following an increase of one unit of the investment in education.

The second term of this condition is the marginal gain in utility incurred by an increase of one unit in the level of investment in education. We see that this second term is increasing in the parameter δ: the higher the weight given to knowledge, the higher the marginal gain in utility associated with the increase in e_t. It should also be noted that the second term of this expression is decreasing in the parameter ε. The higher ε is, the lower the marginal utility associated with an improvement in knowledge (for a given parameter δ).

If there exists an optimal interior level of investment in education e_t, then the two terms of this condition must exactly offset each other in absolute terms, so that the net utility gain from a marginal increase in e_t should be equal to 0, with the gains from deviation exactly offsetting the losses associated with this deviation. In the presence of an optimal interior level of education, the above condition therefore applies equally.

7.4.2   The Second-Order Condition

The condition derived above is a necessary, but not sufficient, condition for the existence of an interior optimum for the variable e_t. Indeed, this condition tells us that the slope of the objective function is zero at the chosen level of the variable e_t, so that infinitesimal movements around this value of e_t do not influence the value of the objective function. This condition is necessarily verified for an interior value of e_t that maximises the objective function. But it is a priori possible that this condition is also true for other values of e_t, which do not maximise the value of the objective function (e.g. by values of e_t that minimise the value of the objective function). We must therefore check that the value of the variable e_t that satisfies the first-order condition is indeed a maximum and not a minimum.

The sufficient condition for the existence of a maximum, called the second-order condition, is that the second derivative of the objective function with respect to e_t is negative:

$$\frac{-\delta(A_t\theta)^2}{(A_t(a + \theta e_t) + \varepsilon)^2} < 0.$$

This second-order condition is satisfied under our hypotheses. Therefore, if there exists a value of e_t that verifies, with strict equality, the first-order condition (and which is therefore such that the slope of the objective function is zero), it is indeed the value of e_t that maximises the value of the objective function.

7.4.3   The Existence of an Interior Solution

Does a strictly positive level of the investment e_t that satisfies the first-order condition with an equality always exist?

The answer is no. To make this clear, it should be noted that the second term of the first-order condition is decreasing in e_t, so that, if the following strict inequality holds true,

$$-1 + \frac{\delta A_t\theta}{A_t a + \varepsilon} < 0,$$

then the condition for the existence of an optimal interior level of education is never verified (with equality), whatever the positive level of e_t. Indeed, under this hypothesis, the first-order condition is not verified in $e_t = 0$, and as the second term of the first-order condition is decreasing in e_t, this condition cannot be verified for any $e_t > 0$ either.

The mathematical intuition behind this result is the following. When the above inequality holds true, the first-order condition cannot be verified with an equality:

instead of an equality between the left and right members of the equation, a strict inequality will remain true *for all possible positive values* of e_t. Therefore, there is no optimal interior level of e_t. In fact, in this case, the optimal solution is simply $e_t = 0$, that is, no investment in education.

The economic intuition behind this result is simple. When the above condition holds true, we know that for all values of $e_t \geq 0$, the net utility gain from a marginal increase in education is strictly negative. It is therefore not possible for the optimal level of education to be strictly positive. The optimal level of education investment must necessarily be zero.

If we have the following equality:

$$-1 + \frac{\delta A_t \theta}{A_t a + \varepsilon} = 0,$$

then the solution is also $e_t = 0$.

Finally, if we have the strict inequality:

$$-1 + \frac{\delta A_t \theta}{A_t a + \varepsilon} > 0,$$

then there necessarily exists an interior solution for the optimal level of e_t. Indeed, in this case, we can see that when $e_t = 0$, the marginal utility gain associated with a small increase in e_t (the second term) dominates the marginal utility loss associated with this increase in e_t (the first term), so that $e_t = 0$ cannot be the solution. Having education equal to zero cannot be optimal: increasing e_t a little will necessarily increase utility. There must therefore exist an optimal level of e_t that is strictly greater than zero. The optimal level of e_t is given by the first-order condition, and is equal to:

$$e_t = \frac{A_t(\delta \theta - a) - \varepsilon}{A_t \theta}.$$

At this point of the reasoning, we can make two important observations.

First of all, the necessary and sufficient condition for reaching an optimal interior level of e_t, which is:

$$-1 + \frac{\delta A_t \theta}{A_t a + \varepsilon} > 0$$

can be rewritten in the following manner:

$$A_t > \frac{\varepsilon}{\delta \theta - a}.$$

In this formulation, the condition corresponds to *a threshold condition* imposed on the variable A_t: the investment in education chosen by the representative individual can only be positive if the stock of knowledge is above a certain critical threshold, given by:

$$\overline{A} = \frac{\varepsilon}{\delta \theta - a}.$$

It should be noted that, in some cases, the critical threshold $\bar{A}$ is negative, so that the interiority condition is necessarily verified. That occurs when ε is negative and $(\delta\theta - a)$ positive, or when ε is positive and $(\delta\theta - a)$ negative.

In the rest of this section, we will examine the most interesting case, in which the critical threshold $\bar{A}$ is strictly positive. We see that if A_t is below the critical threshold $\bar{A}$, individuals do not invest in education $(e_t = 0)$. In that case, the process of learning by doing will be the only mechanism in place and knowledge will grow by a factor of $a > 1$. If, conversely, A_t is above the threshold $\bar{A}$, individuals do invest in education $(e_t > 0)$. In this case, knowledge will grow at the higher rate $a + \theta e_t$.

7.4.4　Determinants of the Optimal Education Level

Our second observation is that, in such a case, the level of education is:

$$e_t = \frac{A_t(\delta\theta - a) - \varepsilon}{A_t\theta}.$$

Let us look at the determinants of this optimal level of investment in education. First of all, the investment increases as a function of the stock of knowledge in t, A_t. The higher the stock of knowledge, the higher the investment (provided of course that A_t stays above the threshold). The intuition behind this result is simple: in terms of future knowledge, the return on education investment depends on the present knowledge stock, through the knowledge accumulation equation. Given that the cost of this investment is constant, it is therefore normal that the greater the knowledge, the higher the value of e_t chosen by the individual.

The optimal level of investment in education e_t increases with δ, the parameter that reflects the individual's interest in knowledge. The greater this interest, the higher the investment in education, all other things being equal. Conversely, the higher the preference parameter ε, the lower the level of education. We also see that the greater the return on investment parameter θ, the higher e_t is, while the learning-by-doing parameter (a) has the opposite effect.

In other words, the formula describing the optimal level of the investment e_t synthesises the different determinants of the level of investment in education chosen by the representative individual. The choice made depends on several dimensions: the individual's preferences (parameters δ and ε), parameters related to knowledge accumulation (parameters θ and a) and, finally, the level of the existing knowledge stock A_t. This last determinant will play a crucial role in the study of long-term dynamics, as we shall see.

7.4.5　Summary

But we must first summarise the principal results regarding the choice of the level of investment in education. Two cases can occur.

- if $A_t \leq \frac{\varepsilon}{\delta\theta-a}$, the solution to the problem is:

$$e_t = 0,$$

- if $A_t > \frac{\varepsilon}{\delta\theta-a}$, the solution to the problem is:

$$e_t = \frac{A_t(\delta\theta - a) - \varepsilon}{A_t\theta} > 0.$$

Both cases are summarised in Figure 7.2. Given a stock of knowledge below or equal to the threshold $\frac{\varepsilon}{\delta\theta-a}$, the investment in education e_t remains at 0. But as soon as the stock of knowledge exceeds the threshold $\frac{\varepsilon}{\delta\theta-a}$, the level of education becomes strictly positive and increases with A_t.

Figure 7.2 shows that if the preference parameter δ increases – which is to say that individuals give more importance to future knowledge – then we see a lowering of the stock of knowledge threshold beyond which investment in education becomes positive. The critical threshold moves to the left and the investment in education will become strictly positive for lower levels of A_t (levels at which investment was previously non-existent). Conversely, if the preference parameter ε increases (which implies a lower valuation of future knowledge gains at the margin), we see an increase in the knowledge threshold beyond which the investment in education becomes positive. In this case, the threshold is pushed to the right and e_t remains equal to zero for a wider interval of A_t values. It should be noted that the critical threshold decreases in θ: the greater the impact of investment in education on future knowledge, the lower

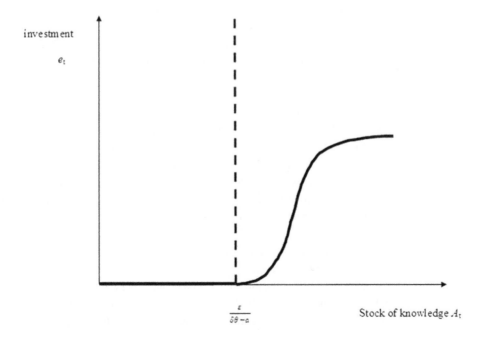

Figure 7.2 Investment in education as a function of the stock of knowledge A_t

the threshold. This critical threshold also increases in a, the factor of knowledge growth linked to learning by doing.

7.5   The Dynamics over the Long Period

In order to be able to describe the dynamics of this economy over the long period, let us assume that the initial level of knowledge A_0 is below the critical threshold $\frac{\varepsilon}{\delta\theta-a}$.

We will furthermore assume that the initial growth in knowledge is only compensated by the population growth:

$$(n)^{1-\alpha} = a.$$

Under these hypotheses, we can demonstrate that the economy is initially in a stagnation regime, in which the output per capita is constant. Indeed, under the hypothesis $A_0 < \frac{\varepsilon}{\delta\theta-a}$, individuals are not investing in education $(e_0 = 0)$, so that knowledge increases by a factor of a. Since this factor is equal to $(n)^{1-\alpha}$, the economy experiences stagnation: output per capita y_t is constant. Total output grows, so do knowledge and population, but the population growth completely compensates for the accumulation of knowledge and therefore output per capita stagnates.

This situation of stagnation is likely to last for some time. As long as the level of knowledge A_t remains below the critical threshold $\frac{\varepsilon}{\delta\theta-a}$, there will be no investment in education and therefore the amount of technological progress will barely compensate for the population growth. For that reason, as long as the level of knowledge remains below the critical threshold, the economy will remain in a stagnation regime.

Nevertheless, even if knowledge is growing slowly, it still continues to accumulate over time according to a factor of a. And, eventually, the variable A_t will reach and exceed the critical threshold $\frac{\varepsilon}{\delta\theta-a}$. This, in turn, will lead individuals to now invest a positive amount in education: $e_t > 0$. From that point forward, the stock of knowledge will no longer increase by a factor of a, but rather by a factor of $a + \theta e_t > a$. Considering that this new factor is greater than the population growth factor of n, the economy will take off: the output per capita can now increase. Exceeding the critical threshold $\frac{\varepsilon}{\delta\theta-a}$ thus enables the economy to exit the stagnation regime and to enter the growth regime. Thanks to the investment in education, we see an acceleration in the accumulation of knowledge, which in turn makes the economy's take-off possible.

The transition point from the stagnation regime to the growth regime depends on the threshold $\frac{\varepsilon}{\delta\theta-a}$ and, therefore, depends both on the individual preferences (parameters δ and ε) and on the technical parameters a and θ. In the case, for example, of a greater interest in knowledge, the threshold will be reached more rapidly, all other things being otherwise equal.

In the growth regime, the growth rate of the output per capita increases with investment e_t, which in turn increases with the stock of knowledge. The economy is thus caught in a kind of "virtuous circle": the higher the stock of knowledge, the greater the investment in education, which in turn leads to a faster accumulation of knowledge. This virtuous circle also entails an ever-faster growth in the level of material living conditions.

Figure 7.3 illustrates the short-run and long-run dynamics of the main variables – output per capita, knowledge and investment in education. In the beginning of the period studied, the stock of knowledge is too small to ensure a sufficient return on the investment in education. Therefore, that investment is equal to zero (lower graph). The stock of knowledge increases (middle graph) but its growth is exactly compensated by the population growth, so that the output per capita stagnates (top graph). The economy is in a stagnation regime.

It seems that nothing, or next to nothing, is happening in this regime. Nonetheless, the stock of knowledge continues to slowly accumulate and, at a certain point in time, it will reach the critical threshold $\frac{\varepsilon}{\delta\theta-a}$. As a result, the level of investment in education becomes strictly positive, which strengthens the accumulation of knowledge. The acceleration in technical progress made possible by education leads to a take-off of the output per capita. The economy is now in a growth regime.

Economic take-off is a regime shift from a stagnation regime in which the population is uneducated $(e_t = 0)$ to a growth regime in which the population is educated $(e_t > 0)$. According to this model, the crucial factor that determines the shift from a stagnation regime to a growth regime is a behavioral change: at a certain point, individuals will start investing in education, thus accelerating the accumulation of knowledge and the improvement of production techniques. From this perspective, the spread of education to the masses is the major change that brought about the take-off of the economy.

It should nonetheless be noted that there are some commonalities between this model and the model from Chapter 4. In both models, the economy takes off once a latent variable exceeds a certain threshold. In Chapter 4, population was the latent variable that would bring about the scale effects that could accelerate knowledge accumulation once it exceeded a certain threshold. In this chapter, the variable that carries the latent dynamics and leads to investments in education that accelerate knowledge accumulation is the stock of knowledge, once it exceeds a certain threshold. So, there are commonalities between the two models: latent variables, critical thresholds and economic take-off.

But a key difference concerns the explanation of the transition from a stagnation regime to a growth regime. Whereas in Chapter 4 the explanation was based on the existence of threshold effects, the thresholds being exogenous, in this chapter, on the contrary, the regime shift is caused by *a change in the behaviour of individuals* (from $e_t = 0$ to $e_t > 0$) and this change in behaviour is analysed by means of microeconomic foundations. These foundations make it possible to identify the determinants of the critical threshold for A_t beyond which the economy experiences a regime shift.

Despite the similarities, the modelling in this chapter is richer than that in Chapter 4, as it uses microeconomic foundations to explain the existence of the stagnation regime, the existence of the growth regime and the transition between these regimes. Behavioural changes are the triggers for regime shift. The introduction of microeconomic foundations enriches the analysis, as it leads to a modelling of the determinants of the critical thresholds that are located both on the side of individual preferences and on the side of accumulation parameters.

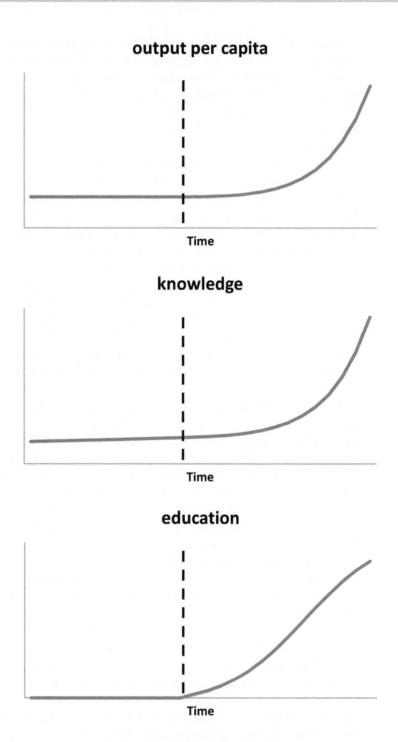

Figure 7.3 Dynamics of output per capita, knowledge and investment in education

In conclusion, it should be noted that introducing individual decisions into the analysis of historical dynamics does not imply that we are free from all forms of social determinism. It remains true, in this model as in that of Chapter 4, that the transition from one regime to another is the product of circumstances, because individual decisions depend on a given, the level of the stock of knowledge A_t. To understand the role played by circumstances, let us recall that individuals living in a stagnation regime and those living in a growth regime are driven by the same interests. However, differences in the environment in which they evolve, more precisely in the level of the latent variable A_t, will lead them to adopt distinct behaviours. These decisions have consequences: a change in behaviour is associated here with nothing less than a regime shift, with the economy moving from a stagnation regime to a growth regime. Decisions to invest in education are influenced by circumstances, but, in turn, they also have an effect on the macroeconomic environment. One of Unified Growth Theory's invaluable contributions is to formalise the influence of the macroeconomic environment on individual behaviour over the centuries and, in turn, the impact of this behaviour on the prevailing economic regime, and on the long-term dynamics.

7.6   International Comparisons

In Chapter 4, we used our model not only to study the process of economic take-off but also to analyse differences in the timing of take-off between economies that differ across several dimensions. In particular, we studied the impact of differences in the initial conditions: population size, knowledge stock and land area.

7.6.1   Differences in Initial Conditions

We can perform the same type of analysis for the present model. Since take-off is associated with the knowledge stock exceeding a certain critical threshold, beyond which individuals will invest in education, differences in the initial knowledge stocks A_0 will lead to differences in the timing of take-off. An economy with a technological lead (a higher initial level of knowledge) will have an earlier take-off than other economies, all other things being equal.

The role of the initial population size is negligible in the framework of the model developed in this chapter, because here the take-off process is based on latent dynamics concerning the stock of knowledge (and not the population as in Chapter 4). Therefore, having a larger or smaller initial population size does not make much difference in terms of the timing of take-off. Similarly, an initial difference in land area L does not have a major impact here. It does affect the level of output per capita – more land leads to a higher output per capita – but there is no effect on the timing of take-off, which depends solely on the accumulation of knowledge, a process that is independent of the land area.

In other words, as far as initial conditions are concerned, it is only differences in the stock of knowledge that lead to differences in the timing of take-off. A country enjoying a technological lead will be able to take off before other countries.

7.6.2   Differences in Structural Parameters (1): Preferences

In addition to the technological lead, other elements can explain differences in the timing of take-off. These other explanatory factors relate to the critical threshold $\frac{\varepsilon}{\delta\theta-a}$. This threshold depends on several types of parameters, related to the preferences (δ and ε) and knowledge accumulation (θ and a) that are likely to vary across countries

Let us first consider variations in individual preferences. Suppose, for example, that individuals in country A have a stronger interest in knowledge accumulation than individuals in country B, which is formalised here by a higher value of the parameter δ. Figure 7.4 compares these two countries A and B that differ only in the value of the parameter δ, but not in the initial conditions or in any other aspects.

For a large number of periods, the situations of countries A and B are exactly the same, in the sense that both countries experience the same dynamics in their output per capita (which is stagnating) as well as the same growth of the knowledge stock, while the level of investment in education is zero in both economies. Therefore, despite the differences in individual preferences between the two countries, there is no divergence during the stagnation regime: economies A and B are indistinguishable during this time.

However, there is a major difference between these two economies: individuals in country A have a greater interest in the future knowledge stock than individuals in country B. A consequence of this greater interest is that the critical threshold $\frac{\varepsilon}{\delta\theta-a}$ takes on a smaller value for economy A than for economy B. Economy A will therefore reach its critical threshold earlier, that is, for a lower level of the knowledge stock A_t. It follows that investment in education will have a positive value in economy A earlier than in economy B (see bottom graph). This early investment in education in country A will accelerate the process of knowledge accumulation in that country (middle graph), allowing the output per capita in that country to take off (top graph).

Meanwhile, nothing new happens in economy B: it remains in the stagnation regime and does not take off. Indeed, in economy B, the stock of knowledge is below the critical threshold so that investment in education remains equal to zero. We therefore see, in the middle of the period studied, a strong divergence between the two economies: while economy A has entered the growth regime, economy B remains in the stagnation regime. This divergence is only due to a difference in individual preferences, in this case in the value of parameter δ.

Much later, economy B will in turn experience a take-off. This take-off occurs when the stock of knowledge reaches the critical threshold specific to economy B. This economy will then, in turn, experience a take-off in investment in education and a take-off in output per capita.

Figure 7.4 illustrates that a difference in individual preferences alone can lead to large discrepancies in the timing of take-off and a large divergence between economies otherwise identical in all dimensions.

It is worth noting that there is a major qualitative shift between the stagnation regime and the growth regime. As long as the two economies are in the stagnation

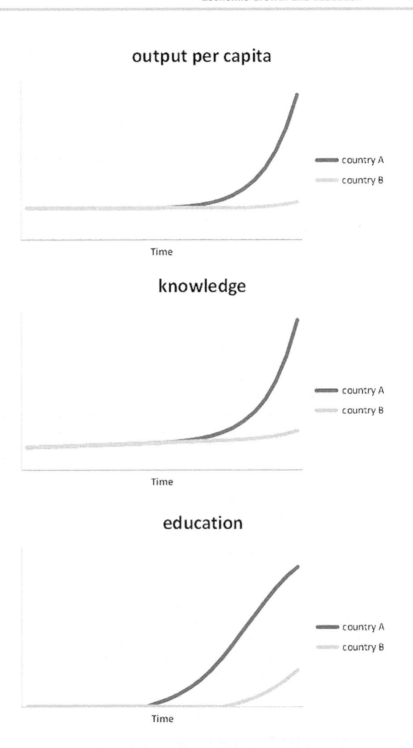

Figure 7.4 Dynamics in countries A and B of output per capita, knowledge and investment in education: different preferences

regime, the difference in individual preferences has no effect: the two economies remain indistinguishable. The difference in preferences is then neutral. But what holds true in the stagnation regime is no longer the case afterwards: this difference in preferences, although insignificant at the beginning of the period, plays a crucial role afterwards, leading to differences in the timing of the take-off and to a divergence between the economies. We witness here a real qualitative change: a parameter that is irrelevant as long as the two economies are in stagnation becomes the key parameter explaining the divergence once one of the two economies emerges from the stagnation regime.

7.6.3   Differences in Structural Parameters (2): Investment and Knowledge

We can also make such comparisons for economies that differ in other ways. Take, for example, the parameter θ that captures the effect of investment in education on knowledge accumulation. The larger the parameter, the greater the effect of education on knowledge accumulation and technical progress.

Figure 7.5 compares two economies A and B that are identical in all respects except for the parameter θ. Economy A has a higher θ parameter. This difference could, for example, be explained by the presence in economy A of a denser network of intermediaries who will experiment, replicate and transmit the new techniques, thus multiplying their effect on knowledge accumulation.

We can see, once again, that the two economies are indistinguishable as long as they are in the stagnation regime. The differences regarding parameter θ have no consequence, because the investment in education is equal to zero, in both economy A and economy B. We can therefore see that the gap between the two economies regarding parameter θ has no impact.

However, at some point, this gap will play an important role. Indeed, the greater value of θ in economy A lowers the critical threshold beyond which the level of investment in education becomes strictly positive in that economy. The greater value of θ thus allows economy A to cross this critical threshold earlier and, as a result, to experience a faster take-off in output per capita. Economy A will therefore grow much earlier than economy B, which will only take off much later.

In other words, differences in the structural parameters of the economies (preference parameters, technical parameters) can have effects that vary greatly depending on the regime considered. While differences in terms of parameters δ and θ are neutral in the stagnation regime, these differences can explain time lags in the timing of take-offs and, subsequently, a strong divergence between economies that are otherwise identical in all dimensions.

7.7   Revisitng the Timing of Economic Take-offs

On the basis of this enriched modelling of economic take-off, can we shed new light on the differences in the timing of the take-off process during the Industrial

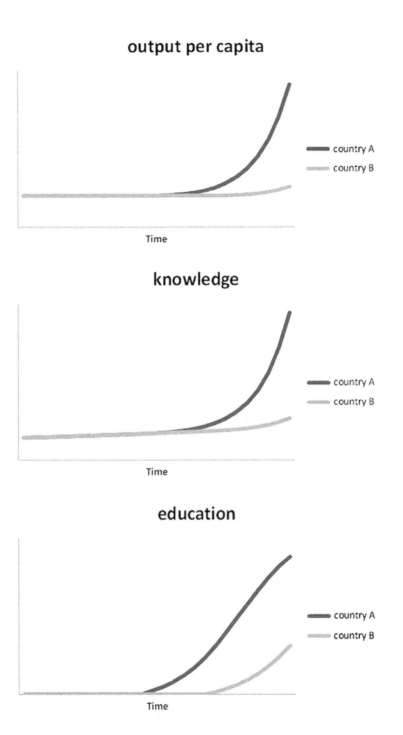

Figure 7.5 Dynamics in countries A and B of output per capita, knowledge and investment in education: different education efficiencies

Revolution? The model studied in this chapter makes it possible to explain the timing of take-off in two different ways.

First of all, we can attribute these differences in the timing of take-off to differences in the initial technological conditions. Indeed, take-off depends on the latent dynamics of the "knowledge" variable. Therefore, the higher the initial level of the knowledge stock, the earlier the take-off will take place, *ceteris paribus*. It follows that a country with a technological lead over its rivals enjoys an earlier take-off. Given that Britain may have enjoyed a certain technological lead in the eighteenth century, this is one explanation for its earlier take-off.

But it is also possible to account for the United Kingdom's early take-off in another way. This stylised fact can be explained by differences in the structural parameters of the British economy compared to those prevailing in other economies. Indeed, as we have shown, differences in preferences or technical parameters can be both insignificant while economies remain stagnant and then become critical when a country takes off. If, for example, the United Kingdom did have a lead in the dissemination of knowledge (a higher θ) in the mid-eighteenth century, this could also explain its early take-off. Such a difference would have had no impact as long as knowledge was below the critical threshold, but would have eventually led to an earlier take-off of the British economy.

In other words, introducing microeconomic foundations considerably broadens the spectrum of explanations for understanding the timing of take-offs. It should be noted, however, that this chapter does not provide a complete answer to this question: one paradox remains unexplained. As Figure 7.1 shows, the Netherlands and Belgium had higher levels of literacy around 1800 than Britain. Yet it was in Britain that the take-off first occurred. This brings us back, once again, to the existence of multiple causes. As we saw in Chapter 5, it is difficult to explain Britain's early take-off without mentioning its advantage at the institutional level. The next chapter will return to this key point.

7.8   Conclusion

This chapter has presented a unified growth model that provides a microeconomic basis for the shift from a stagnation to a growth regime. In this chapter, the regime shift is rooted in a major societal change: *the emergence of mass education*. Whereas, for centuries, the vast majority of the population was illiterate and poorly educated ($e_t = 0$), this has gradually changed and the gradual emergence of mass education ($e_t > 0$) has contributed to the take-off of the economy by accelerating the accumulation of knowledge.

This model illustrates that the transition from a stagnation regime to a growth regime can be linked to *a behavioural change*. As we have seen, the emergence of mass education is not in itself independent of changes in the macroeconomic environment. It is only when the A_t variable (the stock of knowledge) crosses a certain threshold that mass education develops, and not before. Once education takes a positive value $(e_t > 0)$, it will accelerate the accumulation of knowledge, that is, reinforce the growth of A_t. Thus, we are dealing with interactions in both directions between microeconomic decisions (education) and the macroeconomic environment (the knowledge stock).

Finally, it should be noted that the unified growth model studied in this chapter also highlights the existence of *major qualitative changes* between regimes. Differences between economies in the values of certain structural parameters may have no effect on economic quantities when the economies are in the stagnation regime but then, afterwards, cause large differences in the timing of the take-off of these economies and thus cause divergent trajectories.

Appendix 7A.1 Further Reading

This chapter has presented a simplified version of unified growth models (see Galor and Weil 1999, 2000, and Galor 2005, 2010 and 2011). In his treatise, Galor (2011) considers various models that include a larger number of choice variables as well as a larger number of dimensions, compared to the modelling in this chapter. This general theoretical framework allows Galor to replicate more stylised facts, besides the output per capita take-off considered in this chapter, such as the demographic transition from a regime characterised by high mortality and high fertility to one characterised by low mortality and low fertility. Galor also studies the stylised facts about changes in fertility and mortality levels in papers co-authored with Moav (Galor and Moav, 2002, 2005). In these models, the take-off process is linked to the demographic transition. Replication of this single stylised fact requires the introduction of the fertility rate and a factor influencing life expectancy (somatic investment in Galor and Moav, 2005) as the variable of choice.

Other unified growth models include Strulik (2014), who has developed a model based on knowledge accumulation and studies the interactions between knowledge accumulation and economic take-off. Another paper exploring these links is Prettner et al. (2013).

Appendix 7A.2 Exercises

1. Let us consider the model developed in this chapter. Suppose we now have not $\delta\theta > a$, but $\delta\theta < a$.
    a. Derive the optimal level of investment in education.
    b. Explain the relationship between the optimal level of e_t and the knowledge stock A_t.
    c. What happens to the long-run dynamics (regimes, transitions) of output per capita, knowledge stock and investment level?

2. Let us consider the model developed in this chapter, excluding the hypothesis $\varepsilon > 0$. Suppose that the individual preferences are such that $\varepsilon = 0$.

   a. Derive the optimal level of investment in education.

   b. Explain the relation between the optimal level of e_t and the knowledge stock A_t.

   c. What happens to the long-run dynamics (regimes, transitions) of output per capita, knowledge stock and investment level?

3. Consider two countries A and B, equal in all dimensions, except for the knowledge accumulation parameter $a > 0$. Suppose that country A has a greater parameter a than country B.

   a. Compare the optimal levels of investment in education in both countries.

   b. Compare the timing of output per capita take-off in both countries.

   c. In the very long run, which country will enjoy the higher value of output per capita?

4. Consider the economy studied in this chapter, the only difference being that its government decides to subsidise the investment in education at a rate of $0 < v < 1$. The cost of this investment now becomes $(1 - v)e_t$.

   a. Under this new hypothesis, write the problem of the education choice.

   b. Derive the first-order condition.

   c. Under what condition is there an interior optimal level of e_t? To what extent does this condition depend on the level of subsidy v?

   d. What impact does v have on the long-term economic dynamics?

8   The Birth of Institutions

The theoretical framework from the previous chapter provided a microeconomic foundation for the economic take-off process. The regime shift is triggered by a change in lifestyles: the emergence of mass education. In the stagnation regime, the vast majority of the population was uneducated, so that productivity gains were small and they exactly offset population growth. In the growth regime, on the other hand, the majority of the population is better educated, thus accelerating technical progress and allowing for an exit from stagnation. In this transition, the key variable is education. The slow accumulation of knowledge that results from learning by doing seems to have little effect on the economy, but, at some point, the stock of knowledge crosses a critical threshold beyond which people invest in education, leading to an acceleration of technical progress and to economic take-off.

This explanation of economic take-off can be criticised for its lack of emphasis on institutions. In this model, the level of investment in education depends on preferences, technical parameters and the level of the knowledge stock. But the institutional framework has absolutely no impact on the education decision. This is a major limitation of this model: in reality, the emergence of mass education is not solely dependent on the "goodwill" of individuals (the "demand" for education), it also, and above all, depends on the institutional framework. The latter determines the "supply" of education (private or public), the way it is financed (individually or collectively) and therefore the extent to which education is disseminated in society (with education restricted to a small elite or open to the masses). One cannot really study the emergence of mass education and the associated regime shift without considering the role played by institutions.

Generally speaking, economic activity takes place within an institutional framework (laws, constitutions, organisation of powers, regulations, market structure) that constrains the functioning of the economy and defines what is and is not possible by defining the "way the game is played" whose rules individuals must follow. As we saw in Chapter 5, North (1981, 2005) and Acemoglu and Robinson (2013) consider that improvements in the institutional framework have played a fundamental role in the process of economic take-off. According to these authors, institutions that were more balanced or more open provided incentives for individuals to innovate and thereby created an environment conducive to economic growth.

Chapter 5 was devoted to the interaction between the economic development process and institutional dynamics. Using an institutional variant of Kremer's

(1993) model, we showed that it was possible to explain the transition from a stagnation regime to a growth regime on the basis of institutional dynamics. The introduction of a new variable (the quality of the institutional framework) allowed an alternative rationalisation of the economic take-off: at a given point in time, the quality of the institutional framework reaches a critical threshold beyond which technological progress accelerates and makes the growth of output per capita possible.

This model provided a framework for analysing economic take-off from an institutional perspective, thereby "re-embedding" the economic into the social. However, one of the limitations of this model is that it presented the quality of the institutional framework as an aggregate variable whose dynamics followed a given law that was imposed on individuals. However, institutions do not evolve "in a vacuum", independently of citizens; their dynamics are determined by the actions of men and women. This point is clearly underlined by North (1981):[1]

[...] the construction and destruction of these institutions – economic and non-economic – do not occur in a vacuum, but are the result of people's perceptions stemming from historically derived opportunities and values. What is "reality" is relative to people's historically derived rationalizations of the world around them and is fundamentally colored by their views of the rightness or wrongness of the existing customs, rules, and institutions.

The institutions that exist at a given time are, to some extent, the legacy of the past, but their reproduction or replacement over time depends on the actions of individuals, and therefore on their perceptions and motivations.

When studying the dynamics of institutional change, it is crucial to distinguish between, on the one hand, *minor* changes to the existing institutional framework and, on the other hand, *major* changes such as the emergence of new institutions that replace existing ones. Minor institutional changes can occur without the participation of the masses, for example through the normal working of legislative institutions. However, large-scale institutional transformations – the emergence of new institutions – are often only achieved through massive citizen mobilisation. Specifically, major institutional changes take place when citizens decide not to take institutions as something imposed on them (a "given fact"), but strive towards improving them.

One of the major institutional changes is the replacement of a dictatorial political regime by a democratic one. This type of institutional change cannot usually be achieved through the normal legislative process: it usually requires no less than a revolution to overthrow the existing regime. As Figure 8.1 shows, the proportion of the world's population living under different types of political regimes has changed significantly over the past two centuries.[2] In particular, the share of the world's population living in colonies or autocratic regimes has fallen sharply. While democratic regimes were home to only about 1% of the world's population in 1820, this proportion had risen to over 30% by 1970 and to 55% by the year 2000.

---

[1] See North (1981), chapter 2, p. 13.

[2] Since a society can exhibit different degrees of "democratisation" (the degree is dependent not only on the form of political representation, but also on the existence of counter-powers, such as media, trade unions and associations), Figure 8.1 gives a simplified representation of the political situation around the world.

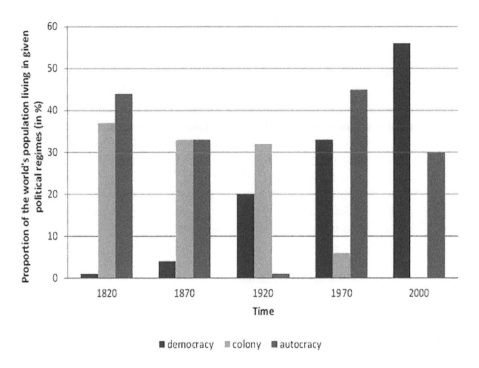

Figure 8.1 Proportion of world population living under different political regimes, 1820–2000 (*source*: *Our World in Data*: ourworldindata.org)

The rise of democratic regimes is a major stylised fact of recent centuries. Many economists, such as Acemoglu et al. (2016), believe that this process of democratisation has contributed to economic growth, by changing incentives for innovation and entrepreneurial initiative.

An institutional transformation such as the overthrow of a colonial or autocratic regime requires the active participation of a large part of the population. Without this participation, it is very difficult to overthrow a regime and establish a democracy. Therefore, in order to study the interactions between institutional change and long-run economic dynamics, it is crucial to look at *the conditions that make institutional transformation possible*, that is, the conditions that will favour the active participation of a large part of the population in the democratic life.

In this chapter, we re-examine the interaction between the process of economic take-off and institutional dynamics, trying to provide a microeconomic foundation for the dynamics of institutional change and the emergence of new institutions to replace existing ones. To this end, this chapter presents a microeconomic model in which individuals decide to participate – or not – in activities aimed at improving the quality of the institutional framework, activities that lead to old institutions being replaced by new ones. We then use this model to shed new light on the links between institutional change and long-term economic dynamics.

In the political sphere, citizen mobilisation can take many forms aimed at bringing about improvements to the institutional framework, such as participation in associations, trade unions, petitions, demonstrations, strikes and even elections. In the economic sphere, the active participation of citizens is also essential for institutions to function properly. For example, a market's efficient performance depends on the efforts of the individuals involved in it: circulation of information, reporting of malfunctions, compliance with competition rules, etc.

This chapter is organised as follows. Section 1 presents a microeconomic model of the choice to participate – or not – in activities aimed at improving the institutional framework (both political and economic). Section 2 then uses the results of this model to investigate the links between citizen participation and long-run economic dynamics. Finally, Sections 3 and 4 will return to the issue of international comparisons in the context of this new theoretical framework.

8.1   Individuals and Institutions

8.1.1   Sources of Institutional Changes

The institutional framework undergoes many changes over time. In this chapter, we will model institutional dynamics by distinguishing between two types of change: minor and gradual institutional change, which is the result of the normal operation of existing institutions, and major and fast institutional change, which is the result of citizen involvement.

Small-scale institutional changes take place in the "normal" course of political life. In contrast, large-scale institutional change requires significant citizen involvement. Indeed, this second type of change corresponds to the birth of new institutions that replace the ones that prevailed until then. Such a replacement of one institution by another does not take place without resistance and can therefore only take place on the condition that individuals participate en masse in the democratic life of their community and stop accepting the institutions in which they live as "given".

In order to formalise this citizen mobilisation, we will introduce a new variable into our analysis, p_t, which represents the participation or involvement of the representative individual or "average citizen" in civic/political life. That variable can be regarded as a measure of citizen participation,

Throughout this chapter, the dynamics of the quality of institutions Q_t will be modelled as follows:

[Hypothesis AR*1]

$$Q_{t+1} = Q_t(q + \rho p_t)$$

in which the fact that $q > 1$ but remains close to 1 accounts for minor institutional change (which does not require active citizen participation), whereas p_t indicates the activity of participating in civic and political life in t. Parameter $\rho > 0$ represents the effects of citizen participation on future institutional quality.

Hypothesis AR*1 tells us that without citizen participation ($p_t = 0$), the quality of the institutional frameworks increases over time but to a limited extent (q being close to 1).

On the contrary, when individuals actively participate in civic life ($p_t > 0$), they help accelerate the process of institutional improvement. We are then in the presence of substantial institutional changes, such as the birth of new institutions that contribute to a faster improvement of the quality of the institutional framework.

8.1.2   Modelling Citizen Participation

Let us consider the choice to participate – or not – in civic/political life. The basic structure of the model is the same as in the previous chapter. Each individual lives for only one period, during which they work and give birth to n children. To simplify the analysis, we will assume that the individual's only decision variable concerns their participation in the democratic life of their community.[3]

This kind of participation entails many costs, because it is easier to settle for the institutions as they are than to advocate for their improvement. We will use the parameter z to express the psychological cost of citizen participation.

Actively participating in the civic life also offers potential benefits: the improvement of the future institutional framework. This improvement is what motivates associative or activist life, and the time horizon considered by these active citizens goes far beyond their short lives. Citizens active in civic/political life get involved and participate in these activities, because they dream of building "a better world" and leaving it as a legacy to their children.[4]

Let us assume that the representative individual decides to participate in the civic and political life while taking into account the effect of his activity on the quality of the future institutional environment. The choice of participation in civic life can be represented as follows: the representative individual chooses participation p_t in such a way as to maximise the following utility function, under the constraint given by hypothesis AR*1.

$$\max{}_{p_t} - zp_t + \sigma\log(Q_{t+1} + \tau)$$

$$\text{under the constraint } Q_{t+1} = (q + \rho p_t)Q_t$$

$$\text{in which } z > 0, \sigma > 0 \text{ and } \tau > 0.[5]$$

Parameter z represents the psychological cost of citizen participation.

---

[3] Here we will deliberately omit the educational choices discussed in Chapter 7. As that chapter looked at the demand side of education and this chapter looks at the "supply" side of the institutional framework, the two chapters are complementary in the study of economic take-off.

[4] For the sake of making the illustration simpler, we assume here that, at the time of their decision at time t, the citizens only take into account the impact of their civic participation on the quality of the institutional environment that their own children will face (during period $t + 1$), but not its effects on the institutions that their grandchildren, great-grandchildren, etc., will face in the subsequent periods $t + 2, t + 3$, etc.

[5] We leave aside the problem of the "free rider", where an individual would not participate in collective action, preferring to place the burden of that action on others, while enjoying the benefits of that action. For simplicity, we consider a representative citizen who does not behave as a "free rider".

Parameter σ accounts for the absolute weight that the representative individual gives to the quality of future institutions, institutions that he will so to speak bequeath to his children.

Parameter τ allows for a varying degree of concavity in the utility gains associated with better future institutions. The higher τ is, the lower the marginal utility gain associated with better future institutions (for a given weight σ). Thus, τ can be interpreted as a parameter that can reflect the conservatism of the individual: the higher it is, the less future institutional improvements will be valued at the margin.

8.1.3   The Problem of the Citizen

By substituting the constraint in the objective function, the utility maximisation problem can be rewritten as follows:

$$\max{}_{p_t} - zp_t + \sigma\log((q + \rho p_t)Q_t + \tau).$$

The first-order condition for an interior optimal level of participation is:

$$-z + \frac{\sigma\rho Q_t}{(q + \rho p_t)Q_t + \tau} = 0.$$

The first term of this condition is the marginal disutility of slightly increasing the level of citizen participation, while the second term is the marginal utility gain associated with such an increase. We see that this second term is increasing with the preference parameter σ, which captures the individual's interest in the quality of future institutions. This second term is also decreasing in the preference parameter τ: the less the individual values, at the margin, institutional improvements (for a given parameter σ), the lower the marginal gain in utility associated with these improvements.

When there is an interior solution to the problem, these two terms must exactly offset each other in intensity, so that their sum must be equal to zero.

The second-order condition of this utility maximisation problem, a sufficient condition for the existence of a maximum, is given by:

$$\frac{-\sigma(\rho Q_t)^2}{((q + \rho p_t)Q_t + \tau)^2} < 0.$$

This condition is verified under our hypotheses. We therefore know that, if there exists a value of the variable p_t for which the first-order condition is verified, that value of p_t maximises the citizen's objective function.

8.1.4   Conditions for a Positive Citizen Participation

From the first-order condition, it is possible to identify another condition, such that, at $p_t = 0$, the marginal disutility of participating a little more will always be greater than the marginal utility of the additional participation, so that, under this condition, positive participation is not optimal. This condition is as follows:

$$-z + \frac{\sigma \rho Q_t}{q Q_t + \tau} \leq 0.$$

The second term of the first-order condition is decreasing in p_t. Therefore, when the above condition holds, the first-order condition cannot be satisfied either in $p_t = 0$, nor for any positive value of p_t. There is then no interior solution to the problem and $p_t = 0$ is optimal.

We can rewrite this condition as follows:

$$Q_t \leq \frac{z\tau}{\sigma \rho - qz}.$$

There exists a critical threshold in terms of the quality of the institutional environment, such that for any Q_t smaller than or equal to this threshold, the individual chooses not to participate in civic life. On the other hand, when Q_t is higher than this threshold, there will be a positive participation because, in this case, at $p_t = 0$ the utility gain associated with an increase in p_t exceeds the marginal utility loss associated with this increase.

Thanks to this reasoning, we can see that two cases are in fact possible:

- if $Q_t \leq \frac{z\tau}{\sigma \rho - qz}$, then $p_t = 0$ (the individual chooses not to participate in civic/political life);
- if $Q_t > \frac{z\tau}{\sigma \rho - qz}$, then $p_t > 0$ (the individual chooses to participate in civic/political life). In this case, the individual's involvement is given by:

$$p_t = \frac{Q_t(\sigma \rho - zq) - z\tau}{z \rho Q_t}.$$

An individual does not automatically participate in civic and political life. When the quality of the institutional framework is below or equal to the threshold $\frac{z\tau}{\sigma \rho - qz}$, individuals choose not to participate in civic/political life. Only when the quality of the institutional framework is above the threshold $\frac{z\tau}{\sigma \rho - qz}$ do individuals participate (see Figure 8.2).

The intuition behind this result is that when the quality of current institutions is too low, it follows from hypothesis AR*1 that there is little to expect in terms of future institutional improvements from active participation in civic/political life. In economic terms, the "marginal return" of this participation is low, so that the representative individual, when comparing this return to the cost associated with participation, decides not to participate. When, on the other hand, the quality of the current institutional environment is sufficiently high, citizen participation can be much more rewarding and it becomes optimal to participate in civic and political life.

The decision for citizens to participate depends on the quality of the current institutional framework Q_t. When this quality is low, individuals do not participate in civic/political life ($p_t = 0$), whereas when this quality is high, individuals do participate ($p_t > 0$). As a result, we are dealing with *hysteresis* or *persistence* in institutional dynamics. A better quality of institutions encourages people to participate

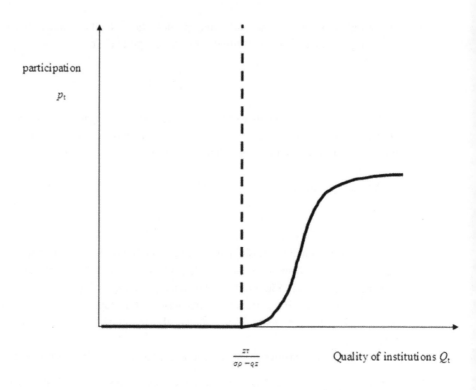

Figure 8.2 The level of political participation as a function of the quality of institutions Q_t

more in civic/political life, leading to faster improvements in institutions. The quality of institutions experiences a self-reinforcing phenomenon: good quality institutions encourage behaviours that further strengthen their quality.

When citizen participation is positive, it depends not only on the level of the quality of the current institutional framework Q_t, but also on the preference parameters σ and τ, as well as the technical parameters q and z. Participation is all the more important if the representative individual has a strong interest in the quality of the future institutional environment, the one he will bequeath to his children. This influence of preferences is formalised by the parameter σ. Moreover, the level of citizen participation decreases with the level of the cost of participation z.

8.2   The Dynamics over the Long Period

8.2.1   Hypotheses

Let us now examine the links between, on the one hand, the decision of individuals to participate in civic/political life and, on the other hand, the economic dynamics over the long period.

According to hypothesis P1, when citizens decide to actively participate in civic and political life ($p_t > 0$), there is an acceleration in the improvement of the quality of institutions. On the contrary, when they do not participate ($p_t = 0$), institutional progress is slowed down. What are the consequences for long-run economic dynamics?

To answer this question, let us first review some hypotheses concerning the accumulation of the factors of production, labour and knowledge.

For labour, to simplify the analysis, we will assume that the population is governed by the following law:

$$N_{t+1} = nN_t$$

with $n > 1$.

For the accumulation of knowledge, we will posit the two following hypotheses, as we did in Chapter 5:

[Hypothesis AR1]

$$\frac{A_{t+1}}{A_t} = \underline{a} > 1 \quad \text{when } Q_t < \overline{Q}$$

$$\frac{A_{t+1}}{A_t} = \overline{a} > 1 \quad \text{when } Q_t \geq \overline{Q}$$

with $\overline{a} > \underline{a}$.

[Hypothesis AR2]

$$\underline{a} = (n)^{1-\alpha} < \overline{a}.$$

For the value of the threshold $\overline{Q}$, we will posit the hypothesis:

[Hypothesis AR*2]

$$\overline{Q} > \frac{z\tau}{\sigma\rho - qz}.$$

Hypothesis AR*2 amounts to assuming that the threshold of institutional quality beyond which technical progress accelerates is higher than the threshold beyond which citizen participation becomes positive.

8.2.2   Economic and Institutional Dynamics

We are now able to study the dynamics of institutional change over the long period, as well as the evolution of the economy as a whole.

Let us assume that initially the quality of institutions is below the threshold $\frac{z\tau}{\sigma\rho - qz}$. There is no citizen participation ($p_t = 0$). The institutional quality grows slowly, according to a factor of q. Since $Q_t < \overline{Q}$, the institutional environment is not conducive to innovations. We therefore have that knowledge accumulates according to the factor $\underline{a}$, which is not sufficient to allow an increase in output per capita. Initially, we are in a stagnation regime: output per capita is constant, because, under hypothesis AR2, technical progress is exactly compensated by population growth.

As the quality of institutions grows very slowly (q is close to 1), the economy will remain in this stagnation regime for a number of periods. Many successive generations will thus experience a regime of economic stagnation.

However, even if institutional progress is slow, at some point the Q_t variable will exceed the critical threshold $\frac{z\tau}{\sigma\rho - qz}$. This will result in a shift from zero citizen participation ($p_t = 0$) to positive participation ($p_t > 0$). This citizen participation will have the effect of accelerating progress in the quality of institutions.

This accelerated growth of Q_t is not, however, sufficient to immediately lead to economic take-off, as the threshold $\frac{z\tau}{\sigma\rho - qz}$ is, according to hypothesis AR*2, below the threshold $\overline{Q}$. Therefore, despite the existence of positive citizen participation, we are still witnessing a stagnation of output per capita. As long as the quality of institutions remains below the critical threshold $\overline{Q}$, the following generations will experience stagnation, despite their efforts to improve institutions.

But because citizen participation has accelerated institutional progress, at some point the quality of institutions Q_t will exceed the threshold $\overline{Q}$, resulting in a much more favourable environment for innovation. This accelerates the accumulation of knowledge and the economy takes off. Thanks to the acceleration of technological progress brought about by institutional progress, knowledge is now accumulating faster than the population is growing, so that there is an increase in output per capita.

The economy has shifted from a stagnation regime to a growth regime. This transition was not directly caused by citizen participation. In fact, it takes a number of periods of citizen participation – several generations of active citizens – before the take-off finally takes place.[6] However, even if it was not the direct cause of the take-off, the emergence of this participation had an accelerating effect on the transition to the growth regime, because it made possible an acceleration of institutional progress, an acceleration that was necessary for faster technical progress.

For illustration purposes, Figure 8.3 shows the dynamics of the output per capita, quality of the institutional environment and citizen participation.

At the beginning of the period under consideration, the economy is in the stagnation regime. Population growth exactly offsets technical progress, so that output per capita stagnates (top graph). Moreover, the quality of institutions is low. It improves over time, but progress is extremely slow (middle graph), because there is no participation in political life (bottom graph).

On the surface, the stagnation regime seems to be in place for all times. However, behind this apparent *status quo*, slow changes are taking place. The quality of the institutional environment is gradually improving and, at some point, the variable Q_t reaches the critical threshold $\frac{z\tau}{\sigma\rho - qz}$ above which the participation of individuals in civic and political life becomes strictly positive (bottom graph). The appearance of citizen

---

[6] This is a major difference from the model in Chapter 7, in which the transition from zero to positive education immediately triggered a regime shift. In the modelling of Chapter 8, the transition from zero to positive political participation does not instantly result in economic take-off, because it all depends on the distance of Q_t from the critical threshold.

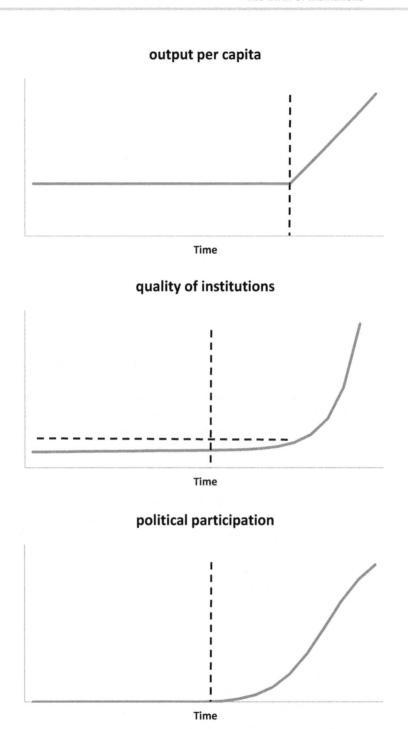

Figure 8.3 Dynamics of output per capita, quality of institutions and political participation

participation has the effect of reinforcing the growth in the quality of institutions (middle graph).

This acceleration of institutional progress caused by citizen participation is *not sufficient* to allow output per capita to take off. Output per capita continues to stagnate because although the quality of institutions is improving, the variable Q_t is still below the threshold $\overline{Q}$ above which the quality of the institutional framework is sufficient to accelerate innovation and technical progress. Although the existence of political participation improves institutions, it is not sufficient to allow the economy to take off.

The take-off will only take place much later, when the institutional quality has reached the critical threshold $\overline{Q}$. At this point, the institutional environment turns a corner and becomes more favourable to entrepreneurs pursuing innovative ventures. This leads to an acceleration in technical progress that allows the economy to achieve output per capita growth despite population growth. This is the take-off phase, which propels the economy into the growth regime.

Citizen participation is not a sufficient condition for an immediate take-off of output per capita. Several periods of participation, several generations of active citizens may be required before take-off occurs. However, citizen participation has played an important role in accelerating institutional progress, which in turn has ultimately made economic take-off possible. Participation in civic and political life has helped to create an institutional environment conducive to growth.

Figure 8.3 also illustrates the concept of qualitative change. The existence of positive and growing citizen participation can be accompanied by stagnation in output per capita (in the stagnation regime) and then growth in output per capita (in the growth regime). The relationship between citizen participation and output per capita is far from simple, given that its nature depends greatly on the quality of the institutions.

When we compare it with the model of Chapter 5, it is tempting to think that the modelling developed in this chapter offers a very limited contribution. Indeed, in both cases, the quality of institutions (the variable Q_t) is the variable that carries the latent dynamics. At first glance, the extremely slow growth in institutional quality seems anecdotal and secondary, but once a certain critical threshold has been exceeded, it is this growth that will allow an acceleration of technical progress and a sustainable take-off of the economy.

However, the modelling in this chapter provides an additional component: the microeconomic foundations of citizen participation, which can enhance the speed of institutional progress and facilitate the transition to the growth regime by encouraging the development of new institutions. Chapter 5 did not provide an explanation for the progress of the institutional framework, which appeared almost as if it were automatic. In this chapter, on the contrary, institutional dynamics are fundamentally linked to the participation of citizens in civic and political life. The more citizens participate, the faster the institutions progress, but at the same time this involvement depends on the institutions already in place. People are therefore both actors of institutional change and dependent on the institutional environment in which they live.

8.3   International Comparisons: Small Gaps, Large Effects

The theoretical framework of this chapter provides a new perspective on international comparisons (see Chapter 2). In particular, our model can be used to examine the effect of differences in the economic structural parameters on the trajectories of various economies.

To that end, let us focus on a single parameter, the σ parameter, which represents the interest that individuals have in transmitting a better institutional environment to the next generation. This parameter accounts for various features of human psychology. For example, we can interpret it as measuring a form of imperfect altruism towards the future generation. Indeed, the higher σ is, the more the individual is willing to participate politically in order to be able to leave better institutions in the future. This motivation to act for the good of one's descendants can be considered as a form of imperfect altruism.[7] Another way of interpreting the parameter σ does not involve the notion of altruism, but simply the notion of concern for justice. If the primary virtue of an institution is to be just, then the parameter σ represents the interest of individuals in promoting justice in general.

These are but two examples, among many, of possible interpretations of the preference parameter σ. Let us now examine the extent to which small gaps between countries in the value of that parameter can influence the economic and institutional dynamics over the long period.

To that end, Figure 8.4 compares two economies, A and B that are identical in all dimensions (initial conditions, structural parameters), except for parameter σ, with members of economy A having a greater degree of (imperfect) altruism or concern for justice than those in economy B.

The top graph of Figure 8.4 shows how small differences in parameters, in this case parameter σ, can lead to large differences in long-run economic dynamics. While economy A experiences a take-off in output per capita after a long period of stagnation, economy B, on the other hand, remains in a stagnation regime over the entire period studied.

How can we explain this difference between the two countries? The two other graphs of Figure 8.4 provide some answers. The bottom graph shows that citizen participation occurred earlier in economy A. In fact, thanks to a higher degree of (imperfect) altruism (or greater concern for justice), the citizens in country A started participating in civic and political life earlier, which, in turn, contributed to an acceleration in institutional progress (middle graph).

This acceleration in institutional progress is not, in itself, enough to trigger economic take-off: for economy A, take-off will occur much later, after several periods of increasing citizen involvement to improve the quality of institutions. But we can see that, eventually, the quality of institutions in country A will reach a certain threshold,

---

[7] Since an individual's utility does not depend on the utility of their children, but only on the future institutional framework they bequeath to them, it is more accurate to speak here of partial or imperfect altruism, or the "joy of giving", rather than "pure altruism" as, for example, in Barro and Becker (1989).

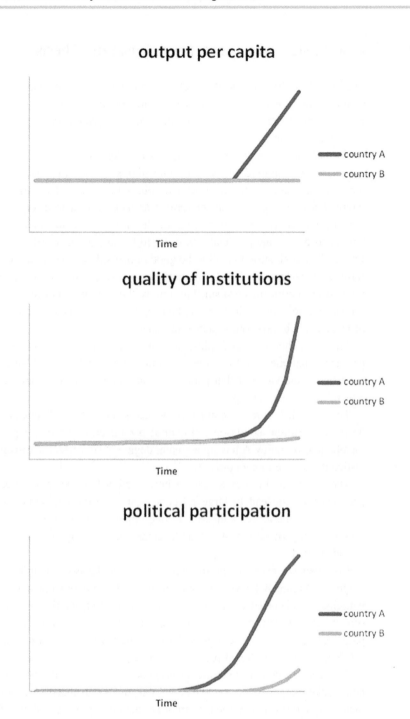

Figure 8.4 Dynamics of output per capita, quality of institutions and political participation in two economies A and B, which differ on parameter σ

which will allow an acceleration of technical progress and, consequently, the growth of output per capita. Economy A then will experience economic take-off.

Meanwhile, economy B remains in a stagnation regime. It does experience a slow improvement in the institutional framework, but in the absence of citizen participation, this improvement is so slow that it is barely perceptible and it does not have any influence on technical progress. Economy B therefore remains in a stagnation regime. In the lower graph, we can see that, at a certain point, economy B sees political participation take off. This is a hopeful sign for this economy: thanks to political participation, the improvement of institutions accelerates and we can hope that in the future, economy B will finally be able to take off.

In other words, Figure 8.4 illustrates that gaps in individual psychological traits across economies can lead to substantial differences in the economic and institutional dynamics over the long period. Figure 8.4 illustrates this point using small variations in the parameter σ, but we could have presented other examples, based on other structural parameters.

Another important observation is that, for very long periods, these differences in structural parameters may turn out to be completely insignificant and have no impact on the dynamics of output per capita. Indeed, Figure 8.4 shows that for 2/3 of the period studied (i.e. tens of successive generations), there is no significant difference between the two economies. It is only when these structural gaps lead to behavioural differences (here with respect to political participation) that they will have an effect on economic dynamics.

8.4   Back to the Industrial Revolution

Can the model in this chapter shed new light on the differences in the timing of take-off? In particular, can this model be used to explain why the Industrial Revolution took place first in the United Kingdom and not in France, China or India?

The model offers two types of answers to this question.

The first answer could already be expressed in Chapter 5. We can assume that the United Kingdom had a considerable lead in its political and economic institutions at the dawn of the Industrial Revolution. This is the thesis formulated by Acemoglu and Robinson (2013). In our model, this amounts to assuming that the United Kingdom had a superior initial institutional quality, namely a higher Q_0 than elsewhere. These favourable initial conditions would have allowed the United Kingdom to reach more rapidly the critical threshold of institutional quality beyond which the institutional environment enhances technical progress. This first explanation, which could already be formulated in Chapter 5, is also compatible with the model of the present chapter.

We can add a second answer that is specific to this chapter. This second answer is predicated on differences in citizen participation, differences that are likely to be rooted in different psychological or cultural traits. Indeed, we have shown that small differences in preference parameters can lead to large differences in the timing of take-off.

According to this second explanation, it is possible to account for a lag in the timing of take-off between countries without having to resort to differences in the initial conditions pertaining to the institutional framework. For example, one could assume that Q_0 had the same level in France and the United Kingdom. In the context of this second explanation, the differences in the timing of take-off would not be due to different initial conditions, but to distinct psychological or cultural traits – the parameters σ, τ, z. These differences would have had no effect throughout most of history, but they would have played a decisive role in explaining why take-off occurred at different points in time.

For example, a minor difference in the degree of (imperfect) altruism or concern for justice – represented by the parameter σ – could explain why take-off occurred at different times. Indeed, the higher this parameter is, the lower the institutional quality threshold beyond which political participation becomes positive. Thanks to this early political participation, the economy can then enjoy an accelerated improvement of its institutions, which, in turn, will enable it to reach the threshold $\overline{Q}$ sooner, $\overline{Q}$ being the threshold beyond which technical progress accelerates, making it possible for the economy to take off.

Differences in preference parameter τ could play a similar role. This parameter quantifies the importance, at the margin, that individuals attach to improving the future institutional framework. Greater conservatism, reflected in a higher value of τ, could explain a delayed economic take-off, by increasing the level of the critical threshold $\frac{z\tau}{\sigma p - qz}$. Indeed, by raising the threshold of institutional quality required for citizen participation, a higher value of τ pushes back the time when the economy will reach this threshold, thus slowing down institutional improvement and postponing take-off.

Finally, a third explanation could be derived from small differences in parameter z, the psychological cost of political participation. The higher this parameter, the higher the critical threshold $\frac{z\tau}{\sigma p - qz}$ above which political participation becomes strictly positive. Consequently, a higher value of z leads to a postponement of the moment when political participation becomes positive and, therefore, slows down the improvement of institutions. This ultimately postpones even further the moment of economic take-off.

In other words, the three preference parameters, σ, τ and z, account for a variety of psychological and cultural dimensions. These parameters are likely to have different values in different countries. This leads us to a second explanation for the differential timing of economic take-offs. This second explanation is based not on differences in initial institutional conditions, but on differences in psychological and cultural traits which, in combination, could suggest that the United Kingdom might have experienced an earlier take-off in political participation, leading to a faster take-off in output per capita.

This is only a second possible explanation that would need to be tested empirically. But the most important point is to show that, compared to the analysis from Chapter 5, by introducing microeconomic foundations to the choice of citizen participation we can considerably broaden the set of possible explanations for the United Kingdom's early take-off.

8.5   Criticisms and Potential Extensions

The model studied in this chapter can be criticised on several levels, and each of these criticisms can lead to extensions of the model.

First of all, this model is predicated on a very optimistic view of citizen participation. Throughout this chapter, we have assumed that citizen participation leads to an improvement in the institutional framework. This is a simplification of reality, intended to make the model as simple as possible. In a more complex model, several types of citizen participation could be introduced, some of which would lead to an improvement of the institutional framework, while others would cause it to deteriorate. As you can see, the institutional framework is itself the result of a whole production process and our hypotheses have simplified this process for the purpose of our presentation.

Furthermore, the model in this chapter presents a monotone dynamic of citizen participation. It is initially non-existent in the stagnation regime, then becomes positive and grows over time. It is important to mention that there are stylised facts that run counter to this trend, such as the decline in trade union participation in Europe at the end of the twentieth century. It should be noted, however, that there are many indicators of participation, and not all of them show the same trends. Moreover, the model in this chapter can very well incorporate these changes by introducing more variables. For example, it is possible to assume that individual preferences have their own dynamics, which can explain certain trends in participation (on cultural models of preference transmission, see Bisin and Verdier 2001).

8.6   Conclusion

This chapter has investigated some of the links between long-run economic dynamics and the way institutions evolve from the perspective of Unified Growth Theory. To do so, we have tried to open the "black box" of institutional change and make it a product of the legacy of the past and of citizen participation.

In this context, it is important to distinguish between, on the one hand, the slow mechanistic evolution of institutions and, on the other hand, the birth of new institutions that change the way society functions by replacing existing institutions. The development of new institutions – and the accompanying qualitative leap – can only occur if there is massive participation of individuals in civic and political life. Without this involvement, the force of inertia will keep existing institutions in place and, as a result, institutional improvement will be extremely slow.

Political participation – the transition $p_t = 0$ to $p_t > 0$ – is usually not enough to make it possible for an economy to shift directly from a stagnation regime to a growth regime. Depending on the values taken by the structural parameters, it is possible that several, or even many, successive periods of participation are needed *before* the economy can experience take-off. This take-off would thus be the product of the actions of many generations that have experienced stagnation and have never seen their efforts bear fruit. However, these efforts are not in vain: by enhancing the improvement of the institutional framework (through the emergence of new institutions), political participation accelerates the transition from the stagnation regime to the growth regime.

A variety of different psychological traits, including (imperfect) altruism, the degree of conservatism and the psychological cost of participation, may have played a significant role in the differences in the timing of take-off between countries. Differences in the psychological/cultural level may have remained insignificant for centuries, with no visible impact, as long as economies remained in the stagnation regime. However, it is possible that, at a given point in time, these differences played a major role in precipitating the emergence of citizen participation, which in turn accelerated institutional progress and led to an institutional environment more favourable to the take-off of output per capita.

Appendix 8A.1 Further Reading

As discussed in Chapter 5, the role of institutions in the process of economic take-off was first studied by Rostow (1960) and North (1981, 2005), both at the level of political institutions (the role of a strong centralising State) and economic institutions (the role of markets and banks). The impact of institutions on the process of research and development, and hence on knowledge accumulation, is examined by Mokyr (2002). The general role that institutions play in economic take-off has also been studied by Acemoglu and Robinson (2013). The article by Acemoglu et al. (2002) investigates the role of institutions in the creation of income inequality at the global level. The impact of institutions on the growth process is also examined in detail in the chapter by Acemoglu et al. (2005) in the *Handbook of Economic Growth*. Finally, within Unified Growth Theory, the role of institutions in the different trajectories of countries is studied in chapters 5 and 6 of Galor (2011).

Appendix 8A.2 Exercises

1. Let us return to North (2005, p. 49).

   There is an intimate relationship between belief systems and the institutional framework. Belief systems embody the internal representation of the human landscape. Institutions are the structure that humans impose on that landscape in order to produce the desired outcome. Belief systems therefore are the internal representation and institutions the external manifestation of that representation.

   a. At what level and to what extent can individual beliefs influence citizen participation in this chapter's model?

    b. Can individual beliefs influence people not to invest in civic participation? If so, under what conditions?

    c. What are the consequences of this lack of participation on long-run economic dynamics (output per capita)?

2. Supposing that two countries A and B satisfy the following hypotheses:

$$Y_t = A_t(L)^\beta (N_t)^\alpha; \quad N_{t+1} = nN_t \quad \text{with } n > 1 \text{ et } Q_{t+1} = (q + \rho p_t)Q_t.$$

[Hypothesis AR1]

$$\frac{A_{t+1}}{A_t} = \underline{a} > 1 \quad \text{when } Q_t < \overline{Q}$$

$$\frac{A_{t+1}}{A_t} = \overline{a} > 1 \quad \text{when } Q_t \geq \overline{Q}$$

with $\overline{a} > \underline{a}$.

[Hypothesis AR2]

$$\underline{a} = (n)^{1-\alpha} < \overline{a}.$$

[Hypothesis AR*2]

$$\overline{Q} > \frac{z\tau}{\sigma\rho - qz}.$$

Supposing furthermore that: $U(p_t) = -zp_t + \sigma\log((q + \rho p_t)Q_t + \tau)$

    Countries A and B are equal in all dimensions (initial conditions and structural parameters). The only difference between countries A and B relates to the preference parameter τ, which takes on a higher value in A than in B.

    a. How do you interpret this difference in preferences?

    b. Can the citizen participation be strictly positive in country A and not in country B? Justify your answer.

    c. Can the citizen participation be strictly positive in country B and not in country A? Justify your answer.

    d. Compare the long-term dynamics of both countries, in terms of output per capita, quality of institutions and citizen participation.

9 Lifestyles and the Natural Environment

As discussed in Chapter 6, taking into account the constraints imposed by the natural environment influences the shape of the economic dynamics over the long period and calls into question the possibility of endless population growth and the likelihood of perpetual improvement in living conditions. The finiteness of the Earth, as well as the extent of environmental damage associated with economic activities, significantly shape the dynamics of the long period.

However, the analyses in Chapter 6 were based on a very simple representation of the pollution process leading to environmental damage. In fact, we assumed as a first approximation that pollution is proportional to population size. This hypothesis is well-founded: the larger the population, the greater the damage it inflicts on the natural environment is likely to be. But the problem with this hypothesis is that it ignores another key determinant of pollution and environmental damage: *lifestyles*.

Indeed, for a *given* population size, the extent of damage linked to economic activity is not independent of the lifestyles adopted by the population. Some lifestyles are, all other things being equal, more favourable – or, at least, less unfavourable – to the natural environment. The term "lifestyle" is a very broad term, potentially covering every action that people take in their daily lives, and it has many dimensions. Here we will focus on the environmental dimension of lifestyle. "Efforts" to avoid environmental degradation take many forms: recycling activities, replacing individual motorised transport with non-motorised transport or public transport, avoiding unnecessary or distant travel, minimising waste, etc.

To illustrate the emergence and extent of lifestyle adjustments in response to environmental damage, Figure 9.1 shows the evolution of recycling activities in the United States since 1960. It shows the proportion of total waste that is recycled for different materials, such as paper, glass and plastic.[1]

Although the proportion of waste that gets recycled varies according to the type of waste, Figure 9.1 shows that there has been a significant change in lifestyles, with unprecedented growth in recycling over the past sixty years. It is no coincidence that the practice of recycling has become widespread in our societies over the last few decades: it is one of many behavioural responses to increasing environmental damage that is threatening the fragile balance that has existed on Earth for thousands of years.

---

[1] These data are available at www.epa.gov.

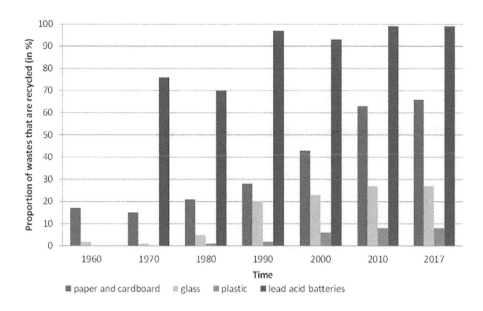

Figure 9.1 Proportion of waste recycled, by type of material, United States, 1960–2017 (*source*: EPA, United States Environmental Protection Agency, *Facts and Figures about Materials, Waste and Recycling*)

Achieving a lifestyle that is more compatible with the natural environment is not without its drawbacks. These efforts to preserve the environment entail constraints and costs. In the (hypothetical) absence of environmental damage, people would probably avoid these efforts, and retain their old lifestyles. However, in the face of environmental emergency, humans are likely to change their habits. We can therefore expect a kind of "adaptation" of lifestyles in the face of environmental damage. The analyses in Chapter 6 did not take this dimension of the problem into account: it was assumed that pollution would increase over time, in line with population growth. No behavioural "adjustment" was modelled.

Taking into account the adaptation of lifestyles in the face of the environmental emergency raises a whole series of questions for economists. First of all, is this transformation of lifestyles likely to materialise and, if so, under what conditions? Second, if the adjustment in lifestyles occurs, how will it counterbalance population growth and reduce pollution? Third, can lifestyle changes prevent the economy from entering the non-regeneration regime, or even the non-reproduction regime?

These are complex issues. Let us just deal with them within the theoretical framework developed in Chapter 6. To do so, we will proceed in three steps. First, Section 9.1 will introduce the environmental effort variable into the model. Section 9.2 will then present a microeconomic model of a representative individual's choice of a lifestyle, or more precisely, of a certain degree of environmental effort. Section 9.3 will use the lifestyle choices studied in Section 9.2 to analyse the evolution of pollution over time, as well as the economic dynamics over the long period.

We will then be in a position to better understand the effect of the "behavioural response" on the evolution of societies over the very long term.

9.1　Pollution and Lifestyles

9.1.1　Modelling Pollution: Behavioural Aspects

As stated above, one of the limitations of the analyses from Chapter 6 pertains to the hypothesis P1, according to which pollution is wholly determined by the population size, without taking into account individual lifestyles.

[Hypothesis P1]

$$P_t = \gamma N_t$$

in which $\gamma > 0$.

In order to account for the behavioural dimension and the potential adjustment in lifestyles in the face of environmental damage, we will replace this hypothesis by an alternate hypothesis, P1*, which takes into account the possible adjustment in lifestyles. The variable x_t indicates the level of environmental effort chosen by individuals. This variable summarises in a single number the "pro-environmental" dimension of the lifestyle of individuals.

Hypothesis P1* amounts to assuming that the link between the extent of environmental damage and the population size is dependent on the level of environmental effort, that is, the extent to which lifestyles are more or less favourable to the preservation of the natural environment. There are many ways of accounting for lifestyles. One simple approach involves varying the parameter γ according to whether the level of environmental effort in the previous generation is zero or positive.

[Hypothesis P1*]

$$P_t = \bar{\gamma} N_t \quad \text{if } x_{t-1} = 0$$

$$P_t = \underline{\gamma} N_t \quad \text{if } x_{t-1} > 0$$

with $\bar{\gamma} > \underline{\gamma} \geq 0$.

According to hypothesis P1*, there exists a critical threshold (in this case, zero) for the level of environmental effort x_t. The strength of the relationship between population size and the extent of environmental damage varies according to whether the level of environmental effort is equal to or strictly above this threshold. When the environmental effort is zero, the link between population size and the level of pollution is strong; this link is represented by the parameter $\bar{\gamma}$. On the other hand, when the environmental effort is positive, the adjustment in lifestyles contributes to a weakening of the relationship between population and pollution. The weakening of this link is formalised by the parameter $\underline{\gamma} < \bar{\gamma}$.

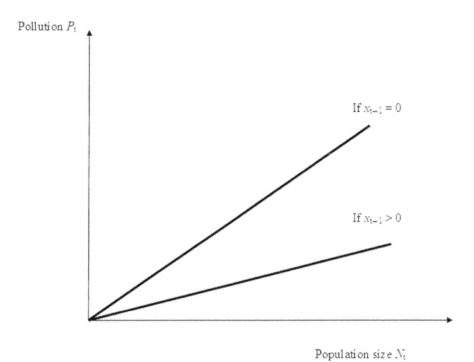

Pollution P_t

If $x_{t-1} = 0$

If $x_{t-1} > 0$

Population size N_t

Figure 9.2 Hypothesis P1*

Figure 9.2 represents hypothesis P1* geometrically in space (N_t, P_t). In this figure, the slope of the diagonal line measures the strength of the relationship between population size (x-axis) and the level of environmental damage (y-axis). In the presence of environmental efforts above the critical threshold, the slope of the line is reduced, reflecting the fact that lifestyle changes weaken the relationship between population size and pollution.

9.1.2   Environmental Efforts and Pollution

For a given population size, the environmental efforts reduce the level of damage linked to human activities. Our model therefore considers investments that prevent emissions (mitigation investments). As the reduction in pollution will also limit the extent of the non-regeneration of the natural environment (by hypothesis P2 which we will return to below), these environmental efforts have the consequence of indirectly reducing the effects of environmental damage.[2]

It should be noted that two distinct scenarios can take place, depending on whether the parameter γ is strictly positive or zero.

---

[2] This distinction between preventive (mitigation) and corrective (adaptation) investment is discussed in Hritonenko and Yatsenko (2013). Our modelling of environmental efforts corresponds to preventive but also, indirectly, corrective investment.

- In the first case $(\gamma > 0)$, lifestyle adaptation has been instrumental in reducing the strength of the link between environmental damage and population size. But lifestyle changes have not been enough to eliminate pollution, nor to break the link between population size and the extent of damage.
- In the second case $(\gamma = 0)$, the adaptation of lifestyles has cancelled out the link between population size and environmental damage, which disappears. This second case corresponds to a radical transformation of lifestyles.

The former is probably the more plausible of these two scenarios. If lifestyle adjustments are likely to reduce the amount of environmental damage for a given population, it is probably too optimistic to think that there can be a total reduction. However, the relative plausibility of the two scenarios depends on what is meant by "environmental efforts". In the case of extreme lifestyle changes, the second scenario may become more realistic. In the remainder of this chapter, we will opt for the first scenario, which at first glance seems more plausible.

9.2   Individuals and Pollution

9.2.1   Modelling the Choice of Environmental Efforts

Let us now consider the choice of the level of environmental effort x_t by the representative individual. Recall that this choice is in fact a very synthetic way of representing the adaptation, or non-adaptation, of individual lifestyles to environmental damage. There are many ways of formalising the behavioural response of humans to such damage. In this chapter, we will opt for a very simple formalisation, in which the individuals' only decision is to adapt (or not) their lifestyles.

The model's structure is very similar to that seen in Chapters 7 and 8. Individuals live for only one period, in which they work and have children. Each person chooses the level of environmental effort that they are willing to make during their own life. The choice is based on purely selfish considerations: the representative individual chooses to adjust their lifestyle or not, by comparing the costs and benefits that this adjustment generates for them, independently of the effects on future generations.[3] The representative individual is assumed to be rational, pursuing a self-centred goal limited to their own existence. This is a simple way of formalising the adaptation of lifestyles.

Adapting one's lifestyle entails some inconvenience. We will model this cost using parameter $\varphi > 0$, which is the psychological unit cost of the environmental effort x_t. Besides this cost, there are also utility gains generated by the change in lifestyle. The weight given by the individual to these gains is not independent of the extent of the environmental damage. The greater the damage, the greater the environmental emergency, and the greater the importance individuals place on the gains associated with lifestyle adaptation.

---

[3] For more sophisticated models of intertemporal optimisation, see Hritonenko and Yatsenko (2013).

We will assume that the individual's utility function can be formulated as follows:[4]

$$-\varphi x_t + \omega P_t \log (x_t + \varepsilon)$$

in which $\varphi > 0$, $\omega > 0$ and $\varepsilon > 0$ are preference parameters. This function formalises the elements mentioned above in a simple fashion.

Parameter φ accounts for the psychological cost of the environmental effort. Waste sorting activities, greener travel, etc., require effort, which results in a loss of utility, all other things being equal.

Parameter ω formalises the absolute weight assigned by the representative individual to the benefits associated with the efforts the individual makes. Working for the preservation of our Planet is also a source of satisfaction.

Finally, parameter ε offers a simple way to vary the degree of concavity of the function associated with the benefits of environmental efforts. The higher ε is, the lower the marginal utility gains associated with increases in the level of effort *ceteris paribus*.

9.2.2 The First-Order Condition

The choice of the level of environmental effort x_t can be written as the following utility maximisation problem:

$$\max{}_{x_t} - \varphi x_t + \omega P_t \log (x_t + \varepsilon).$$

The first-order condition, that is, the necessary condition for the existence of an interior optimal level of x_t associated with this problem, is:

$$-\varphi + \frac{\omega P_t}{x_t + \varepsilon} = 0.$$

The first term is the marginal loss of utility resulting from an increase in environmental effort, while the second term is the marginal gain in utility resulting from an increase in this effort. We can see the greatest utility gain associated with a marginal increase in environmental effort the greater the parameter ω (significant weight given to the valorisation of environmental effort), the higher the current level of environmental damage ("environmental emergency") and the lower the parameter ε (high valorisation, at the margin, of the increase in effort).

9.2.3 The Second-Order Condition

The above condition is a necessary condition for an interior optimum, that is, a condition that must necessarily be satisfied by the interior value of the effort x_t that maximises the individual's objective function. It should be noted, however, that we

---

[4] Of course, there are many other formalisations of the environmental effort choice. In particular, we could imagine an individual who takes into account, in their decision to make an effort, the effect of their decision on the quality of the natural environment in the future, at periods $t + 1$, $t + 2$, etc. The formalisation adopted in this chapter has the undeniable advantage of being simpler.

cannot exclude a priori that other values of x_t may also satisfy this condition, yet not lead to the maximum value for the objective function. In order to ensure that we are indeed in the presence of a maximum, we need to check that the second-order condition is satisfied.

The condition is as follows:

$$\frac{-\omega P_t}{(x_t + \varepsilon)^2} < 0.$$

This condition is verified. We can then infer that if a value of environmental effort x_t satisfies the first-order condition, then this value of x_t leads to the maximum value of the individual's objective function (and thus to the maximum utility).

9.2.4   Conditions for a Positive Environmental Effort

There does not necessarily exist an interior optimal level of x_t. In other words, the first-order condition is not always verified for a value of $x_t > 0$. To understand this point, note that, if, at $x_t = 0$, the following inequality is verified:

$$-\varphi + \frac{\omega P_t}{0 + \varepsilon} \leq 0.$$

Then, as a consequence, for $x_t = 0$, the marginal disutility of increasing the environmental effort by a little (the first term) is, in absolute terms, higher than the marginal gain in utility resulting from this increase in the level of effort (the second term). It is therefore better to remain at $x_t = 0$ and not attempt any increase in the level of environmental effort.

Since the second term of the first-order condition is decreasing in x_t, and if the above inequality is true in $x_t = 0$, it will also be true for any positive value of x_t. It is therefore never optimal to have a positive level of environmental effort when the above condition is true.

However, when we have, instead,

$$-\varphi + \frac{\omega P_t}{0 + \varepsilon} > 0$$

we then see that at $x_t = 0$, the utility gain associated with a marginal increase in environmental effort is necessarily higher than the utility loss associated with this increase, so that it is now optimal to choose a strictly positive environmental effort.

Two scenarios can therefore occur, depending on whether

$$-\varphi + \frac{\omega P_t}{0 + \varepsilon} \leq 0 \quad \text{or} \quad -\varphi + \frac{\omega P_t}{0 + \varepsilon} > 0.$$

This condition can be rewritten as follows:

$$P_t \leq \frac{\varphi \varepsilon}{\omega} \quad \text{or} \quad P_t > \frac{\varphi \varepsilon}{\omega}.$$

If the level of pollution is below a certain critical threshold, the representative individual will choose not to make any environmental effort and will maintain a polluting lifestyle. However, if the extent of the pollution is higher than this critical threshold, the agent then opts for a positive level of effort and changes lifestyles.

Our modelling reflects the fact that the adaptability of lifestyles is not independent of the level of "environmental emergency". Depending on the extent of environmental damage, individuals tend to adapt their lifestyles or not, according to their own objectives.[5]

9.2.5   Summary

In summary, two distinct scenarios can occur:

- if $P_t \leq \frac{\varphi \varepsilon}{\omega}$, the individual chooses not to make any environmental effort: $x_t = 0$;
- if $P_t > \frac{\varphi \varepsilon}{\omega}$, the individual chooses to make an environmental effort: $x_t > 0$. The level of this effort is given by:

$$x_t = \frac{\omega P_t - \varphi \varepsilon}{\varphi}.$$

Both scenarios are summarised in Figure 9.3.

We have emphasised above the importance of the level of environmental damage, as the representative individual will not adapt their lifestyle if this damage is below a certain threshold. However, it is useful at this juncture to point out that the level of this threshold depends on the psychology of the individual. More precisely, this threshold depends on three preference parameters that reflect the importance of the psychological cost of lifestyle adjustment (φ), as well as the importance that the individual places on the gains induced by this adjustment in absolute terms (ω) and in marginal terms (ε).

In other words, the microeconomic modelling we have developed in this section takes into account the fact that beyond a certain level of environmental damage, individuals can react to this damage by changing their behaviour and lifestyles.

---

[5] It should be noted that the adjustment (or non-adjustment) of lifestyles in the face of environmental urgency is considered here to be "rational" in the precise sense that it is optimal for the individual *given the objective being pursued*. If one were to adopt another conception of "rationality", for example "collective" or "social" rationality, the optimal level of effort would probably take on different values than those studied here. This conflict between individual and collective rationality is common in economics. In the context of intergenerational externalities, there is no guarantee that the individual's choices correspond to what would be optimal from the point of view of a social objective. As this book focuses exclusively on the positive economic analysis of the long period, we will not address these normative issues here.

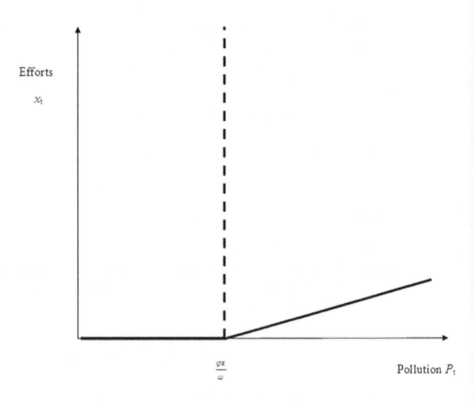

Figure 9.3 Environmental efforts as a function of the level of pollution

However, this change in behaviour only occurs above a certain threshold, which depends on individual preference parameters.

9.3   The Dynamics over the Long Period

9.3.1   Hypotheses

In this section, we will study the economic dynamics over the long period in relation to the evolution of environmental damage. As explained above, we will take into account the possible adjustment of lifestyles in the face of the environmental emergency. To this end, we will replace hypothesis P1 by P1*.

However, we will keep hypotheses P2 and P3 from Chapter 6.

[Hypothesis P2]
There exists a pollution threshold P^L such that:

$$L_{t+1} = L_t \quad \text{if } P_t < P^L$$

$$L_{t+1} = jL_t \quad \text{if } P_t \geq P^L$$

with $0 < j < 1$.

[Hypothesis P3]

There exists a second pollution threshold, $P^N > P^L$, such that:

$$N_{t+1} = n\, N_t \quad \text{for } P_t < P^N$$

$$N_{t+1} = r\, N_t \quad \text{for } P_t \geq P^N$$

with $0 < r < 1 < n$.

Since the decision to adapt one's lifestyle depends on a critical pollution threshold $P^x = \frac{\varphi \varepsilon}{\omega}$, we have to complete these hypotheses with another hypothesis, concerning the relative importance of the different thresholds. Note that the pollution threshold P^x is reached for a population size $N^x = P^x / \bar{\gamma}$. The hypothesis P4 imposes inequalities on the different critical thresholds in terms of population size.

[Hypothesis P4]

The population thresholds satisfy the following condition:

$$\overline{N} < N^L < N^x < N^N < N^C.$$

in which $\overline{N}$ is the threshold for seeing positive scale effects, N^L the threshold for non-regeneration of the natural environment to occur, $N^x = P^x / \bar{\gamma}$ the threshold for the emergence of lifestyle adaptation, $N^N = P^N / \underline{\gamma}$ the threshold for the onset of non-reproduction of the population and N^C the congestion threshold.

According to hypothesis P4, the population threshold above which the economy benefits from positive scale effects is lower than the population threshold above which the cultivable area is reduced by environmental damage, which is itself lower than the extreme thresholds of non-reproduction of the population and congestion. Compared to Chapter 6, the novelty here consists of assuming that the population threshold associated with behavioural adaptation, N^x, occupies an intermediate position between these thresholds. It is higher than the threshold beyond which a contraction of the natural environment appears, but remains lower than the extreme thresholds of non-reproduction of the population and congestion. Hypothesis P4 thus formalises the idea that if behavioural reactions, lifestyle adaptations, can occur, they only do so at sufficiently high levels of population size – and consequently of environmental damage.

We must also add another hypothesis here, a non-reswitching property hypothesis that prevents a shift from period to period from a situation of positive environmental effort to a situation of zero environmental effort. This hypothesis is necessary because, without it, it could theoretically be possible to see individuals change from positive to zero environmental effort decisions generation after generation, in succession.

This case is indeed theoretically possible, as decisions to adjust lifestyles are specific to each successive generation. We are not dealing here with a benevolent social planner who would take into account in their decision all the social consequences of their actions on every generation. Instead, we are looking at a succession of generations of individuals who make decisions according to their own objectives (limited to their own lifetimes, without taking into account the lives of later generations). In this context, situations where one goes from a positive environmental effort to a zero effort and vice versa cannot be excluded, as the decision to make an environmental effort varies according to the level of pollution, which in the following period depends on the environmental effort made. Since the decision to make efforts positively depends on the level of pollution and since that level will decrease when we go from $x_{t-1} = 0$ to $x_t > 0$, an additional hypothesis is needed to prevent the occurrence of the type of behavioural cycles that reflect a transition from $x_{t-1} = 0$ to $x_t > 0$ to $x_{t+1} = 0$.

If the individual chooses to make an effort in t (when there was no environmental effort in $t - 1$), that means that the following inequality is verified:

$$P_t > \frac{\varphi \varepsilon}{\omega} \leftrightarrow N_t > \frac{\varphi \varepsilon}{\omega \bar{\gamma}}.$$

The case of a behavioural "reversal" in the next period, in $t + 1$, occurs if:

$$P_{t+1} \leq \frac{\varphi \varepsilon}{\omega} \leftrightarrow nN_t \leq \frac{\varphi \varepsilon}{\omega \underline{\gamma}},$$

when the population is below the congestion threshold (the case we are interested in when the lifestyle adjustment appears).

We can therefore avoid a behavioural reversal by imposing hypothesis P5:

[Hypothesis P5]

$$n\underline{\gamma} > \bar{\gamma}.$$

According to hypothesis P5, while lifestyle adaptation helps to reduce the strength of the link between population size and the extent of environmental damage, it is not sufficient to bring down the level of pollution in the next period given the population growth.

This hypothesis may seem pessimistic, but it is necessary if we want to reach a sustainable adjustment in lifestyles. In the absence of this hypothesis, we would have a situation where lifestyle adaptation would take place in every other generation, and would not take place in every generation. We would have, for example, lifestyle changes in even-numbered periods, and no lifestyle changes in odd-numbered periods. Hypothesis P5 avoids this type of implausible result.

9.3.2   Revisiting the Dynamics over the Long Period

Let us now consider the dynamics of the economy over the long period. To do so, we will assume, as in Chapter 6, that knowledge accumulation follows hypothesis K1.[6] We will also assume, as in Chapter 6, that $(n)^{1-\alpha} = \underline{a}$.

Initially, the population size is small and below the threshold $\overline{N}$. The economy does not benefit from positive scale effects and population growth according to the factor n

---

[6] For the sake of simplicity, the adverse effect of congestion on knowledge accumulation discussed in the first part of Chapter 6 will be omitted here.

exactly offsets the accumulation of knowledge. The output per capita is constant. This is the stagnation regime.

This stagnation regime is associated with a certain level of pollution. Indeed, the population size is positive and according to hypothesis P1* this will lead to environmental damage. However, this damage is too small to trigger a change in lifestyles, because we have $N_t < \overline{N} < N^x$. The damage is also too small to prevent a regeneration of the natural environment from one period to the next.

However, during the stagnation regime, the population does experience growth and, sooner or later, it will reach the threshold $\overline{N}$. At that threshold, scale effects appear and enable an economic take-off. Indeed, these scale effects bring about an acceleration of the technical progress (hypothesis K1) and, since $\overline{a} > (n)^{1-\alpha}$, the output per capita begins to grow. The economy takes off and enters the growth regime.

In this second regime, the population size keeps on increasing but remains under the thresholds N^L and N^x. There is therefore neither non-regeneration of the natural environment, nor behavioural adaptation. But the continuous increase in population size is such that, at some point, the threshold N^L is reached, and consequently the arable land area is now smaller because of desertification and rising sea levels associated with climate change. The economy moves then into the non-regeneration regime.

As in Chapter 6, several scenarios are possible regarding the dynamics of the output per capita in this third regime:

- if $\overline{a} \, j^\beta > (n)^{1-\alpha}$, the economy experiences output per capita growth, but at a lower rate than during the growth regime;
- if $\overline{a} \, j^\beta = (n)^{1-\alpha}$, the economy experiences output per capita stagnation because the accumulation of knowledge only compensates for the non-regeneration of the Earth, without any surplus;
- if $\overline{a} \, j^\beta < (n)^{1-\alpha}$, the economy enters a phase of decreasing output per capita because the accumulation of knowledge is not sufficient to compensate for the non-regeneration of the Earth.

The non-regeneration regime is characterised by either, in the best-case scenario, a slowdown in the growth of output per capita, or by a stagnation or, in the worst-case scenario, by a decrease in output per capita. The decrease in output per capita occurs when the accumulation of knowledge is not rapid enough to compensate for the erosion of the natural environment.

Hypothesis P4 implies that the existence of this non-regeneration regime is not impacted by a potential adaptation of lifestyles. Indeed, according to this hypothesis, the lifestyle adjustment only occurs for a population size large enough to lead to greater environmental damage than the damage associated with the shift to the non-regeneration regime.

But population growth is such that at some point the population size will reach the threshold N^x, beyond which individuals make changes to their lifestyles and decide to make environmental efforts. The economy then enters a regime that we could label as the "adaptation regime".

As a result of the economy entering the adaptation regime, the link between population size and the extent of environmental damage becomes weaker (hypothesis P1*). Lifestyle adjustments are, however, insufficient to decrease the total level of pollution (hypothesis P5), but will considerably slow down the increase in pollution. It should be noted that because the level of pollution does not go down, the natural environment still cannot fully regenerate in this adaptation regime. Therefore, as with the non-regeneration regime, the economy experiences either low output per capita growth, stagnation or decline.

However, it would be wrong to assume that lifestyle adaptation is not important. Lifestyle adaptation plays a crucial role: by slowing down the growth of environmental damage, lifestyle adjustment postpones the occurrence of the depopulation regime to later periods.

Indeed, the depopulation regime sets in when environmental damage reaches the threshold P^N. Thanks to lifestyle adaptation, the link between population size and environmental damage is weakened, which leads to an increase in the level for which population is compatible with the pollution threshold P^N. Since that population threshold is higher, it will therefore not be reached as rapidly. *Lifestyle adaptation makes it therefore possible to postpone the onset of the depopulation regime.*

This is the fundamental difference brought about by the adaptation of lifestyles. Of course, this adaptation does not prevent the economy from experiencing the regime of non-regeneration, nor from seeing the growth of output per capita either slow down or become zero or even negative. However, the adaptation of lifestyles will lengthen the period during which environmental damage remains below the threshold P^N. Once the depopulation regime is reached, the dynamics will resemble those studied in Chapter 6, with the appearance of regime cycles, depending on the extent of the demographic adjustments resulting from the environmental damage.

9.3.3   Regime Cycles Revisited

Several types of regime cycles can occur, depending on the extent of the demographic adjustment (parameter r). Here are some examples of the possible regime cycles:

- cycle A: stagnation regime $\rightarrow$ growth regime $\rightarrow$ non-regeneration regime $\rightarrow$ adaptation regime $\rightarrow$ depopulation regime $\rightarrow$ stagnation regime;
- cycle B: growth regime $\rightarrow$ non-regeneration regime $\rightarrow$ adaptation regime $\rightarrow$ depopulation regime $\rightarrow$ growth regime;
- cycle C: non-regeneration regime $\rightarrow$ adaptation regime $\rightarrow$ depopulation regime $\rightarrow$ non-regeneration regime;
- cycle D: adaptation regime $\rightarrow$ depopulation regime $\rightarrow$ adaptation regime.

Cycles A and B are unlikely because they imply making huge adjustments in the population size. However, cycles C and D are much more plausible. The occurrence of C-type cycles implies that, immediately after the demographic correction, several generations abandon the adaptation of lifestyles, albeit temporarily, because eventually population growth would bring the environmental damage back to a level above the threshold beyond which the adaptation of lifestyles takes place. For illustrative purposes, Figure 9.4 presents a numerical example of a type C cycle.

In Figure 9.4, we can see that the economy is initially in the stagnation regime: the output per capita is constant (top graph) because technical progress is exactly offset by population growth.

Once a certain critical population size has been reached, the economy benefits from powerful scale effects that will bring about an acceleration of technical progress, leading to the take-off of output per capita. The economy then enters the growth regime (upper graph, middle). Throughout this period, environmental damage tends to increase as the population grows (middle graph). On the other hand, in these first two regimes, no environmental effort is made (bottom graph). The reason is that the environmental damage remains too low to elicit a behavioural response from the population.

The continuous growth of pollution will eventually lead the economy to reach the threshold P^L, beyond which the natural environment cannot regenerate completely from one period to the next. The economy then enters the non-regeneration regime, which is characterised here by a slowdown in output per capita growth (top graph). But entering the non-regeneration regime does not slow down the growth of pollution. Environmental damage continues to increase.

At some point, pollution will reach a second critical threshold, P^x, at which point individuals will modify their behaviour and start making efforts to save the planet. The economy then enters the adaptation regime. The adaptation of lifestyles is shown in the bottom graph of Figure 9.4. This behavioural response has the effect of reducing the growth rate of pollution (middle graph).

Despite this behavioural response, pollution continues to increase and, at some point, it will reach the threshold P^N, beyond which the population will no longer be able to reproduce. The economy then enters the depopulation regime. The contraction in the population size reduces pollution below the threshold P^x, thereby causing the environmental efforts to disappear (bottom graph). The economy thus reverts to the non-regeneration regime. The growth rate of pollution increases again (middle graph), and it follows that eventually the economy will once again reach the threshold P^x, generating new environmental efforts (adaptation regime), and then back to the threshold P^N, leading to population contractions (depopulation regime).

In this numerical example, we can therefore see that the economy enters at some point a type C cycle, where the non-regeneration regime is followed by the adaptation regime, then by the depopulation regime, which then brings the economy back into the non-regeneration regime through population contraction, and so on.

The numerical example in Figure 9.4 does not assign a major role to the behavioural response, which occurs very late – too late – when the level of environmental damage is already extremely high. In other words, the threshold P^x is, under this parameterisation, too close to the threshold P^N. It follows that the behavioural response cannot really significantly postpone the emergence of the depopulation regime, because it comes much too late in the process.

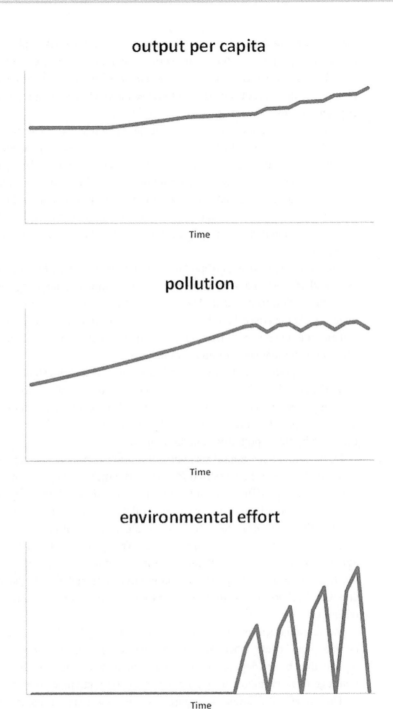

Figure 9.4 Dynamics of output per capita, pollution and environmental efforts: an example of a type C cycle

By way of comparison, Figure 9.5 shows a slightly different calibration of the parameters, which leads to a much earlier behavioural response. The numerical example in Figure 9.5 is in fact a case of type D cycle.

Here again, the economy starts in the stagnation regime. It then reaches the growth regime, followed by the non-regeneration regime once the environmental damage reaches the threshold P^L. The non-regeneration regime is once again characterised by a slower growth of the output per capita in comparison to its level in the growth regime.

The main difference with the previous numerical example is that here the preference parameters are such that the threshold P^x is much lower than before, which leads to a faster behavioural response. The adaptation regime therefore occurs earlier, which has the effect of slowing down the growth of the pollution more rapidly. This postpones the depopulation regime to later periods.

Since the depopulation regime comes later, its population size is larger. Therefore, the contraction in population size that takes place in this regime no longer brings the economy below the threshold P^x (as in Figure 9.4), but above it. In other words, the population contractions caused by pollution do not return the economy to the non-regeneration regime, but only to the adaptation regime. We can thus see, on the lower graph, that the level of environmental effort, although fluctuating, remains positive (once that effort has begun).[7] The economy is therefore in a type D cycle, where it moves from an adaptation regime to a depopulation regime and so on, without having to go through the non-regeneration regime again.

By comparing Figures 9.4 and 9.5, we can see that, by modifying the level of the critical threshold P^x, variations in the calibration of the preference parameters can affect not only the timing and magnitude of the behavioural response to pollution, but also influence the long-run dynamics, by modifying the size of the cycles it faces once the depopulation regime is reached.

In other words, this section illustrates that the adaptation of behaviours in the face of the environmental emergency has an important effect on long-term dynamics. This lifestyle adaptation is certainly not sufficient, either to prevent damage from causing non-regeneration of the natural environment or to avoid the future advent of the depopulation regime; however, by weakening the link between population size and environmental damage, it makes it possible to postpone the depopulation regime to more distant periods. This is a fundamental influence. Therefore, the introduction of a behavioural response to the environmental emergency is far from neutral when describing long run dynamics.

9.4   Criticisms

Even though the modelling presented in this chapter is enhanced compared to that in Chapter 6, it is nonetheless open to criticism on several levels.

---

[7] Fluctuations in environmental effort are due to the fact that this effort increases with the level of pollution, which in turn fluctuates due to contractions in population size.

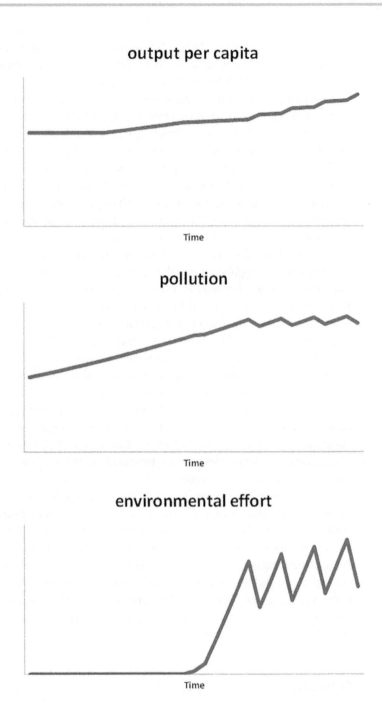

Figure 9.5 Dynamics of output per capita, pollution and environmental efforts: an example of a type D cycle

A first criticism concerns the reliability of the long-run dynamics under our hypotheses, especially with respect to the level of the various critical thresholds. For example, what would happen if we had $N^x < N^L$, namely if the adaptation of lifestyles occurred earlier – that is, for a lower pollution level – than the non-regeneration of the natural environment? In this case, the adaptation of lifestyles would make it possible, by slowing down the growth of pollution, to postpone the advent of the non-regeneration regime. Adapting lifestyles would postpone the period when output per capita either slows down, stagnates or even decreases. However, here again, this delay would not prevent the economy from eventually reaching the non-regeneration regime. The difference here would still relate to the timing of regime shifts, but this is a crucial difference.

A second criticism relates to the modelling of the effect of lifestyle changes. The analyses conducted in this chapter incorporate lifestyles, which helps to weaken the link between the extent of environmental damage and population size. However, they still give population growth a key role in the process of degrading the natural environment. Conversely, we could make environmental damage more dependent on lifestyles, or on output per capita, rather than on population. We could introduce additional modelling refinements along these lines to further enrich the analysis with new effects and mechanisms. But even in this more general model, population size would still play a central role. This is true for all species: the extent of their effect on the natural environment depends on their number. The human species is no exception to this rule.

9.5   Conclusion

This chapter has applied Unified Growth Theory to the issue of environmental emergency. By adapting the model from Chapter 6, we have introduced the possibility that humans might change their lifestyles in the face of threats to our planet. To do so, we have introduced a choice variable, environmental effort, and have studied the conditions under which such a change in lifestyle could take place, as well as the effects of this change on the economic dynamics over the long period.

Our results are mixed, to say the least. Admittedly, the introduction of lifestyle adaptation leads to the emergence of a new regime, the adaptation regime, whose main characteristic is to postpone, in time, the emergence of the depopulation regime by weakening the link between population size and the extent of pollution. This is a significant factor. But unfortunately, adapting lifestyles does not prevent environmental damage from undermining the regeneration of the natural environment and thereby from clouding the long-term prospects of societies.

Appendix 9A.1 Further Reading

This chapter is largely inspired by the environmental economics literature on behavioural responses to pollution. This literature has several distinct components. First, there is a substantial empirical literature on the relationship between lifestyles and environmental damage. See for example Christensen (1997). At the theoretical level, Hritonenko and Yatsenko (2013) study, in chapter 11 of their book, the response strategies to environmental pollution in a neoclassical growth model, through two types of investments: on the one hand, investments aimed at reducing industrial greenhouse gas emissions (mitigation investments); on the other hand, investments aimed at reducing the negative impact of climate change (adaptation investments). This dilemma between mitigation and adaptation is also studied in the article by Bréchet et al. (2013).

Appendix 9A.2 Exercises

1. Consider the model developed in this section, keeping all the hypotheses, except for hypothesis P4. The population critical thresholds satisfy:

$$N^L < \overline{N} < N^x < N^N < N^C$$

in which $\overline{N}$ is the threshold for scale effects, N^L the threshold for non-regeneration of the natural environment, $N^x = P^x/\overline{\gamma}$ the threshold for lifestyle adaptation, $N^N = P^N/\underline{\gamma}$ the threshold for non-reproduction of the population and N^C the threshold for congestion.

   a. Describe the long-term dynamics of the economy, in terms of output per capita, population size and level of environmental effort. What regimes does the economy go through?
   b. Repeat a. if the population critical thresholds satisfy:

$$N^L < N^x < \overline{N} < N^N < N^C.$$

2. The quality of institutions can affect the ability of a society to solve the challenges posed by environmental damage. Suppose that the choice of the level of environmental effort can be written as the following maximisation problem:

$$\max{}_{x_t} - \varphi x_t + \omega \log(Q_t x_t + \varepsilon)$$

in which Q_t is the quality of institutions, which follows the law $Q_{t=1} = q Q_t$ with $q > 1$.
   a. Derive the first-order condition for the optimal level of environmental effort.
   b. Under what condition is the optimal level of environmental effort strictly positive? Does this condition depend on the level of the quality of institutions? If so, how?
   c. Derive, under hypotheses P1* and P2 to P4, the long-run dynamics for the output per capita, pollution, quality of institutions and environmental effort.

3. Suppose that space exploration leads to the discovery of a habitable exoplanet, and that over time humans develop new technologies to reach this exoplanet. Suppose that these discoveries take place when the population size N_t has a level $N^x < N_t < N^N$. In each period, a fraction $0 < b < 1$ of the population will go to this planet. The population dynamics thus becomes, below the threshold N^N, $N_{t+1} = (n - b) N_t$, with $n - b > 0$.

   a. What is the impact of the discovery of this exoplanet on the Earth's population size? Distinguish between different cases, depending on whether $n - b$ is greater than, equal to or less than 1.

   b. What is the impact of the discovery of this exoplanet on the level of environmental effort made on our planet?

   c. Describe the long-term dynamics of the output per capita, population size, pollution and environmental effort.

   d. Compare these dynamics with those occurring had the exoplanet not been discovered.

Conclusion: Continuity and Discontinuity in History

This book presents, in a simple and pedagogical way, Unified Growth Theory, its concepts, its workings, its specific mechanics. Developed over the last twenty years, Unified Growth Theory proposes to study, using *a single* model, the conditions of transition between various regimes, each regime being characterised by its own relationships between economic, demographic and technological variables.

The applications of Unified Growth Theory are numerous, and go far beyond those studied throughout this book. Unified Growth Theory can be used in areas as diverse as technological, demographic and cultural change, institutional transformations and environmental issues. These are just a few of the many possible applications of this general theoretical framework.

In each of these applications, the historical process is described as determined by *a latent dynamic*: one variable (or several, depending on the complexity of the model) tends to grow over time, generating only quantitative changes, while the shape of the relationships between the variables is left unchanged. It is only when the latent variable reaches a critical threshold that social transformation takes place: the form of the relationships between the variables is changed (qualitative change). We are then in the presence of a change of regime. *According to Unified Growth Theory, historical dynamics can be interpreted as a succession of distinct regimes, each regime having its own laws and regularities.* This explanatory pattern can be applied to many social developments, over periods of varying lengths, and lead to the identification of a greater or lesser number of distinct regimes.

By way of conclusion, it seems useful to us to distance ourselves a little from Unified Growth Theory, in order to put this product of contemporary economic thought into a double perspective. First of all, we would like to come back to the main contribution of Unified Growth Theory to the economic analysis of the long period. Then, we will identify the many remaining problems when studying long time horizons, which are future challenges for Unified Growth Theory, as well as for the economic analysis of the long period in general.

How to Think about Historic Discontinuity

At first glance, one might think that the main contribution of Unified Growth Theory to the economic analysis of the long period lies in its greater *generality* compared to previous theoretical frameworks, in particular with regard to growth theories (exogenous or endogenous).[1] The thesis of Unified Growth Theory's greater generality could be defended on the basis of the extended time period it studies: far from being confined to "modern" industrial societies, this theory also generally relates to earlier periods spanning several centuries or even millennia.[2]

However appealing this idea may be, it does not stand up to closer analysis. As Solow (2000) pointed out in his review of half a century of scientific research on economic growth, *all* modern growth theories include three elements: initial conditions, rules of evolution and parameters. Unified Growth Theory is also based on these elements and therefore does not differ in nature from earlier growth theories. *In all of these models, we have initial conditions, rules of evolution for variables and parameters.* On the basis of this observation, it seems difficult to defend that Unified Growth Theory's main contribution lies at the level of its greater generality. Unified growth models are dynamic systems (among other systems) replicating certain stylised facts (among the set of facts to be explained).

In our view, the major contribution of Unified Growth Theory does not lie in its greater generality, but elsewhere. Its main contribution can be found at the conceptual level, in its formal representation of the historical process. More precisely, Unified Growth Theory's main contribution to the economic analysis of the long period lies in *its capacity to offer an original formalisation of the articulation between continuity and discontinuity in the historical process.*

Thinking about discontinuity in history is a tremendous challenge, both for economists as well as all social scientists. Societies have life horizons that go far beyond individual lifetimes. Since the length of each human life is extremely short compared to that of societies and civilisations, it is naturally very difficult for humans to think of societies in their own temporality and to grasp the changes they are undergoing. However, just as humans, societies can change, age or even disappear.

In an article from 1950, the historian Braudel invited economists to think about the discontinuity in social change:[3]

Now, what is a social discontinuity, if not, in historical language, one of those structural ruptures, of those deep, silent, supposedly painless breaks. We are born with a state of the social (i.e., at the same time, a mentality, frameworks, a civilisation and especially an economic civilisation) that several generations have known before us, but everything can collapse before our life ends. [...] This passage from one world to another is the very great human drama on which we would like to shine a light. [...] I don't want to be given a philosophy of these catastrophes [...], but a multi-light study of discontinuity. Sociologists are already discussing it, historians are discovering it; can economists think about it? [...] These deep-seated ruptures

---

[1] See for example Solow's (1956) modern growth theory, studied in Chapter 1.

[2] Some articles, such as Galor and Moav (2005), use unified growth models to study a period going back to the agricultural revolution (8,500 years before the common era), that is a period lasting more than 10 millennia.

[3] See Braudel (1969), p. 132 [translated by Colette J. Windish]. Braudel is one of the leaders of l'École française des Annales, which initiated a shift in the historical discipline, moving from a history of "events" (wars, revolutions) to a history of everyday life. Pirenne (1963) is generally considered to be one of the inspirations for this shift.

cut off one of the great destinies of humanity, its essential destiny. Everything it bears on its momentum is collapsing or at least being transformed. [. . .] The political economy that we have, as best we can, assimilated to the lessons of our good masters, will not serve us in our old age. But precisely, about these structural discontinuities, even at the price of hypotheses, do economists have nothing to say? To tell us?

Discontinuity in history is nothing less than the "transition from one world to another", with all the upheavals that such a transition implies, at the level of representations, beliefs and behaviour. Economists, according to Braudel, do not think in terms of the "long period": they generally study *a single* form of society and thus disregard social discontinuities in their analyses. This reproach can be expressed with regard to many economic theories of the long period, which presuppose a continuity in the general form of social organisation and its laws: Marx's work being a notable exception of that tendency.[4]

Unified Growth Theory can be interpreted as an attempt to *think about societies in their own temporality* – well beyond the temporality of human lives – in order to account for the discontinuities in the historical process, the "transitions from one world to another". It provides a formal framework for analysing the articulation between continuity and discontinuity in history. Let us return to the main components of this theoretical framework.

Continuity is represented by the notion of economic regime: within an economic regime, laws and regularities do not change. More precisely, within a regime, the relationships between economic, demographic, and other variables are invariant. This invariance prevails as long as the society remains within this regime.

Within Unified Growth Theory, the concept of economic regime formalises what lasts, what is stable and invariant. The life span of a regime is also the life span of a given society. This life span can very well exceed a generation, reaching durations of a few centuries or even several millennia. *The economic regime is the concept that makes it possible to think about the long term, the very long life of societies.*

However even the oldest, strongest structures can one day disappear. At times, discontinuities arise and what had remained true for dozens of generations can suddenly cease to be true. It is the notion of regime change that formalises the discontinuity in the historical process, within Unified Growth Theory.

When one or more latent variables reach a critical threshold, the economy changes regime and a historical discontinuity occurs: the shape of the relationships between economic, demographic, institutional or environmental variables changes. Laws and regularities are modified. Society leaves the world in which it was evolving and enters a new world. *The change of regime represents the discontinuity in history, the "structural break" that modifies all aspects of life.*[5]

---

[4] One could also mention Schumpeter (1942) as an exception.

[5] Despite a regime change occurring, an important source of continuity in the models discussed above is that the interests of individuals (represented by the utility function), as well as their rationality, remain *unchanged*, and remain robust to regime changes. It follows that, while regime change is associated with behavioural change, the reasons behind those behaviours are themselves invariant. It may, however, be possible to consider alternative models in which some aspects of individual preferences are variables that evolve as regimes change. Such models include Galor and Moav (2002, 2005).

Unified Growth Theory makes it possible to formalise continuity in history and episodes of discontinuity. This formalisation also sheds new light on an old problem: the problem of the relativity of economic and social laws. These laws are not as universal as the laws of physics or chemistry, but they nevertheless exist. The only difference from the laws of the so-called "hard" sciences is that economic and social laws are *relative* to a given regime. Within a regime, these laws are invariant and have an unlimited scope. However, once the regime is replaced by another regime, it is possible that old economic laws are no longer true.

In short, if there is one major contribution of Unified Growth Theory, it is that it offers a theoretical framework for thinking about the articulation of continuity and discontinuity in history in history. From this point of view, the fundamental conceptual elements of this articulation are those of "latent dynamics" and "critical thresholds". As long as the latent variables remain below the critical thresholds, the economy remains in its regime and continuity reigns: the relationships between the variables are invariant. However, once the critical thresholds have been reached, there is a change of regime, a short episode of discontinuity in history, what Braudel called a "world change". This formalisation of the continuous and discontinuous in history is undoubtedly one of the major contributions of Unified Growth Theory to the study of the long period.

The Challenges of the Long Period

While Unified Growth Theory provides a theoretical framework for thinking about the long period – in particular the articulation between the continuous and discontinuous in history – it does not, however, provide answers to all the questions posed by the long period. Three major challenges remain: (1) how to measure economic variables over (very) long time periods; (2) how to "section" or "partition" history; (3) how to forecast future dynamics.

Let us begin with the first challenge posed by the long period: the difficult measurement of economic quantities/variables over long time horizons. As discussed in Chapter 2, Unified Growth Theory aims to explain or "rationalise" what econometricians call "structural breaks" in long time series, especially the series pertaining to gross domestic product, population size and output per capita. Unified Growth Theory is thus closely linked to the existence of long statistical series for economic quantities/variables.

While considerable progress has been made in the construction of long statistical series during the twentieth century, it is difficult to exaggerate the scale of the difficulties involved in constructing such series. The long period remains today a continent to be explored, a territory about which little is still known. The work on the "very long term" undertaken by Kondratiev (1928) for a period extending from the end of the eighteenth century to the beginning of the twentieth century, and continued in particular by Braudel (1990) for a period extending from the fifteenth to the eighteenth century, mainly concerns *price* series, and not quantity or volume series (with a few exceptions). The measurement of the long dynamics of production, although the subject of numerous studies, remains a work in progress.

"When it comes to production, in truth, we know very little about it" admits Braudel (1990).[6] The long statistical product/output series constructed by Maddison (2001, 2003), on which the Unified Growth models are based, provide a quantification of the dynamics of production over the long run, but these series rely on a number of assumptions, extrapolations and approximations.[7] Making a list of them would go far beyond the scope of this book, but it is important to remain somewhat humble about how much we still do not know about the long period.[8]

All of this has consequences for the descriptive contribution of Unified Growth Theory. Are there other, as yet unknown, regimes to be discovered? Will future work by historians not call into question the division of Unified Growth models in terms of regimes? For example, does the Malthusian regime, the true foundation of Unified Growth models, not constitute a "first approximation", which could hide a large number of distinct economic regimes that remain too little documented? Only the future will be able to provide answers to these questions. However, these questions should lead us to put the contribution of Unified Growth Theory into perspective as to how precisely it describes the historical process.

The second challenge posed by the long period is related to the first one, and concerns *the "sectioning" or "partitioning" of history*. This problem constitutes one of the major challenges for the economic theory of the long period and, far beyond, for the historical discipline in general. Within Unified Growth Theory, this problem of the partitioning of history takes the form of a problem of regime identification. Since regimes formalise historical continuity and regime changes reflect discontinuity, identifying regimes amounts to a kind of "partitioning" of history, which offers a certain representation of history in terms of continuities and discontinuities.

This challenge of partitioning history is a general one. As Foucault (1969) noted in his *Archaeology of Knowledge*, the historian – whether a historian of facts or a historian of ideas – is confronted with a tremendous number of elements, which need be "isolated, grouped together, made relevant, put in relation to each other, gathered into coherent sets".[9] The historian's role is to *create series* of elements and to describe the relationships between the different series. Organising archival material into series is extremely difficult: how does one partition, divide this number of elements into groups and sub-groups? On what grounds does one make these groupings of some elements rather than others?

---

[6] See Braudel (1990), p. 129 [translated by Colette J. Windish].

[7] See, for example, Le Roy Ladurie (1973) for a critical evaluation of Toutain's (1961) construction of series on agricultural output in France between 1700 and 1958.

[8] The main measurement problems include, in addition to the simple local availability of data (and the difficulties created by the extrapolation, from those local data, of production over larger territories), the problem of variations in the quality of goods and services over the centuries, as well as the difficulties arising from various goods and services appearing and disappearing over time.

[9] See Foucault (1969), p. 15 [translated by Colette J. Windish].

Two dangers are constantly present when constituting these series. The first danger faced by the historian is that he may create, through his analyses, continuities between the studied elements, continuities which do not exist in reality, but which a scientist introduces (more or less consciously) into his work, so as to constitute a theory with a broad enough scope. The second danger lies, on the contrary, in the risk of creating or amplifying, through the divisions made, discontinuities between the elements, discontinuities which do not exist in reality, but which appear as a result of the historian's desire to classify, to separate, to distinguish.

Let us illustrate these two dangers in the field of economic analysis of the long period. A first temptation, for the economist, could be to try, by his choice of divisions, to "bring in" the greatest possible number of societies into a single analytical framework, thus denying the specificities of the societies studied. This criticism has often been levelled at economists, and was in particular made against Rostow's theory of the stages of economic growth (see Chapter 1). A second temptation would be, on the contrary, for the economist of the long period to amplify, through his classifications, the differences between the societies studied, so as to present them as incomparable and incommensurable entities. The incommensurability of societies is an extreme case: in this case, there is no "common standard" to compare the societies studied.

Economists have often been accused of the sin of excessive generalisations – an excess of continuities. What can we then say about Unified Growth Theory? What balance does it find between continuities and discontinuities in history? Unified Growth Theory cannot escape the difficulties raised by Foucault (1969), difficulties which will remain, for a long time, at the heart of the analysis of the long period.

Finally, a third challenge in looking at the long period is the potential for future *forecasting*. Beyond the intrinsic interest in understanding the past, the mechanisms that have governed the movement of societies over the centuries, the economic theory of the long period – as all scientific theories – also has the ambition to enlighten us about the future. Understanding the past in order to better anticipate the future is one of the motivations behind the study of the long period.

From this perspective, Unified Growth Theory makes a paradoxical contribution, to say the least. By definition, each economic regime is characterised by its own laws, by its own regularities. These laws or regularities are specific to each regime studied, in the sense that their validity is limited to the prevailing regime. It is therefore difficult, on the basis of these laws, to extrapolate, to predict *beyond the existing regime*. This limits the contribution of Unified Growth Theory to long-term forecasting.

It would be wrong, however, to infer from the relative nature of economic laws an absolute impossibility of foreseeing anything about the future movements of our societies. Unified Growth Theory makes an important contribution regarding the *nature* of forecasting methods that are likely to be "valid" over the long period. Given that the economic laws are relative to the prevailing regime, a quantitative extrapolation from existing trends (extending curves under certain assumptions) is unlikely to be useful in predicting future developments. Therefore, rather than a *quantitative* extrapolation, Unified Growth Theory suggests that a forecast should start first from a *qualitative* extrapolation. Such an extrapolation involves identifying the latent variables at work in the economy and the potential critical thresholds associated with these variables. Then, on the basis of these elements, it becomes possible to think about the eventuality and temporality of a possible future regime change.

However, if the methodological contribution of Unified Growth Theory is indisputable, the fact remains that the difficulties posed by long-term forecasting remain substantial, not to say (almost) insurmountable. Indeed, while it is possible to identify several latent variables likely to govern future societal evolutions, forecasting also requires something much more complex, that is quantifying the critical thresholds associated with these variables. The problem is that it is often only a posteriori that such thresholds can be measured, whereas they are almost impossible to measure a priori. Beyond this difficulty, another problem remains, and it is a major one. While the identification of latent variables and the quantification of critical thresholds are necessary, they are by no means sufficient for forecasting over the long term. It is still necessary to have an idea of the new form of relationships that will be established in the future between economic variables, that is, to give an outline of the "new" regime.

These words have particular resonance at the time of completion of this text. In this spring of 2021, the Covid-19 pandemic has forced over the past year most of humanity into some form of imposed lock-down. The lock-down is not only contributing to an unprecedented economic crisis, but the consequences are not restricted to that crisis and are still mostly unknown. Will this unique episode in recent history lead to a questioning of representations, behaviours and lifestyles, thereby leading to changes in the relations between economic variables and, ultimately, to a real regime change? Or is this pandemic only an acute crisis, which will leave the shape of the relationships between economic variables unchanged? These questions illustrate the difficulty of forecasting, not only in the short term, but also – and even more so – in the long term.

Three Lessons

What should be the take-away from this book, beyond the key concepts of Unified Growth Theory, that is, economic regime, quantitative and qualitative changes, critical thresholds or latent dynamics?

Three main lessons can be derived from our analyses.

The first lesson is intrinsically linked to the very concept of economic regime. While the analysis of time series of periods lasting several decades may bring to light the existence of "empirical regularities" or "economic laws", extending the horizon for our analysis to a longer period of time may erase those "regularities" or "laws". That is what happened with the Malthusian principle of population. For decades, it was presented by writers such as Ricardo, Nassau Senior or Mill as one of the basic postulates or axioms of economic analysis. That principle ceased being valid during the last quarter of the nineteenth century and, above all, during the twentieth century. One must therefore be cautious when discussing the scope of "economic laws" or how universal those laws are. Unified Growth Theory teaches us that economic laws are not absolute, but rather relative to a given economic regime.

The second lesson is linked to the first. It is that a variable may, at a given time in history, constitute an obstacle to the process of economic development and, at a different time, become the driving force of that process. Such is the case with population size: rightly presented as a phenomenon that impedes the take-off of output per capita, population growth has for centuries been an obstacle to improving living conditions. Nonetheless, it is that very population growth which later led to a population size large enough for the economy to benefit from strong scale effects, effects that accelerated technical progress and enabled output per capita to take off.

The third lesson should be read very cautiously: Unified Growth Theory teaches us that slow and quantitatively minor changes in a variable, may originally seem anecdotal, but can, if repeated over a long length of time, become the latent dynamics that will govern, at a given time, the transition to a different economic regime. Once again, that is the case for population size, as seen above. However, population size is not the only "latent" variable which can lead to regime changes. It is also the case for the quality of economic and political institutions. Those institutions took centuries to form, in a very slow process. That slowness does not mean that they have not, at a given time, played a decisive role in the transition from a stagnation regime to a growth regime. Furthermore, environmental damage also experienced very slow movement over the centuries. And yet, when one looks toward the future, one cannot but wonder if it is not exactly that variable that is governing and will govern in the future, a number of regime changes. Unified Growth Theory calls therefore for some caution: it is not necessary the most "mobile" variables that are the most important in the long run.

If these lessons are proved right, then this book shall be replaced, over time, by other books that will present other regimes, other transitions, governed by other latent dynamics. The economic analysis of the long period is only just starting.

References

Acemoglu, D. "Oligarchic versus democratic societies", *Journal of the European Economic Association*, 6 (2008), pp. 1–44.

Acemoglu, D. *Introduction to Modern Economic Growth* (New York: Princeton University Press, 2009).

Acemoglu, D., S. Johnson and J. Robinson, "Reversal of fortune: Geography and institutions in the making of the modern world income distribution", *Quarterly Journal of Economics*, 118 (2002), pp. 1231–1294.

Acemoglu, D. S. Johnson S. and J. Robinson, "Institutions as the fundamental cause of long-run growth", in P. Aghion and S. Durlauf (eds.), *Handbook of Economic Growth* (Amsterdam: North-Holland, 2005).

Acemoglu, D., S. Johnson, J. Robinson and P. Yared, "Income and democracy", *American Economic Review*, 98 (2008), pp. 808–842.

Acemoglu, D., S. Naidu, P. Restrepo and J. Robinson, "Democracy does cause growth", *Journal of Political Economy*, 127 (2016), pp. 47–100.

Acemoglu, D. and J. Robinson, *Why Nations Fail: The Origins of Power, Prosperity, and Poverty* (London: Penguin Books, 2013).

Aghion, P. and P. Howitt, *Endogenous Growth Theory* (Cambridge, MA: MIT Press, 1998).

Allen, R. *Global Economic History: A Very Short Introduction* (Oxford: Oxford University Press, 2011).

Arrow, K. "The economic implications of learning by doing", *Review of Economic Studies*, 29 (1962), pp. 155–173.

Bairoch, P. *Mythes et paradoxes de l'histoire économique* (Paris: La Découverte, 1993).

Barro, R. "Government spending in a simple model of endogenous growth", *Journal of Political Economy*, 98 (1990), pp. 103–125.

Barro, R. and G. Becker, "Fertility choice in a model of economic growth", *Econometrica*, 57 (1989), pp. 481–501.

Barro, R. and X. Sala-I-Martin, *Economic Growth* (New York: McGraw-Hill, 1995).

Bisin, A. and T. Verdier, "The economics of cultural transmission and the dynamics of preferences", *Journal of Economic Theory*, 97 (2001), pp. 298–319.

Blaug, M. *Economic Theory in Retrospect* (Cambridge; New York: Cambridge University Press, 1985).

Boisguilbert, P. Le Pesant. *Le détail de la France* (1697) in E. Daire. (ed.), *Economistes Financiers du XVIIème siècle* (Osnabrück: Otto Zeller, 1843; Paris).

Boisguilbert, P. Le Pesant. *Le factum de la France* (1707), in E. Daire. (ed.), *Economistes Financiers du XVIIème siècle* (Osnabrück: Otto Zeller, 1843; Paris).

Botero, G. *Sur les causes de la grandeur des villes* (1588; Paris: Editions Rue d'Ulm, 2014).

Boulding, K. "Earth as a spaceship", Washington State University Committee on Space Sciences, 1966.

Braudel, F. *Écrits sur l'histoire* (Paris: Flammarion, 1969).

Braudel, F. *La dynamique du capitalisme* (Paris: Flammarion, 1985).

Braudel, F. *Écrits sur l'histoire II* (Paris: Flammarion, 1990).

Bréchet, T., N. Hritonenko and Y. Yatsenko, "Adaptation and mitigation in long-term climate policy", *Environmental and Resources Economics*, 55 (2013), pp. 217–243.

Cantillon, R. *Essai sur la nature du commerce en général* (1755; Paris: INED, 1952).

Challier, M.-C. and P. Michel, *Analyse dynamique des populations. Les approches démographiques et économiques* (Paris: Economica, 1996).

Christensen, P. "Different lifestyles and their impact on the environment", *Sustainable Development*, 5 (1997), pp. 30–35.

Clark, G. *A Farewell to Alms. A Brief Economic History of the World* (New York: Princeton University Press, 2007).

Condorcet, N. *Esquisse d'un tableau historique des progrès de l'esprit humain* (1795; Paris: Masson et Fils, 1822).

Cournot, A. *Recherches sur les principes mathématiques de la théorie des richesses* (1838; Paris: Dunod, 2001).

Crafts, N. and T. Mills, "From Malthus to Solow: How did the Malthusian economy really evolve?", *Journal of Macroeconomics*, 31 (2009), pp. 68–93.

Darwin, C. *On the Origin of Species* (1859; London: John Murray, 1902).

Dasgupta, P. and G. Heal, *Economic Theory and Exhaustible Resources* (Cambridge: Cambridge University Press, 1979).

de la Croix, D. and P. Michel, *A Theory of Economic Growth. Dynamics and Policy in Overlapping Generations* (Cambridge: Cambridge University Press, 2002).

Denis, H. *Histoire de la pensée économique* (Paris: PUF, Quadridge, 1966).

Eltis, W. *Classical Theories of Economic Growth* (London: Macmillan, 1984).

Engels, F. *Outlines of a Critique of Political Economy*, in K. Marx *Economic and Philosophic Manuscripts of 1844* (1844; London: Lawrence and Wishart, 1970).

Engels, F. and K. Marx, *The Communist Manifesto* (1848; Minneapolis: Lerner Publishing Group, 2017).

Foley, D. and T. Michl, *Growth and Distribution* (London: Harvard University Press, 1999).

Forrester, J.W. *World Dynamics*, Second edition (Cambridge, MA: Wright-Allen Press, 1973).

Foucault, M. *L'archéologie du savoir* (Paris: Gallimard, 1969).

Galor, O. "From stagnation to growth: Unified Growth Theory", in: P. Aghion and S. Durlauf (eds.), *Handbook of Economic Growth*, Vol. IA, (Amsterdam: Elsevier North-Holland, 2005).

Galor, O. "The 2008 Lawrence R. Klein Lecture – Comparative economic development: Insights from Unified Growth Theory", *International Economic Review*, 51 (2010), pp. 1–44.

Galor, O. *Unified Growth Theory* (New York: Princeton University Press, 2011).

Galor, O. and O. Moav, "Natural selection and the origin of economic growth", *Quarterly Journal of Economics*, 117 (2002), pp. 1133–1191.

Galor, O. and O. Moav, "Natural selection and the evolution of life expectancy", Working Paper, (Providence, RI: Department of Economics, Brown University, 2005).

Galor, O. and D. Weil, "From Malthusian stagnation to modern growth", *American Economic Review*, 89 (1999), pp. 150–154.

Galor, O. and D. Weil, "Population, technology, and growth: From Malthusian stagnation to the demographic transition and beyond", *American Economic Review*, 90 (2000), pp. 806–828.

Geary, R. *An International Comparison of National Products and Purchasing Power of Currencies* (Paris: OEEC, 1958).

Gide, C. and C. Rist, *Histoire des doctrines économiques depuis les Physiocrates jusqu'à nos jours* (Paris: Dalloz, 1944).

Godwin, W. *Enquiry Concerning Political Justice* (London: G.G.J. & J. Robinson, 1793).

Harris, B., R. Floud, R. Fogel and S.C. Hong, "Diet, health and work intensity in England and Wales, 1700–1914", *NBER Working Paper* 15875 (2010).

Harrod, R. "An essay in dynamic theory", *Economic Journal*, 49 (1939), pp. 14–33.

Heilig, G. "How many people can be fed on Earth?", in W. Lutz (ed.), *The Future Population of the World. What Can We Assume Today?* International Institute for Applied Systems Analysis (1994).

Hicks, J. "Mr Keynes and the Classics: A suggested interpretation", *Econometrica*, 5 (1937), pp. 147–159.

Hritonenko, N. and Y. Yatsenko, *Mathematical Modelling in Economics, Ecology and the Environment* (New York: Springer, 2013).

Jevons, W. S. *The Theory of Political Economy* (1871; London: Penguin Classics, 1971).

John, A. and R. Pecchenino, "An overlapping generations model of growth and the environment", *Economic Journal*, 104 (1994), pp. 1393–1410.

Jones, C. *Introduction to Economic Growth* (New York: W. W. Norton and Company, 1998).

Jones, C. and P. Romer, "The New Kaldor Facts: ideas, institutions, population, and human capital", *American Economic Journal: Macroeconomics*, 2(1) (2010), pp. 224–245.

Kaldor, N. "Capital accumulation and economic growth", in F. Lutz et D. Hague (eds.), *The Theory of Capital* (New York: St Martin's, 1961).

Kaldor, N. *Economics Without Equilibrium* (Cardiff: University College Cardiff Press, 1985).

Keynes, J. M. *The General Theory of Employment, Interest and Money* (1936; London: McMillan, 1939).

King, G. *Of the People of England, republished in Several Essays in Political Arithmetic* by Sir William Petty (London: Printed for Robert Clavel at the Peacock, and Henry Mortlock at the Phoenix in St. Paul's Church-Yard, 1699).

Kondratiev, N. D. "The concepts of economic statics, dynamics and conjuncture", *Sotsialisticheskaya Ekonomika*, #4 (1924), republished in *The Works of Nikolai D. Kondratiev*, translated by Stephen S. Wilson, edited by Matalia Makasheva, Warren J. Samuels and Vincent Barnett, assisted by Jan Reijneders, Solomos Solomou and Andrew Tylecote, Vol. 1, "Economic Statics, Dynamics and Conjuncture" (London: Pickering & Chatto, 1998).

Kondratiev, N. D. *Long Cycles of Economic Conjuncture* (1928) in *The Works of Nikolai D. Kondratiev*, translated by Stephen S. Wilson, edited by Matalia Makasheva, Warren J. Samuels and Vincent Barnett, assisted by Jan Reijneders, Solomos Solomou and Andrew Tylecote, Vol. 1, "Economic Statics, Dynamics and Conjuncture" (London: Pickering & Chatto, 1998).

Kremer, M. "Population growth and technological change: One million BC to 1990", *Quarterly Journal of Economics*, 108 (1993), pp. 681–716.

Kuhn, T. *The Structure of Scientific Revolutions* (Cambridge, MA: Harvard University Press, 1962).

Kuznets, S "Economic growth and inequality", *American Economic Review*, 45 (1955), pp. 1–28.

Le Roy Ladurie, E. *Le territoire de l'historien* (Paris: Gallimard, 1973).

Lee, R. "The demographic transition: Three centuries of fundamental change", *Journal of Economic Perspectives*, 17 (2003), pp. 167–190.

Lucas, R. "On the mechanisms of economic development", *Journal of Monetary Economics*, 22 (1988), pp. 3–42.

Maddison, A. *The World Economy: A Millenial Perspective* (Paris: OECD, 2001).

Maddison, A. *The World Economy: Historical Statistics* (Paris: OECD, 2003).

Malthus, T. *An Essay on the Principle of Population* (in St Paul's Church-Yard, London: J. Johnson, 1798). Quotes from the version edited by A. Flew (London: Pelican Books, 1970).

Malthus, T. *A Summary View of the Principle of Population* (1830) republished in *An Essay on the Principle of Population*, edited by A. Flew (London: Pelican Books, 1970).

Marshall, A. *Principles of Economics* (London: McMillan, 1890).

Marx, K. *Grundrisse. Foundations of the Critique of Political Economy (Rough Draft)* (1858; London: The Pelican Marx Library, 1973).

Marx, K. *Capital: A Critique of Political Economy* (1867; New York: The Modern Library, 1906).

Marx K. and F. Engels, *German Ideology* (1846; Electric Book Company, 2000).

Michel P. and G. Rotillon, "Disutility of pollution and endogenous growth", *Environmental and Resource Economics*, 6(3) (1995), pp. 279–300.

Milanovic, B., P. Lindert and J. Williamson, "Preindustrial inequality", *Economic Journal*, 121 (2011), pp. 255–272.

Milanovic, B. *Global Inequality. A New Approach for the Age of Globalization* (Cambridge MA: The Belknap Press of Harvard University Press, 2016).

Mill, J. S. *Principles of Political Economy* (London: J.W. Parker, 1848).

Mokyr, J. "Malthusian models and Irish history", *Journal of Economic History* (1980), pp. 159–166.

Mokyr, J. *The Gifts of Athena: Historical Origins of the Knowledge Economy* (New York: Princeton University Press, 2002).

Morishima, M. *Marx's Economics* (Cambridge: Cambridge University Press, 1973).

Morishima, M. *Ricardo's Economics* (Cambridge: Cambridge University Press, 1989).

Myrdal, G. *Asian Drama: An Inquiry into the Poverty of Nations* (London: Penguin Press, 1968).

Niveau, M. *Histoire des faits économiques contemporains* (Paris: PUF, 1976).

Nordhaus, W. "Optimal greenhouse-gas reductions and tax policy in the 'Dice' model", *American Economic Review*, 83 (1993a), pp. 313–317.

Nordhaus, W. "Rolling the 'DICE': an optimal transition path for controlling greenhouse gases", *Resource and Energy Economics*, 15(1) (1993b), pp. 27–50.

Nordhaus, W. "New directions in national economic accounting", *American Economic Review*, 90(2) (2000), pp. 259–263.

Nordhaus, W. "Economic aspects of global warming in a post-Copenhagen environment", *Proceedings of the National Academy of Science*, 107 (2010), pp. 11721–11726.

Nordhaus W. and J. Tobin, *Is Growth Obsolete?* NBER 50th Anniversary Colloquia, Colloquium n° 5 (1972).

North, D. *Structure and Change in Economic History* (New York: W.W. Norton and Company, 1981).

North, D. "Economic performance through time", *American Economic Review*, 84 (1994), pp. 359–368.

North, D. *Understanding the Process of Economic Change* (New York: Princeton University Press, 2005).

Oparin, D.I. *Critical Analysis of Professor Kondratiev's Long Cycles of Conjuncture* (1928) in *The Works of Nikolai D. Kondratiev*, translated by Stephen S. Wilson, edited by Matalia

Makasheva, Warren J. Samuels and Vincent Barnett, assisted by Jan Reijneders, Solomos Solomou and Andrew Tylecote, Vol. 1, "Economic Statics, Dynamics and Conjuncture" (London: Pickering & Chatto, 1998).

Petty, W. *Several Essays in Political Arithmetic by Sir William Petty* (Saint-Paul Church-Yard: Robert Clavel at the Peacock and Henry Mortlock at the Phenix, 1699).

Piketty, T. *Le capital au 21ème siècle* (Paris: Editions du Seuil, 2013).

Pirenne, H. *Histoire économique du moyen-âge* (Paris: Presses Universitaires de France, 1963).

Prettner, K., A. Prskawetz and H. Strulik, "The past and future of knowledge-based growth", *Journal of Economic Growth*, 18 (2013), pp. 411–437.

Ricardo, D. *The Principles of Political Economy and Taxation* (1817; London: Dover Edition, 2004).

Romer, P. "Endogenous technical change", *Journal of Political Economy*, 98 (1990), pp. 71–102.

Rostow, W. *The Stages of Economic Growth: A Non-communist Manifesto*, 3rd ed. (1960; Cambridge: Cambridge University Press, 1990).

Rostow, W. *The Economics of Take-Off into Sustained Growth* (London: Macmillan, 1963).

Schumpeter, J. *Capitalism, Socialism and Democracy* (New York; London: Harper & Brothers, 1942).

Schumpeter, J. *History of Economic Analysis* (New York: Oxford University Press, 1954).

Smith, A. *An Inquiry into the Nature and Causes of the Wealth of Nations* (1776; Electric Book Company, 2000).

Solomou, S. *Phases of Economic Growth 1850–1973. Kondratieff Waves and Kuznets Swings* (Cambridge: Cambridge University Press, 1987).

Solow, R. "A contribution to the theory of economic growth", *Quarterly Journal of Economics* (1956), pp. 65–94.

Solow, R. *Growth Theory. An Exposition*, 2nd ed. (New York: Oxford University Press, 2000).

Sraffa, P. *Production of Commodities by Means of Commodities* (Cambridge: Cambridge University Press, 1960).

Strulik, H. "Knowledge and growth in the very long-run", *International Economic Review*, 55 (2014), pp. 443–458.

Toutain, J. C. "Le produit de l'agriculture française de 1700 à 1958. 1ère estimation du produit au XVIIIème siècle", in J. Marczewski (ed.), *Histoire Quantitative de l'Économie Française, Cahiers de l'Institut de Science Économique Appliquée*, 115 (1961), pp. 1–216.

Turgot, A. R. J. 1766, *Réflexions sur la formation et la distribution des richesses*. Initialement publié dans les *Ephémérides du Citoyen* (1769, tomes XI et XII, et 1770, tome I), repub-lished in *Formation et distribution des richesses*, textes choisis et présentés par Joël-Thomas Ravix et Paul-Marie Romani (Paris: GF Flammarion, 1997).

Vauban, S. *Projet d'une dîme royale* (1707) in E. Daire (ed.), *Économistes Financiers du XVIIème siècle* (Osnabrück: Otto Zeller (1843); Paris).

Walras, L. *Eléments d'économie politique pure* (Lausanne: L. Corbaz et cie, 1874).

Weil, D. *Economic Growth* (London: Routledge, 2005).

Weyland, J. *Principles of Population and Production* (London: Printed for J. Hatchard, 1815).

Withagen, C. "Pollution, abatement and balanced growth", *Environmental and Resource Economics*, 5 (1995), pp. 1–8.

Wrigley, E. A. *Population and History* (New York: McGraw-Hill, 1969).

Xepapadeas, A. "Economic growth and the environment" in K. G. Mäler & J. R. Vincent (ed.), *Handbook of Environmental Economics, edition 1*, Vol. 3, Chapter 23, pp. 1219–1271 (Amsterdam: Elsevier North-Holland, 2005).

Index

CPSIA information can be obtained
at www.ICGtesting.com
Printed in the USA
BVHW012105160822
644726BV00005B/20